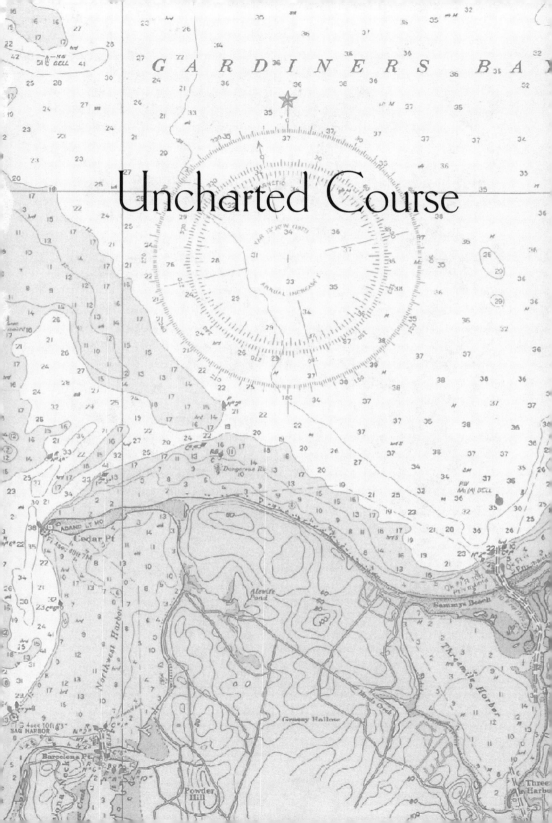

Uncharted Course

Uncharted Course

The Voyage of My Life

Anthony Drexel Duke

with Richard Firstman

THE BAYVIEW PRESS
NORTHPORT • NEW YORK

ISBN 10: 0-9793032-0-6
ISBN 13: 978-0-9793032-0-3

Library of Congress Control Number: 2007922549

Published by the Bayview Press, Northport New York.

Jacket and text design by Joe Gannon.

Photographs in the text are from the personal collections of Anthony Drexel
Duke and Cordelia Biddle Robertson and the archives of Boys & Girls Harbor,
with the following exceptions: Duke family photographs on pages 10 and 11
courtesy of Duke University Archives; photograph of Paul Moore on page 189
from his personal collection.

The background map illustration used on the jacket and the halftitle page is
from the Image Archives of the Historical Map & Chart Collection/Office of
Coast Survey/National Ocean Service/NOAA.

6 5 4 3 2 1

Produced by
Mulberry Tree Press, Inc.
Northport, NY

For my mother in heaven,
Cordelia Biddle Robertson

A note from the children of
Anthony Drexel Duke

A S HIS FRIEND GEORGE PLIMPTON used to say, "Get ready! Hold your hats! Let the show begin!" You are about to read a unique story by a one-of-a-kind man. It is the story of Tony Duke Sr., our father, a down-to-earth but larger-than-life superhero to thousands of children of all ages.

When we were kids, one of the prayers he taught us contained these hopes: "Grant, oh Lord, that we may never forget to be kind. Help us to be unselfish in friendship, thoughtful of those less fortunate than ourselves and eager to bear the burdens of others." These were words he truly lived by. He first learned them while a student at St. Paul's School, and not for a day has he stopped applying them, particularly in his lifelong devotion to disadvantaged children. For more than seven decades, he has used his uncanny, almost magical, perhaps God-given ability to work with young people, most notably those he has come to know and love through his beloved institution, Boys & Girls Harbor—his legacy, his gift to the world.

What follows are Dad's words; his memories, his impressions and images of a life fully lived. It is a life that spans most of the Twentieth Century and the beginning of the Twenty-first, a nearly epic tale of world war and high adventure, personal struggle and unflagging humor, kindness, and massive good will. He is a father figure to thousands, a man with a common touch, and a gifted leader of the first order, whether serving as a twenty-seven-year-old commander of a fleet of LSTs in the South Pacific or as an eighty-something gentleman escorting a gaggle of Harbor kids to Yankee Stadium. Each of

5

us feels lucky to have a piece of him in us, and in our own children, his grandchildren. We love him and we salute him! He's our Dad, Daddy, Dads, Pa, Papa, Popi, Pops.

He's Tony. A man with a hell of a good story to tell.

Anthony Drexel Duke, Jr.
Nicholas Duke
Cordelia Duke Jung
Josephine Duke Brown
December Duke McSherry
John Duke
Barclay Duke (in memoriam)
Douglas Duke
Lulita Duke Reed
Washington Duke
James Duke

CONTENTS

A note from the children of Anthony Drexel Duke 🍃 5

ONE: The Happiest Millionaire and the Tobacco Kings 🍃 9

TWO: Roaming Youth 🍃 43

THREE: A Real Education 🍃 78

FOUR: The First Boys 🍃 99

FIVE: To Sea on the 530 🍃 124

SIX: From the Great War to a Great Experiment 🍃 174

SEVEN: Three Mile Harbor 🍃 196

EIGHT: Bright Days and Dark 🍃 230

NINE: Miracle on 104th Street 🍃 260

TEN: Passages 🍃 291

ELEVEN: Onward 🍃 309

TWELVE: All My Children 🍃 322

Acknowledgements 🍃 330

Index 🍃 332

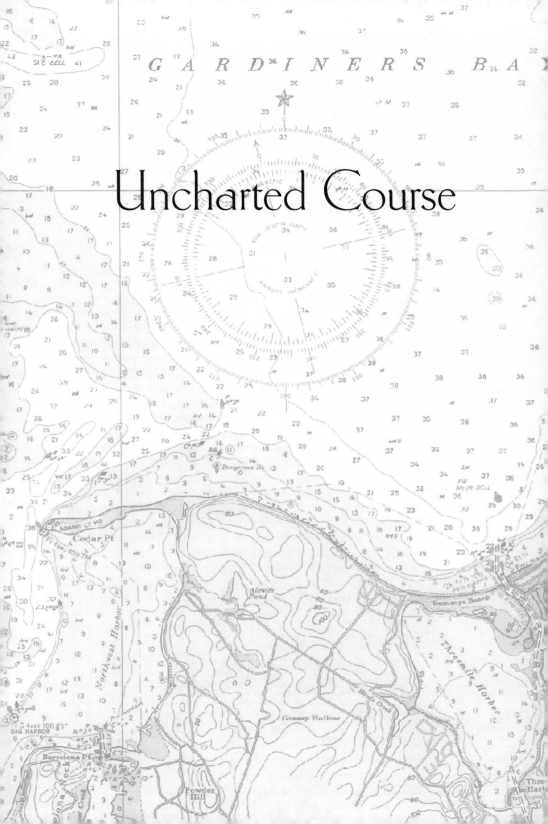

Uncharted Course

ONE

The Happiest Millionaire
and the Tobacco Kings

I WAS ALMOST BORN on a Ferris wheel—but that's another story. Allow me first to tell you a few things about what came before.

I have lived, so far, eighty-eight years. This prompts the chronological curiosity (if you don't want to be too technical about it) that my parents were born two centuries ago. My father arrived on the scene in 1884; my mother fourteen years later. Each came from a family worthy of a book itself, and, indeed, two books have been written. On my father's side there is *The Dukes of Durham 1865–1929*, by Robert F. Durden, a history professor at the university in North Carolina which bears the family's name, and whose press published that volume. On my mother's side there is *My Philadelphia Father*, a bouncy memoir published in 1955 by Cordelia Drexel Biddle, a magnificent woman who once nearly gave birth on a Ferris wheel.

The story of my mother's Philadelphia father is an excellent place to begin to tell you the tales of my own personal history, for Granddaddy Biddle was truly unforgettable. He was a larger-than-life figure who was one of the great presences in my life. Anthony Joseph Drexel Biddle was an author and publisher, an amateur boxer, religious movement founder, and a phenomenally awful opera singer. He joined the United States Marine Corps at the age of forty-two and taught hand-to-hand combat at sixty-seven. But it was on the Philadelphia home front where he became known for the antics that made him worthy of a book, which begat a Broadway show that was turned into a movie in which Granddaddy was played by Fred MacMurray. The movie was produced by Walt Disney, who renamed the story "The Happiest Millionaire," and gave Granddaddy's tale the full Hollywood treatment. That my grandfather was probably just shy of being a millionaire—he inherited a house and some money from his father—hardly mattered. He acted like one, and an eccentric one at that.

The house at 2104 Walnut Street, a huge Philadelphia brownstone with a dining room that could easily seat forty guests, featured gaudy statues in every corner. It was always the scene of one peculiar activity or another. It was there that Granddaddy conducted the Drexel Biddle Bible Classes, which combined boxing and hymn-singing. And it was there that he kept his collection of live alligators, which he'd caught himself in the Florida Everglades. Of this my mother commented, "We were proud of being the first private alligator owners in Philadelphia, but were aware that, socially, the distinction was dubious."

Granddaddy was born in 1874 to parents who united two of the most prominent families of Philadelphia society: the Biddles and the Drexels. The former was one of the city's oldest families; the latter one of its wealthiest.

The Biddles traced their descent to William Biddle, a onetime shoemaker who left England for America in 1861 with his wife, Sarah, and their two children. After holding a commission in Oliver Cromwell's army, William had become a Quaker, for which he was imprisoned under "most difficult circumstances" at the notorious Newgate prison. His captivity delayed the family's passage to America, where William had five years earlier arranged to purchase, from William Penn and others, a parcel of land in the "Province of West Jersey."

After making the voyage to the New World, William eventually increased his holdings to forty thousand acres in what is now Burlington, New Jersey, and in Pennsylvania. William found there was more tolerance for Quaker tolerance in America than in England. In 1688, Quakers in Germantown took a public stand against slavery—a declaration believed to be the first stirring of the abolitionist movement in America. The independent-minded Biddles were also among the few families from Philadelphia to fight for the colonists in the American Revolution.

The Drexels arrived later in America by better than a century. But they made up for lost time by being among the earliest, shrewdest, and most vigorous pursuers of what was yet to be called the American dream. Francis Drexel, a native of Austria, sailed to Philadelphia from Europe in 1817, after wandering the continent to escape Napoleon's compulsory draft. A talented painter, Francis spent a few years traveling in South America, selling his portraits of political leaders. Then he returned to America and became an entrepreneur of a different sort.

The young nation's financial system was still largely unformed, which created a need for individual "currency brokers." Francis saw the opportunity and prospered. Eventually he turned his operation into a private bank that specialized in the risky area of railroad financing. His sons, Francis Jr. and Anthony, learned as teenagers by his side. Eventually they took over the business.

In 1851, the first son, Francis Jr., got Gold Rush fever, and left Philadelphia to open an office in San Francisco. Meanwhile, as the Civil War approached, his younger brother Anthony became active in financing the Union. His efforts were pivotal to the North's victory.

When Ulysses S. Grant became President in 1869, he asked Anthony Drexel to be secretary of the treasury. But Anthony had other ideas. He initiated a partnership with John Pierpont Morgan to form Drexel, Morgan and Company, planting the seeds for what would become the first and most influential dynasty of modern American finance.

At a time when the United States did not have a central bank, it was financiers like Drexel and Morgan who raised the enormous sums necessary to build railroads and factories and fight wars. Though J.P. Morgan has been treated more reverentially and famously in popular history, it is my great-great-grandfather, Anthony Drexel, whom many financial historians now credit with being the real genius of the outfit. The primary catalyst for this change of perception is a 2001 biography by Dan Rottenberg. After twenty years of research, Rottenberg put his conclusion in the title: "The Man who Made Wall Street: Anthony J. Drexel and the Rise of Modern Finance."

It was shortly after Anthony Drexel and J.P. Morgan formed their golden partnership that Edward Biddle joined the Drexel firm in

Philadelphia. And it was shortly after Biddle joined the firm that he began to court the boss's daughter.

Edward was a handsome, headstrong man who knew what he wanted, and he wanted Emily Drexel. The ensuing wedding, an inevitably extravagant affair attended by President Grant and social celebrities from all over the East Coast, gave rise to the prodigious Drexel-Biddle branch of our family tree.

Though he descended from the tolerant Quaker, William Biddle, Edward apparently had none of the same tendencies.. He developed instant and irreversible mother-in-law issues, and he felt no compunction about complaining that he'd married himself into a business he didn't much like. Eventually, Emily's father had no choice but to arrange other employment for his dyspeptic son-in-law.

This occurred after an incident that came to be known in family lore as "the million-dollar punch." In the narrow confines of the bank vault one day in 1879, Edward and a junior clerk bumped against one another, prompting the clerk to tell Edward to watch where he was going—adding, somewhat gratuitously, "you clumsy ox."

It was probably that last part that caused Edward to knock the clerk to the floor with a single wallop. "The man offended me and I knocked him down," he explained to his father-in-law. "I think now it is a question of his going or my going."

"In that case, Edward," Drexel replied, "I think it will have to be you. I'm afraid you're not cut out for a banker."

"I'm certain I'm not," Edward agreed. They stared at each other in silence until Drexel offered an alternative. "I think I can arrange for you to study law in Logan Bullitt's office."

If Edward wasn't quite the crown prince in the eyes of his in-laws, he insisted on being the king of his castle—even if the castle, a three-story red brick house on Locust Street, had been given as a gift from the true king. "At home, Edward was the unquestioned monarch," my mother recounted in her book, "a martinet who ruled with stately arrogance and majesty. He did the family marketing, on the theory that only superior man could thwart the swindling grocer and butcher. He was the one who sat erect and silent at the dinner table mixing the salad dressing, another task fit only for man. Edward arranged all the fetes and played the imperturbable host. When a controversial subject arose that Edward considered improper, he peremptorily ordered the matter dropped. It was into this household that my father was born in 1874, and modern psychiatrists will certainly claim that his asthma was psychosomatic in character."

Granddaddy, whose asthma I will get to in a moment, was the first of three boys born to Emily Drexel Biddle, before she died in a most bizarre and inexplicable way. Emily was both a fine pianist and a one-time tomboy who was proud of her strength. On a dare from a friend, she tried to lift up the end of the grand piano in her living room. As the story goes, the strain was too much for her heart, and she died soon after. Under the circumstances, to paraphrase my mother, modern psychiatrists may be forgiven for claiming Emily's premature departure was psychosomatic in nature.

Having long ago worn out his welcome with the Drexels, Edward found that his wife's untimely death put him in a precarious position. Just how precarious became clear when he and Mr. Drexel met nine days after Emily died. "If my daughter hadn't died, you probably would have had seven million dollars," Mr. Drexel told Edward. "But she did die, and I know you're too much of a gentleman to expect anything further."

Edward agreed. But the new arrangements weren't just about money. Edward's father-in-law had some ideas about the children. He told Edward that while nine-year-old Anthony should continue to live with him, he felt that the two younger boys would be better off with their grandparents.

"Naturally," Drexel said, "I'm going to provide for Anthony, as well as Livingston and Craig. When they reach the age of twenty-one, they will each get the income from a million dollars."

It was an unfortunate arrangement for the boys. But, although Edward's posture was ramrod straight, he lacked the backbone to stand up to the great man, and to insist on keeping his boys together with him. Perhaps he wanted to avoid jeopardizing the financial arrangements being offered. And so my grandfather's home was broken up. Within a couple of weeks he had lost his mother, and, in a sense, his younger brothers (though both homes were near one another).

Now, about Granddaddy's asthma. It was with him from the start. But by the time he was fourteen, it was so severe that doctors warned it would affect his heart unless he was taken to a better climate. This advice happened to come just as his father was about to remarry, and so Granddaddy went with Edward and his new wife on their honeymoon to Europe. After landing on the continent they sailed to the Madeira Islands, a popular health resort in the North Atlantic that was a part of Portugal, but situated off the coast of Morocco. They wound up staying there for more than a year, and Granddaddy became fascinated with the history and culture of the Madeirans. Their way of life was rugged, poverty-stricken, and strangely beautiful. This experience was at the root of Granddaddy's love of people of all kinds. According to my mother, "He played with the dark-complexioned boys and girls and never afterward had any feeling about color."

Granddaddy was a natural-born writer—if not a great writer, at least a prolific and passionate one—but his formal education was somewhat patchy. After Madeira, his father and stepmother took him with them to Switzerland, where he spent two years at an English school that specialized in French. His encounters with a group of rough English boys there led him to take up boxing.

From Switzerland the trio went to Germany, where Granddaddy attended the university at Heidelberg. He came home to Philadelphia at age nineteen, expert in French, German, boxing, and fencing, and worldlier than most his age. He hoped for a job as a newspaper reporter, and his father got him one with the Philadelphia *Public Ledger*, which his grandfather, Anthony Drexel, had resuscitated years earlier. "The city editor was less than overjoyed at having this pampered pet fobbed off on him," my mother wrote, but he quickly demonstrated to the editor and everyone else in the city room that he was anything but a dilettante.

His first job was covering the docks. From that post he graduated to the city morgue, the aldermen's courts, and the police stations. What helped him—aside from his good right punch, and a willingness to use it—was his fascination with the seamier side of Philadelphia life, and his sympathy for the squalid life immigrants had to bear.

"He went among the poor and the foreign-born without condescension and with the kindness that was to characterize him all his life," my mother wrote. He loved to listen to the different ways people spoke—it was like music to him—and from this experience Granddaddy acquired an extraordinary facility with dialects. "He was never much at repartee," Mother recounted, "but for a party he could turn on a seemingly endless stream of Swedish, German, and French anecdotes. He did hilarious takeoffs in a jumbled kind of Pennsylvania Dutch. That knack got him into the Pen and Pencil Club and broke down the last barriers against him as a 'society dandy.' He turned out to be a favorite entertainer."

He parlayed that status into access to the people he wanted to meet—most especially the top prizefighters of the day. One of the first was Bob Fitzsimmons, an Irishman who was then the world middleweight champion. Many years later, my mother asked Fitzsimmons if he remembered the first time he'd met her father.

"I'll never forget it," Fitzsimmons said. "He was nervous, and talked to me like a professor. 'I have an aptitude for boxing ever since I reached man's estate,' he says. He didn't look to me as if he'd reached man's estate, but I guess he had. We went out to the big barn back of his father's house and there in the loft, with hay all around, he had fitted up a ring. 'I want to learn the solar plexus punch,' he says, and I taught it to him. 'It's right here,' I told him, pointing under the heart. Then he squares off. 'Look out!' he shouts at me. I thought the hay was falling and up went my hands. He caught me good and square and two pitchforks in the corner looked like four. 'Bob, old man,' I says to myself, 'you're going to take a nap if another like that comes your way.' I taught Mr. Biddle no more new ones that day."

Granddaddy talked the Gladstone Hotel janitor into letting him put up a ring in an unused area off the boiler room in the basement. The two of them spent many nights socking one another. One such match was witnessed by a bunch of reporters. They later portrayed it as one of the epic battles of the time. The pedigreed Drexel Biddle and the Negro janitor pounded each other for four rounds before the match was stopped, with the janitor helpless on the ropes—though not before he scored three knockdowns and a wicked cut over Granddaddy's right cheekbone.

The fight firmly established Tony Biddle's reputation among his fellows in the press corps, especially after the story of the punch he'd landed on Bob Fitzsimmons' solar plexus somehow got around (though the part about it being a sucker punch somehow got dropped from the accounts). The Pen and Pencil boys pushed Granddaddy to arrange a real match with the champion, and so he did. The bout attracted fifteen hundred spectators, some of whom might have felt snookered. In the meticulous record he kept of his fights, Granddaddy could not bear to write the word "defeat." He merely noted, "Biddle stayed 2½ rounds."

After a year or two at the *Ledger*, Granddaddy decided to go out on his own as an independent writer for magazines and newspapers. One summer in Atlantic City, he had a passing but memorable encounter with a girl named Cordelia Bradley, whose family was from Pittsburgh. Months later, he had a story published in a Pittsburgh newspaper. When Cordelia saw the byline, "A.J. Drexel Biddle," she dispatched a congratulatory telegram. In response Granddaddy sent her a massive bulldog. The growling gift terrorized her family but certainly got Cordelia's attention. How could she say no when Tony Biddle asked her to marry him?

After a lavish Pittsburgh wedding, the couple settled in Philadelphia in an inherited house on Walnut Street. There the bride found herself co-hosting weekly "boxing matinees." The guests, who included some of the best-known prizefighters of the era, would first spar a few rounds with Granddaddy in the hayloft, then repair to the house for a buffet spread with the family. This accounted for such renditions of grace as Bob Fitzsimmons' memorable prayer, "May the good God 'elp us to eat all wot's on the tyble." With their gloves on, most of the guests pulled their punches with the host—all except a heavyweight from California named Al Kaufmann, who knocked my grandfather out with one punch.

But he was indefatigable, always seeking out better fighters to challenge. In 1909, Granddaddy went out to Merchantville, New Jersey, where Jack Johnson, the first black heavyweight champion, was training for his upcoming title fight against Philadelphia Jack O'Brien.

In those days fighters had no regular sparring partners. Small-time fighters who wanted to pick up a few extra bucks would show up at a fighter's camp, sit on a long bench, and wait their turn to be smacked around by the champ. Granddaddy went out to Merchantville, calling himself "Tim O'Biddle," and took a seat on the bench. Johnson spotted him and said, "You there, boy." Granddaddy, as usual, came out fast and furious. Johnson pushed him off, urging him, "Now, you boy there, don't get yoself stirred up." But to Granddaddy, being stirred up was a way of life. Johnson finally had to whack him on the side of the head.

In his twenties, Granddaddy's love of boxing evolved into a passion for muscle-building, and then a fascination with the many styles of hand-to-hand combat. Somehow his strong religious convictions got mixed up with his obsession with physical fitness, and he began to practice what he described as "athletic Christianity." He formed a Sunday school class at Holy Trinity Church on Rittenhouse Square. Accompanied by Philadelphia Jack O'Brien, he taught children that Christ had been an athlete "who went into the jungle for forty days to train for a match with the Devil." Inexplicably, Granddaddy's peculiar amalgam of the spiritual and the roundhouse became an actual religious movement. "Drexel Biddle Bible Classes" spread across the country and even overseas. By 1910 there were said to be 300,000 members worldwide.

In addition to boxing there was a lot of singing in athletic Christianity, and this stimulated Granddaddy's grand aspiration to be an opera singer. "He demonstrated by his own rollicking attack on ancient hymns that nothing elevated the soul so pleasantly as a good community sing," my mother recalled in My Philadelphia Father (which she wrote with the assistance of Kyle Crichton). In an attempt to hasten his operatic career, Granddaddy had two or three teachers work on him simultaneously. What's more, he booked for his debut nothing less holy than the Philadelphia Academy of Music, where Caruso had sung and the Philadelphia Symphony Orchestra played. "He sent out a thousand announcements with order blanks and waited," Mother wrote. "The sparse and straggling returns would have discouraged anybody else and perhaps resulted in a cancellation of the concert. Father merely let it be known that the presence of all Biddles, Drexels, and affiliated relatives would be expected, and filled the other seats with members of the Bible classes.

"There was a warm reception for Father when he appeared before the curtain. For each number, he held before him a small sheet of paper, probably containing the words of the song. He twisted this paper while he sang, and at the end it was in shreds. The applause became more scattered as he neared the end."

Afterward, someone asked my mother's Aunt Sally what she thought. "Excruciating," she replied. This was the general opinion, but unfortunately Granddaddy made the recital an annual agony for the Drexel-Biddles. "Several weaker members arranged excursions out of town as the event neared," Mother recalled, "but most of them appeared like condemned prisoners."

One summer, the Manhattan Opera Company was performing a season at Atlantic City's Steel Pier, and Granddaddy somehow got himself attached to the troupe. The background is sketchy, but apparently the company was struggling and thought the Biddle name would help the box office. Granddaddy was content to sing a few minor roles, but when "Pagliacci" was announced he declared he would sing the tenor role. The director politely but firmly informed Mr. Biddle that Charles Dalmores, an internationally famous star of the time, would sing the role as planned. Imagine his surprise when Dalmores then announced he would cede the role to Mr. Biddle. Furious, the director demanded to know what was going on. "Nothing," Dalmores replied nonchalantly. "He merely said that if I opened my mouth and sang one note, he'd throw me over the rail into the ocean. I'm convinced he would do it." Granddaddy always recalled his performance fondly, but according to my mother, it was generally agreed that it was the worst Canio ever sung in the Western Hemisphere.

Granddaddy found that he and his new brother-in-law, Alexander Bradley, shared an interest in the publishing business. Together they revived *The Philadelphia Sunday Graphic*, with Bradley running the business side of things and Granddaddy serving as editor. The venture lasted only a year, though. Granddaddy decided books would be more profitable and launched the Drexel Biddle Publishing Company. Besides publishing the works of others, he wrote books of his own. Over the course of his life he wrote many, ranging from a very popular children's tale called *Froggy Fairy Tales* to *Do or Die: Military*

Manual of Advanced Science in Individual Combat. He also published a collection of his stories about hardscrabble Philadelphia life, called *Shantytown Tales.* But perhaps his biggest success was something he toiled at for fifteen years: a two-volume history of the Madeira Islands that sold well, brought critical attention, and won him an appointment as a Fellow of the Royal Geographic Society of London. This was among his proudest accomplishments, and from then on he signed his books, "A.J. Drexel Biddle, F.R.G.S."

Along with writing, boxing, singing opera and herding alligators, Granddaddy found yet another passion in a new invention. He was one of the first Americans to own an automobile, and he later become such an expert that, for years, he wrote for the famed *Blue Book* of the American Automobile Association. To him, there was only one way to drive, and that was fearlessly and as fast as possible. At one point he set a Philadelphia-to-New York record of just over seven hours, and he was widely hailed for making it from Philadelphia to Atlantic City in just four hours. (Usually, though, the Atlantic City trip took all day, which annoyed his brother Livingston. "Tony was crazy about cold bathing," he once recalled in a letter to my mother, "and he knew every little pond on the way to Atlantic City.")

As cars become more commonplace, Granddaddy saw no reason to adjust his driving style to accommodate his fellow travelers, or even to acknowledge their presence. "He sat bolt upright behind the wheel, drove straight ahead, with a damn-the-torpedoes attitude," my mother later recalled. He drove offensively, too fast, and almost always while distracted by the animated conversation he carried on with my grandmother (or whomever was accompanying him). "If a thing struck him as exciting or amusing, he would throw up his hands in delight," Mother wrote. "What saved him and everyone else were his lightning reflexes; he could always yank the car back on the road after one of those outbursts." My grandmother never learned to drive, but eventually insisted on a unique innovation. Whenever Granddaddy bought a new car, she insisted the factory install two horns: one for him, one for her. So when she saw a close shave coming, she would honk long and loud.

Granddaddy always seemed to have some new irons in the fire. When World War I broke out in 1914, he opened a camp outside

Philadelphia where he trained four thousand young men in military maneuvers. He used long hours of calisthenics and gymnastics to prepare them for advanced training. When he judged them ready, he taught them how to use a machete, saber, dagger, bayonet, and hand grenade. He also taught them the techniques of jiu-jitsu, and a potentially lethal French punch-and-kick sport known as *savate*.

In 1917, at age forty-two, he joined the Marine Corps himself. Commissioned as a captain, he was assigned to training bases in Port Royal, South Carolina (renamed Parris Island a few years later), and Quantico, Virginia. He went on to Europe, touring British and French training bases, and upon his return to headquarters he convinced the commandant of the Marine Corps to make boxing part of the regular training regimen for American recruits.

At Quantico, Granddaddy met a twenty-year-old New Yorker named Gene Tunney. Tunney had learned to fight on the streets of Greenwich Village, but Granddaddy Biddle is credited with giving Tunney his first formal training as a boxer. By the end of the war Tunney had acquired his nickname, "the Fighting Marine" and was the light heavyweight champion of the American Expeditionary Forces. After the war, Granddaddy could often be found in Tunney's corner. He would be there on September 23, 1926, when Tunney would take the world heavyweight title from Jack Dempsey before 120,757 fans at Philadelphia's Sesquicentennial Stadium.

But my grandfather's most enduring contribution to boxing came in 1920, when he went up to New York and enlisted the support of Tammany Hall to pass a law in the New York State Legislature to legalize gloved boxing. The law, sponsored by State Senator and future Mayor Jimmy Walker, created the New York State Athletic Commission. It would lead to similar actions by other states, and it paved the way for boxing to become a major American spectator sport.

In addition to his contributions to Marine training, Granddaddy saw action toward the end of the war, fighting at the Battle of Belleau Wood. Better than any war story was the one he told about meeting and befriending his counterpart in the British army, a man who was a member of the House of Lords. This Peer of the Realm invited Granddaddy to come with some of his men to his home in the country when

*Granddaddy Biddle squaring off with Young Jack O'Brien
as old Jack looks on.*

*Granddaddy with Gene Tunney during World
War I. Tunney credited my grandfather with
turning him into a professional prize fighter.*

the battles were over. When the time came, Granddaddy selected a few deserving Marines, and they were given an elegant dinner by the lord and his wife in one of Britain's most ancient country houses. Granddaddy was seated to the hostess's right at a very long table and discovered very early on that she was suffering from some sort of gastrointestinal disturbance. Being the Philadelphia gentleman that he was, each time the lady broke wind, Granddaddy took responsibility, murmuring an apology to the rest of the guests. Just before they left the table, the lady released one final major assault, at which point a British gentleman at the other end of the table called to Granddaddy, "I say, Colonel, let this one be on me."

IT WAS INTO THE ANTHONY BIDDLE CIRCUS that three children were born, starting with Anthony Joseph Drexel Biddle—Tony Junior—a week before Christmas of 1896. He was followed in close succession by his brother Livingston and sister Cordelia. Granddaddy was close with all of them, not in the least because of his own experience of having lost his mother and then being separated from his younger brothers. My mother recalled a time when she played the piano for her father and he suddenly burst into tears. "I want you to be happy," he said. "When I was a boy I was such a lonely little boy."

Of course, by then he was lonely no more—and his only daughter was in no danger of being unhappy. My mother grew up merrily hearing the sound of heads being bumped in the hayloft that was the center of activity in the house on Walnut Street. Like any child of Anthony Drexel Biddle, Cordelia learned first things first in life: the left jab, the right cross, and the solar plexus punch. Instead of dolls, she liked to say, she played with barbells. Instead of hopscotch and ring-o-leevio, she learned to patch up cuts under the eye. She and her brothers Tony and Livingston were a happy threesome. They boxed, hunted, and fished together, and they took turns feeding the alligators.

The turning point in her young life came when she was thirteen and spending the summer of 1911 in Atlantic City. On the boardwalk she encountered a boy who suggested they enter a dance contest, which they did, and which they won. "What's your name, kid?" the manager of the dance hall asked. When she said "Cordelia Biddle," his eyes lit up and the next day her name was in the papers. This was apparently something of a minor scandal in certain corners of the family. It led Aunt Mary Drexel, the matriarch of the Drexel side, and the self-appointed protector of the family name, to summon Cordelia's father to her estate in Bryn Mawr.

"Anthony," she said to Granddaddy, "I'm ashamed of you. Allowing that dear little girl to run wild down there in that awful place." Whether he wanted it or not, she offered the opinion that Cordelia's life so far was "hardly fitting for a girl with her social position." What was needed, Mary Drexel suggested, was for Cordelia to be sent off to boarding school. Her father didn't disagree, and her mother found the idea positively inspired. As my mother later described her mother's situation, "She had almost more than she could tend to at home. Much as she would have liked to raise us, her main job was raising father."

The only one involved who was not so enamored of the idea was Cordelia herself. Preparing to be shipped off to a place called Miss Walker's School in Lakewood, New Jersey, she was sure she'd be stuck with "silly girls who wouldn't know the first thing about the rabbit punch," as she put it to John Lawless, the family's coachman. With her parents away on a motor trip, John had the sad duty of taking Cordelia to school by train.

Miss Walker welcomed Cordelia warmly—until she noticed that, in addition to bringing her Irish coachman, John, she'd brought her Irish terrier, Pat. "Turn that dog over to your man immediately," Miss Walker demanded, "and get it out of here."

My mother had hidden Pat on the train, fully intending to have him with her at school. "Pat is the dearest thing in the world to me," she told Miss Walker. "I would rather die than part with him!" If Pat went, she insisted, so would she. Miss Walker ignored her and looked around for John. But he was gone. She rushed to the front porch in time to see him already far down the road. Mother won the battle: Pat stayed and she stayed. For a while, anyway.

The place was torture for my mother because she was so ill-prepared, her education to this point having been mostly in pugilism and other facets of Biddle-ism. "I was captain of the basketball team and the best rider, but that didn't hide the fact that I was academically retarded," she wrote. "I'm afraid I became a problem child." In this little place where report cards listed "orthography" for spelling, the only time she got a good grade was when she copied from a classmate. And she found the rules illogical and stifling. She caused an uproar when she left the room in the middle of a piano recital. Besides finding Miss Walker's an entirely foreign culture, Mother felt lonely and isolated from her fellow Biddle Musketeers. Tony, her older brother, was basically incommunicado up at St. Paul's, a boarding school in Concord, New Hampshire. And her younger brother, Livingston, broke her heart with his letters detailing how marvelous a time he was having at home—all about the latest dogs their father had brought home and the famous guests he invited to dinner.

Once a week the girls of Miss Walker's School got a half hour of freedom. They marched down the road like prisoners to the Lakewood drugstore, where they had ice creams and picked up postcards before marching back. Granddaddy gave Mother far more allowance than she could possibly spend, and by the end of two months she had squirreled away a considerable nest egg. On one of these furloughs soon after her arrival, Mother decided to make a break for it. While the teacher who had escorted them was in the back of the drugstore getting her large-size Phillips Milk of Magnesia, Mother took Pat in her arms and started for the railroad station. She made the afternoon train back to Philadelphia, arriving home to a mixture of welcome and rebuke. She insisted she wouldn't go back to Miss Walker's. "It's a terrible place!" she said. "It's a jail!"

This hit a nerve with Granddaddy, whose latest interests included prison reform, particularly at New Jersey's notorious Trenton State Prison. But my grandmother insisted Miss Walker's was nothing of the sort. "It's a lovely school," she told Cordelia, "and you couldn't be with a finer woman than Miss Walker." They drove her back to Lakewood and made her promise she wouldn't even think about running away again.

What made Miss Walker's School palatable for my mother during the next couple of years was that Lakewood had a vibrant summer scene—and the most famous summer residents, Mr. and Mrs. George

Jay Gould, happened to be relatives of relatives. George Gould, the son of railroad magnate Jay Gould, had built one of the showplaces of America for his wife, a former actress. Gould called this palace and its grounds Georgiancourt. The main building was made to resemble Hampton Court in England, only much bigger, and the Goulds entertained as if it were Buckingham Palace. The estate featured the only private "court tennis" layout in the country. (Court tennis, or *jeu de paume* in the original French, is an ancient game from which modern tennis is descended. With features reminiscent of the Basque sport jai alai, it's played on a court meant to replicate the monastery cloisters where it was played, mainly in France, in the 1500s and earlier.)

Mother's connection at the Gould estate was that her cousin, Tony Drexel Jr., was married to Marjorie Gould, one of George Gould's eight children. Tony and Marjorie spent long periods at Georgiancourt and began to include Mother, their bouncy and talkative teenage cousin. "They couldn't have been nicer in pretending I belonged there," Mother recalled. "The girls at school were jealous, which made the pleasure all the greater."

Mother soon found yet another house to escape to when her closest aunt and uncle, Gladys and Bill Thaw, also bought a summer house in Lakewood. Aunt Gladys and Uncle Bill had riotous weekend parties, which Mother described memorably: "Uncle Bill met the trains in a huge Pierce-Arrow limousine—the old type where the driver seemed to be about fifteen feet off the ground—and the procession through town was like General MacArthur's later return from Tokyo. Bill's local friends rushed out of their stores and stood on the pavement like a guard of honor. In the midst of the turmoil, Aunt Gladys sat as calm and happy as a Buddha. She needed it all with Uncle Bill, whose idea of life was to enjoy it quick before the final curtain fell."

Every party turned into a dance. At this Mother excelled beyond her years (fifteen at this point), as she had demonstrated at the contest in Atlantic City that had gotten her shipped off to Miss Walker's in the first place. A man of any age who wanted a whirl at the tango, the maxixe, the one-step, or the hesitation waltz—Cordelia Biddle was the girl for him. (She was also known to favor the bunny hug and the turkey trot.) All this fun had a singular effect on Mother: it made her hate school all the more. It was agony for her to go back to Miss Walker's after a tea dance at Georgiancourt, or another boisterous party at Aunt Gladys' and Uncle Bill's. Especially the day Angier Duke swept down from New York in his open Rolls-Royce.

ANGIER BUCHANAN DUKE OWED his comfortable station in life to the collective diligence, acumen, and ambition of three men: his grandfather, his father, and his uncle. The patriarch, Washington Duke, was a hard-working, twice-widowed man who was born in hardscrabble North Carolina in 1820, and spent most of his early life behind a plow on land he did not own. His poor fortune continued when he was drafted into the Confederate Navy for the last year of the Civil War, when he was a forty-four-year-old widower with four children. He survived, only to be captured by Grant's army during the very last week of battle. He was imprisoned for two weeks before being sent by ship to a military base on the Carolina coast. From there he had to walk a hundred and thirty miles to return to his home in the Piedmont Mountains. He arrived there with a single half dollar and two blind mules.

Reunited with his children—sons Brodie, Benjamin, and James, and daughter Mary—Washington Duke found the family farm stripped bare except for a small quantity of dried tobacco he had stored away, and which was still in decent condition. He hitched the blind mules to a wagon left behind by Sherman's army and headed out for the small towns of North and South Carolina to sell his tobacco.

In the parlance of the day, he was a "drummer," a traveling salesman, which meant he had to leave his children in the care of an unmarried sister of his late wife's. The children, primarily ten-year-old Ben and nine-year-old James (nicknamed Buck), worked in the farm fields and in a crude log shed near the house, where they beat the tobacco with wooden flails, sifted it by hand, and packed it in cloth bags. The tobacco was labeled with the brand name "Pro Bono Publico," and Washington Duke headed out to peddle it. He later remembered that in the years immediately after the war, he and his sons could process more than four hundred pounds of smoking tobacco in a day. They cleared a handsome profit of thirty or forty cents a pound when it was sold. The tiny factory gradually expanded into a two-story building, and within seven years of the end of the war, the Dukes were producing some 125,000 pounds of tobacco a year.

The senior Duke covered thousands of miles as he sold the family's various brands to tobacconists from Maine to California. In *The Dukes of Durham*, Robert Durden tells of a merchant in Missouri who remembered, years after the Duke name had become famously associated with tobacco, that his first contact with the company had been with the founder himself, the indefatigable traveling salesman Washington Duke. According to Durden, "As the Missourian recalled it, one cold morning an elderly gentleman, wearing a broad brim hat and soberly dressed, opened the door to the tobacco shop in St. Louis, walked half way down to the office, turned deliberately, and walked back to shut the door. Then, speaking slowly in a droll, broad accent, he said, 'Good morning. I did shut the door and I'm from North Carolina.' After putting down his worn black carpetbag, Washington Duke continued, 'I've got some mighty good smoking tobacco in here and believe you could sell a heap of it if you had some of it in your store.'"

By the early 1870s, the teenaged Buck Duke, the youngest of Washington Duke's three children, was letting it be known that he had high ambitions, which included running the little family company. "At the age of fifteen," said one account of the company's history, "Buck Duke lifted the cares of business off his father's back by the simple expedient of taking the company away from him."

As Durham was becoming a bustling burg promoted as the "Chicago of the South," Buck pushed his father to sell the farm and move into town. They built a new factory on Main Street, on the spot where a large Liggett and Myers plant would stand a century later. Buck and Ben, his older brother by a year, had complementary interests and talents but were different in temperament. And they had opposing approaches to the business. Ben—my grandfather— was slight in stature, a scholarly sort who was very much for running the business carefully and properly. Buck, meanwhile, was very much for taking what their father had started and turning it into as big and profitable an enterprise as possible. Buck was a large, physical man with little patience for formal education. Ben enjoyed going away to the New Garden School, a Quaker academy near Greensboro later renamed Guilford College. Buck missed the farm and factory and did not last long.

Though reasonably successful, W. Duke, Sons and Company was only one of about a dozen tobacco manufacturers in Durham. The enterprise lagged far behind the company that first made Durham famous: W.T. Blackwell and Company, makers of the world-famous Bull Durham brand. But the ambitious Buck Duke was always looking for ways to help the company move ahead. At one point he wanted to make rum-flavored tobacco. What eventually changed everything was the consumer product that burst onto the American scene in the late 1870s: the cigarette.

A European invention, cigarettes had first been produced in the United States near the end of the Civil War. They caught on first in New York, which became the first center of the industry. This changed when major manufacturers John F. Allen and Lewis Ginter moved their business to Richmond, Virginia, to be closer to the bright-leaf varieties of tobacco grown in North Carolina and Virginia that were ideal for use in the cigarette. Buck Duke was convinced that cigarettes were the future, and in 1881—by which time his father had sold his shares in the company and retired to Durham—he plunged the Duke Tobacco Company into the industry full speed. He and his brother brought more than a hundred skilled hand-rollers, many of them Jewish immigrants from eastern Europe, to Durham. In their first year they produced 9.8 million cigarettes. It was still only about three percent of the number made by manufacturers in New York, but by the end of that decade, aggressive marketing made their three brands—Duke of Durham, Pin Head, and Cross-Cut—among the best sellers in the country.

In 1884, Buck Duke made a decision that would revolutionize the tobacco industry. Four years earlier, Allen and Ginter had tried to use a machine, invented by a clever eighteen-year-old named James Bonsack, that could make cigarettes. But Bonsack's machine had proved unreliable. Allen and Ginter had given up on it and gone back to hand-rolling.

Buck, though, wanted to give the machines a try. If they worked, they could do the work of forty-eight men. He leased two of them, and when they broke down, as he thought they might, he got Bonsack to send a mechanic named William T. O'Brien to the Durham factory. Together Buck and O'Brien were able to get the machines working smoothly. Automating cut the cost of making cigarettes in half. Believing that the Bonsack machine would eventually eliminate hand-processing altogether, Buck went up to New York and opened a factory there. He also decided to move his family to the city. The company benefited from its exclusive rights to the Bonsack machine by enjoying unprecedented production. This led Buck, in 1890, to make a bold move: He brought in several other companies to form the largest tobacco manufacturer in the world, which he named American Tobacco Company.

While Buck went about making himself one of the most powerful business and industrial leaders of his time, his brother Ben and sister Mary turned their attentions toward philanthropy. Their father, Washington, was an active Methodist, and in the tradition of that church, Ben and Mary gave substantial aid toward education in North Carolina at a time when there was no public welfare. They financed the Lincoln Hospital for Negroes in Durham, as well as a grade school and college for blacks, an orphanage, and two colleges for women. In 1887, Ben Duke also began giving to Trinity College, a mainly Methodist institution with some Quaker roots located in Randolph County. With Ben's encouragement, his father, sister, and eventually his brother Buck also contributed. A substantial gift from Washington Duke helped the college move to Durham in 1892.

After leaving the tobacco business to his sons and their partners and retiring to Durham, Washington Duke had also become involved in the local Republican Party. The party was founded on anti-slavery principles, and its second candidate for President had been Abraham Lincoln. North Carolina's Democrats, meanwhile, were then the party of racism. They warned of a coming domination by black people, and howled when Trinity College invited the distinguished black educator Booker T. Washington to speak on the campus. For their support of racial equality, Republicans like Washington and Ben Duke were vilified in the newspapers, and privately despised. But their wealth and power protected them; others were sometimes hounded from their jobs

111 Fulton St.

LEFT: *The Dukes of Durham, around 1903. In front row starting at far left is my grandfather Ben, his father Washington Duke, and brother James, better known as Buck.*

BELOW, LEFT TO RIGHT:

Washington Duke around 1880.

Benjamin Newton Duke, my grandfather, as a young man.

Sarah Pearson Angier Duke, my grandmother, known as Sally to friends and Ga-Ga to us.

James Buchanan Duke in 1881, when he was twenty-five. Uncle "Buck" was the driving force behind the family tobacco business. My cousin Doris Duke was his daughter.

or homes. Blacks in Durham knew they had friends in the Duke family, and in 1892 a large delegation of them came to Washington Duke's home to thank him for his unwavering support.

My grandfather Ben, meanwhile, fought his own racial battles at Trinity. In 1903, a courageous professor named John Spencer Basset published in a college publication an article entitled "Stirring the Fires of Racial Antipathy." The article denounced racial hatred and espoused and predicted equality. On the Board of Trustees, Ben Duke alone defied public opinion and backed Basset, who was being derided as "a slobbering lover of blacks," in the words of an editorial writer at one racist North Carolina newspaper. When reaction on campus boiled up into a move by some trustees to fire Basset, my grandfather insisted that the college stand up for free speech, free thought, and equality for people of all races. The trustees ultimately voted to retain Basset and defend Trinity's dedication to free speech. Ben Duke was quoted as saying, "I felt prouder of Trinity than ever before." The crowning moment came in 1905, when President Theodore Roosevelt came to Trinity and praised the institution's dedication to academic freedom.

Washington Duke died that year, at age eighty-four. By then, the vicious racial politics of North Carolina had led many of the more progressive whites of the state to move to friendlier environments in the north. Buck Duke was one of them. He built a mansion on Fifth Avenue at Seventy-eighth Street in New York. Buck's driving energy was also moving the family into a new business interest: electric power. Buying up good locations for dams on Carolina's rivers, the new company—Southern Power Company, later named Duke Power—constructed hydroelectric plants and soon began making more money than the tobacco business ever had. This was a good thing for the family fortune, since by then federal trust-busters had broken the monopoly of the American Tobacco Company. In 1924, the phenomenal success of Duke Power allowed Buck to create a family philanthropic foundation called the Duke Endowment. Its main provision was a major expansion of Trinity College. As a tribute to his father, Buck arranged for the college to be renamed Duke University.

Ben Duke had married Sara Pearson Angier (Sally to her friends) in 1877, and they had three children. The first, George Washington

Duke, died at two. The next, Angier Buchanan Duke, was born on December 8, 1884, and Mary three years later. They raised their children primarily in Durham, but like his brother, Ben drifted north as the family business expanded, and in 1901 he built a home in New York.

Angier, my father, grew up in Durham. In 1905 he graduated, naturally, from Trinity College. In school he was a right-handed pitcher for the baseball team, but soon after graduating he became left-handed. I mean this quite literally. He lost his right hand in a hunting accident that fall. About the mishap I know only that he went on a duck hunt somewhere in the mountains of North Carolina—don't hold me to the duck; it may have been pheasant or grouse, or even quail—and some sort of malfunction caused his shotgun to explode, blowing off his trigger hand. His mother would knit him socks to cover the stump, but after a while people didn't think much of it because he was so agile with his remaining hand. In any event, his lost extremity seemed to faze him very little.

It has been said that, perhaps more than any other member of the family, Angier enjoyed the style of life that great wealth made possible in the years before the First World War. "Although helping to manage his father's affairs, Angier Duke felt no economic need to work," Durden wrote. Instead, my father indulged his enthusiasm for the elite new mode of transportation known as the motor car. In the summer of 1905, just after finishing up at Trinity, he set out to drive from New York to Durham. But the road only went as far as Charlottesville, Virginia, so from there he shipped his car by train. My grandfather had an eye for the autos as well, and he was smitten by one his brother Buck had purchased from the Fiat company in Italy. Ben was so besotted with the car, in fact, that he wrote to Fiat to order a version for himself. He requested a "24–32 H.P. car, fitted with a Demarest Limousine body, similar to the one built by Rothschild on Mr. J.B. Duke's 28 H.P. 'Mercedes.'" The car arrived in dark maroon and black, with red running gear and monogrammed panels, among other luxuries. The sticker price was a staggering $9,500. But Ben's infatuation didn't last, and he soon switched to a Rolls-Royce. Angier's favorite was a specially built five-seat Torpedo-Phaeton featuring "speed and brake levers."

My father was handsome, sociable, and very comfortable with his privilege. The leisurely bliss of his extended bachelor years are exemplified by a note he sent the family's executive secretary in 1913, when he was twenty-nine, making arrangements for a return trip north while visiting the hot springs of western Virginia. "I expect to leave here Thursday night for Philadelphia, and go from there to the Princeton-Harvard Foot Ball Game at Princeton," he wrote. "I should like you to instruct Fox [the chauffeur] to bring the Rolls-Royce Limousine Car to Princeton, and be at the Princeton Inn not later than one o'clock on Saturday, as I am going to motor to the Rumson Country Club after the game that afternoon, and will want that car."

Angier had friends everywhere, and among these were Gladys and Bill Thaw, whose spectacular summer house in Lakewood, New Jersey, had always been the scene of lively parties. One day Angier drove the Rolls down and wound up dancing the night away with a beguiling young woman. Very beguiling, and very young. Not yet sixteen, she was little more than half his age, but my mother's dance moves and social aplomb apparently led my father to believe she was at least in the ballpark. For her part, Mother said, "I won't say the Rolls-Royce won me over, but it did no harm."

On one of Angier's next visits to Lakewood, Cordelia was by his side in the Rolls when they drove into town and happened to encounter the girls from Miss Walker's coming out of the drugstore after their dreary chocolate sodas. The girls couldn't believe what they were seeing, but Cordelia merely nodded to them as they went by.

"I hate that school," she told Angier.

"Why don't you leave it?" he replied.

"*How* can I leave it?"

"Well, you can marry *me*."

"I can hardly wait," Cordelia said.

"Do you mean it?" Angier asked.

"Certainly I mean it. Do you?"

"Of course I do," he said. "I meant it the first minute I saw you."

They drove right over to Miss Walker's, where Mother packed her suitcase and left before Miss Walker figured out what was going on. "When she found out, she acted hurt," Mother later said, "but I think she was relieved. One more year and I'd have ruined her school."

Arriving home in Philadelphia, my mother caught her parents off guard, to say the least. "What are you doing here?" Granddaddy asked.

"I've come home to get married," Mother said.

"*Married!*" cried Granddaddy, furious.

"Now, Anthony," my grandmother said, putting a hand on his arm. "Let the girl talk. Now what's this, Cordelia?"

"I'm going to marry Angier Duke," Mother said forthrightly. "He's outside."

Granddaddy ran outside, but the prospective groom wasn't there. Angier, who knew by now just how young Cordelia was, had wisely decided that it would be better if Cordelia smoothed the way and introductions were made later.

Granddaddy came back in and declared there would be no marriage. "It's out of the question!"

"You're only fifteen," my grandmother agreed.

Realizing that his wife was on his side, Granddaddy instantly reversed himself.

"She'll be sixteen next month," he said—not yet aware that his prospective son-in-law, at twenty-nine, was only ten years younger than him.

"It'll mean giving up school," said my grandmother.

"Oh, school," Granddaddy said dismissively.

"How can you think of marriage when you haven't even come out socially?" asked my grandmother.

"Well, by Jove, she *will* come out," Granddaddy declared. "I'll see to that."

And so my grandmother acquiesced, although not without quite a bit of worry about what people might be thinking about the Rolls-Royce that was parked outside the house every day. She also worried what they would think when they realized that Cordelia was out, unchaperoned, with a man twice her age. The newspaper society columns reported the arrival in Philadelphia of "Angier Duke, an heir to the Duke tobacco fortune and one of the richest young men in the country," attributing his stay to visits with friends. Meanwhile, he was squiring Cordelia to the Poconos and the Jersey shore before

The Biddle Family of Philadelphia:
My grandparents and mother
seated, with uncles Livingston and
Tony standing.

My parents, Angier Buchanan Duke
and Cordelia Drexel Biddle,
before their marriage in April 1914.

returning each night to Walnut Street, where they sat in the living room and held hands.

Perhaps it was customary in those days for a man to woo his beloved by giving her a huge dog. Just as Granddaddy had initiated his courtship of Grandmother by sending a menacing bulldog to the Bradleys in Pittsburgh, Angier one day brought a German police dog named Hans to the Biddle household on Walnut Street. Granddaddy loved dogs, of course, but in this case the feeling was hardly mutual. When he first discovered the dog, he put out a solicitous hand—which Hans nearly had for lunch. He tried seducing the dog with some sweet words, but all he got in return was a vicious growl. "Get this damnable dog out of here!" he yelled finally.

The two of them, father and dog, managed to co-exist over the next few days. But with revenge on his mind, Granddaddy decided to introduce Hans to the alligators, who had a habit of opening their jaws and hissing at strangers, human or otherwise. Granddaddy was sure they would send Hans running for his life. He brought the dog into the conservatory and lifted one of the gators out of the tank. Right on cue, it opened its jaw and hissed. Whereupon Hans turned around and bit Granddaddy in the leg.

"This is the end!" he shouted. "This blasted dog has got to go!"

"It will not go!" Mother answered.

"What sort of man is this Angier Duke," Granddaddy said, "bringing a villainous dog like that in here!" He proceeded to accuse his future son-in-law of sending the dog over for the express purpose of biting him. It was all a plot, he said, muttering something about "smart New Yorkers."

Granddaddy calmed down soon enough, perhaps soothed to learn that he and his presumed son-in-law shared a passion for motor cars. He got over the row with Hans the dog and continued making arrangements for what he fully intended to be the coming-out party of all coming-out parties. Though it might well have been kept to a modest scale (since it was essentially a preamble to the wedding), Granddaddy spared no extravagance for his only daughter. He rented the Rose Garden of the Bellevue-Stratford Hotel and spent thousands redecorating it.

"What he probably had in mind," Mother later observed, "was that the Dukes of North Carolina and New York were not going to outshine the Biddles of Philadelphia. He might have only a puny million to stack against their multimillions, but in those contests where he had a fair chance he was not going to be outdone. He insisted on an invitation list that finally included everybody who had once nodded to him on the street." According to Mother, Granddaddy "had only one philosophy: people, people, and more people. He liked them individually, in small groups, and in the mass."

Though such affairs usually featured the young lady of honor attended by droves of friends, Mother found herself surrounded by girls she didn't know. Her life before Miss Walker's School had been centered around the boxing ring in the stable, so while most of the people her parents knew had girls around her age, they were decidedly not her type—"dainty creatures who would have fainted at the sight of a bloody nose," as she put it. Nonetheless, at the height of the festivities, Anthony J. Biddle climbed up on a table, called for order, and announced the engagement of his teenaged daughter to the handsome and refined Angier Buchanan Duke of Durham, North Carolina and New York City.

The revelation caused a great sensation, and marked the beginning of an exhausting period of pre-wedding parties given by Dukes, Drexels, Biddles, and assorted other branches of the two families in both Philadelphia and New York. To my mother, it seemed like a contest to see who could throw the most elaborate party. Meanwhile she struggled to keep the Duke connections straight, while Angier did the same with all the Drexels and Biddles. This included all the nicknames. My father's mother was Sarah Pearson Angier Duke. Her friends called her Sally, while she answered to an even more unceremonious name within the family. "Now let's not stand on ceremony," she told her future daughter-in-law. "Everybody calls me Ga-Ga and you might just as well get used to it."

Worn out by the unrelenting fanfare, Mother kept threatening to run away. Angier finally said that's just what she should do. He had a house in Palm Beach. He suggested she and her mother should get away for a couple of weeks while he stayed in Philadelphia and helped her father supervise the final details of the wedding. And so they did, traveling to Florida in Angier's private railroad car, which featured a combination cook-steward who looked after them from their own kitchen. Mother was so tired from all the entertaining and wedding preparations that she slept all the way from Philadelphia to Daytona Beach.

Removed from the Philadelphia scene and bathed in the Florida sunshine for two weeks, Mother returned to Philadelphia rejuvenated—only to find Granddaddy nearly out of his mind. The trouble had started when two of his best friends had mysteriously snubbed him at the Philadelphia Club. When he asked what he had done to offend them, one of them said, "We thought you were our friend, Tony." Granddaddy was devastated. "I *am* your friend," he said. "I am your devoted and forever friend." He really did talk that way.

As it turned out, the friends were upset because it seemed that everyone in town had received an invitation to the wedding, except them. "But you *have* been invited," Granddaddy insisted. "I took the invitations to the post office myself."

Granddaddy stormed down to the main post office and confronted the postmaster. "I've been checking on that, Mr. Biddle," he said, "and find that, for some reason, the only ones missing are those addressed to persons whose names begin with S, M, and B."

At this, Granddaddy was apoplectic. "Do you know what my name is?" he shrieked. "Do you know how many members of my family begin with B?!"

"W-w-we're checking, Mr. Biddle," the postmaster kept repeating.

Since it would be nearly impossible to determine which of the two thousand invitations hadn't reached their destinations, it was decided that the entire list would receive a second mailing. Inevitably, the story got into the papers. The Philadelphia *Evening Bulletin* reported, "General interest in the forthcoming Biddle-Duke wedding was heightened today by a peculiar mix-up in connection with the invitations to the ceremony and reception . . ."

The wedding finally came off on a chilly day in April of 1914. The *Bulletin* devoted a good percentage of that afternoon's front page to an enormous picture of the wedding party and a story that read, in part:

Miss Cordelia Biddle, slender and white and demure, stood, a girlish figure, at the chancel steps in Holy Trinity Episcopal Church this afternoon and gravely repeated the words that made her the bride of Angier Buchanan Duke, of New York. More than 1200 persons, many of them the socially elect of this city, New York, Baltimore and Washington, thronged the big church on Rittenhouse Square to see the beautiful sixteen-year-old daughter of A.J. Drexel Biddle become the wife of the young New Yorker, a member of one of the richest families of the South. . . .

Those who had been unable to enter the church, lacking cards of admission, stretched in a closely packed line from 19th and Walnut Streets, near to Locust. Across from 19th street, on the border of the verdant square, were banked other hundreds. The throng so choked traffic that even the trolleys were stopped.

Anticipating such a crowd and dissatisfied with the police chief's offer of a mere contingent of mounted police, Granddaddy had hired a dozen private detectives in plain clothes "to protect the wedding presents at the house and later mingle with the crowd to see that bomb throwers were discouraged," my mother later wrote. She learned of the extra detail only when her father whispered it to her mysteriously as they neared the church. Mother couldn't help but laugh—with their Irish faces, red ties, and black derbies the undercover men could be picked out from a block away. But she and Granddaddy were both glad for the mounted police when the car stopped and the crowd surged around them. As Mother, her parents, and my father's sister Mary Duke, the maid of honor, alighted to the canopy that ran from the curb to the front door of the church, the crowd followed. The canopy swayed, and Mother later recalled being not frightened so much as fascinated, watching the scene like a disinterested passerby. The police managed to calm the crowd and save the canopy. Reported one of the newspapers the next day: "The bride was not a bit perturbed. She

The wedding was the major social event of the year in Philadelphia, attended by more than 1,200 people.

My father, mother, and Aunt Mary Duke (my father's sister, who later married my mother's brother Tony).

smiled as she entered the church on her father's arm. Mr. Biddle seemed gratified by the demonstration. 'It's a great tribute,' he said."

After the ceremony, the cars carrying the wedding party crept through the crowds and made their way back to the house on Walnut Street. Mother's most enduring memory was the sight of a grinning John Lawless, the family coachman who had taken her to Miss Walker's School only three years earlier, surrounded by huge wooden tubs filled with champagne and ice. The reception line dragged on for hours.

California was the honeymoon destination, and to get there my father had his railroad car standing by in the Philadelphia rail yards. Off they went, but by the time they reached Chicago, Mother felt the urge to escape the private car and see something other than her new husband and the passing scenery. She loved being alone with him, she told him, but she was more than a little her father's daughter, and she needed to be around people. She asked if he wouldn't mind if they took the regular train the rest of the way to California. My father happily agreed. He'd taken the private car because he felt it was expected of him, he said later, but he was nearly as eager as she was to escape that island on rails.

Returning east weeks later, the newlyweds set up housekeeping in my father's house on Fifth Avenue in New York. Philadelphia and New York were rivals in those days. Mother had been secretly smitten by the big city a hundred miles to Philadelphia's north ever since she had gone up with some classmates from Miss Walker's to see one girl's father, a famous stage actor, perform in "Kismet." So the question of where Mr. and Mrs. Angier Duke would live was really no issue at all. Mother was a New Yorker now, and she relished it.

TWO

Roaming Youth

A T AGE SIXTEEN-AND-A-HALF, my Philadelphia mother was living the life of a New York society matron. The wife of a man who lived on a healthy allowance from the family trust, she made herself at home in his magnificent house at the corner of Fifth Avenue and Eighty-second Street, directly across the street from the Metropolitan Museum of Art. The mansion had five stories, two elevators (and, in 2006, a price tag of $45 million). Mother rode horses in Central Park and tried to play the role as she imagined it. The great dressmakers of the day brought her their latest designs, from which Mother ordered a vast wardrobe. Aside from the great art museum, the neighbors included John Philip Sousa and the Carusos, Enrico and Dorothy. Mrs. Caruso became my mother's good friend.

My parents' marriage turned out to be just the first of two Biddle-Duke mergers. Even before the wedding on Rittenhouse Square, it had been announced that my father's sister, Mary, would marry my mother's brother, Tony. How it happened was this: Mother had met Mary soon after she'd first started seeing Angier, and they had quickly become close friends. All Mother's bragging about her brother Tony piqued Mary's interest. When he sent Mother a picture of the St. Paul's School football team, Mary zeroed in on the dashing Tony, and said, "I have to meet that handsome boy"—though here again there was a big age difference, only in reverse. At twenty-eight, Mary was a full decade older than Tony. When Mother planned a visit to Tony up in New Hampshire, Mary insisted on tagging along. They watched Tony captain the school's varsity Halcyon crew to victory over the Shattuck Boat Club, after which his fellow crew members carried Tony on their shoulders, delivering him to the spot on the riverbank where Cordelia, Angier, and Mary were watching. Mary fell in love on the spot. Tony, it seems, had no objections.

Though it meant another of his children would be married to someone much older—the bride being the cradle robber in this case—Granddaddy gave the couple his hearty endorsement. In fact, based on my mother's account, it seems as if Granddaddy was the one in love with Mary. She was an attractive, serious woman, but it was music that won his heart. Mary had a beautiful voice, and she and Granddaddy would sit together at the organ, playing and singing duets. "Do you know this one, Mary?" he would ask, crooning a few notes of a song, which Mary would invariably finish without missing a beat. "Did you hear that, Cordelia?" he would ask Mother. So when my grandmother protested the marriage—"But he's still in preparatory school!"—Granddaddy cut her off, making it clear that school was a sorry reason for Tony not to marry this wonderful girl.

With the wedding of Mary and Tony planned for just a year after that of their siblings, Mother took on the job of coordinating the event. The venue would be my Uncle Buck Duke's country manor in Somerville, New Jersey. My mother's simple theory was that "the Durham crowd would be happy to get to New York and the New York crowd would rather die than traipse off to some unknown place called North Carolina." And so preparations were made for my aunt and uncle to be married on the 2,200-acre estate known as Duke's Farm, about forty miles west of the city.

According to Mother, the place was "trimmed and cultivated and landscaped to within an inch of its life," but that didn't stop her mother-in-law, a passionate horticulturist, from redesigning it for the wedding. Mother loved to tell the story of how my grandmother Ga-Ga hired a landscape contractor, walked him to the foot of the rose garden, and declared, "I want you to build me a mountain."

"A what?" said the contractor.

"A mountain," Ga-Ga repeated. "Right here."

As Mother later put it: "Not only was the mountain built, it was covered with huge fir and pine trees transported at fabulous cost from somewhere. Since the whole job had to be done in a few months' time, the operation was something like building the pyramids. Buck Duke showed his true character by never once flinching when his beloved grounds were filled with machines, trucks, and an army of workmen. It was stated officially that the mountain reared itself one hundred feet above the ground, and I can testify that Ga-Ga had planned it with astuteness. Seen from the garden, the hill gave the impression of being one of a series of peaks that perhaps formed part of the Appalachian range."

As my parents' wedding had made news in Philadelphia, so, too, did this second Biddle-Duke union. My mother was matron of honor and Buck Duke's two-and-a-half-year-old daughter, Doris, served as flower girl. By the time of the wedding in June of 1915, Mother was nearly halfway through her first pregnancy.

My brother Angier was born that November, almost during that year's Army-Navy football game at the Polo Grounds (Army 14, Navy 0). That close call was topped only by my arrival three years later, almost on a Ferris wheel. The story is that my parents went out for a day to Long Beach, Long Island, and were somewhere near the top of the circle when—reacting perhaps to either the altitude or the swinging motion—I decided to make my entrance a couple of weeks ahead of schedule. After Mother's close call with Angier at the football game, Granddaddy had given her hell for gallivanting about at such a critical time. So when nearly the same thing happened with me—in midair, no less—he would have been fit to be tied had he not been in France with the Marines at the time.

In any event, my parents got off the ride and found their way to a nearby hospital in time for me to make my debut in more appropriate surroundings. Being the first-born, my brother had been named after our father, who in turn had been given the maiden name of his mother, Sarah Pearson Angier. (I should say here that throughout his life my brother, like my father, was happy to be called "Angie." But while he was fine with the sound of it, my brother detested its spelling. He felt "Angie" in print had a female connotation. I'm not sure why it didn't have the same association when spoken. In any event, the only complication involving my name was one of redundancy. I was given the name of my grandfather and uncle, becoming the newest Tony in the family.

Mother was a doting sort who wanted her sons to be second to none. But her desire for well-turned-out boys, combined with her wide-eyed gullibility, led to some unusual child-rearing techniques. When Angier was two, he still didn't have much hair, at least not as much as the other toddlers Mother saw in the park. She saw an article in the *Police Gazette,* a sensational periodical of the time, about a bald child who suddenly sprouted a full head of hair after his mother sprinkled sugar on his head. Mother thought this was a fabulous idea. But why not grow even more hair by mixing sugar with honey? She covered Angier's head in the syrupy mixture, then put him in his carriage and parked it outside in the sun. When she looked out the window a while later, she couldn't believe it: Angier suddenly had a shock of dark hair! Mother ran to get her Brownie camera and snapped a picture, which became a highlight of her scrapbook collection. When she went outside to get him, though, Angier was bawling. It was then that Mother discovered that it wasn't hair on Angier's head, but flies and maybe a bee or two. When Angier sprouted a fine head of hair a year later Mother still attributed it to the treatment. She felt it would have worked a lot sooner if not for the flies.

Mother had a marvelous capacity to see life as amusement. She considered fear and worry useless emotions and taught us to confront obstacles head-on, either by using our wits to overcome them or by simply laughing at them and moving on. There was the time, for instance, when we traveled to Florida by rail and our train derailed somewhere in Georgia. After a terrifying few moments our car came to rest on its side. But there was Mother, picking me up and dragging Angier out of the wreckage, roaring with laughter and declaring, "What fun!"

Mother's fearlessness was an enduring theme of our childhood, perhaps not surprising given her own upbringing. Angier and I and some other kids were skating on a pond one winter when suddenly—crack!—the ice broke and my brother disappeared. Everyone scurried to safety, yelling and running around looking for rope, logs, anything. Out of nowhere came Mother. She ran along the cracking ice and

Angier as a baby, around 1916, with our parents and Duke grandparents,
Granddaddy Ben and Ga-Ga.

Mother and sons:
That's me as a baby
and Angier at three.

grabbed Angier, and when the ice broke beneath them, she simply walked to the shore, carrying Angier to safety with the water up to her neck. Then there was the time our wirehaired fox terrier, Zing, found himself in the jaws of our neighbor's huge Great Dane, a dog with a bad reputation who looked to me as though he would swallow Zing whole at any moment. Mother literally flew at the Great Dane, flailing at him with her fists, kicking him, yelling at him until he dropped Zing and fled. I can't count the number of times I saw her break up a dog fight just in time to save the loser.

THOUGH I DON'T REMEMBER THEM too well, we made annual summer trips to North Carolina to visit the Duke side of the family when I was very young. My mother would have gladly foregone these excursions. She felt the southern wing of the family had it in for northerners, including her. Only years later did she realize that gently taunting Yankees was just a southern amusement, and that rather than taking it personally, she should have joined the game and come back with something snappy herself. Mother also had problems with the food. The chicken was all right, but she couldn't bring herself to take a bite of Ga-Ga's specialty: broiled squirrel. (A few years later, in advance of the first trip south my brother and I would take alone, Mother wrote to Ga-Ga: "The boys go regularly these days to Central Park to play, and they love the squirrels there. We don't eat them up here—the squirrels, that is. Please don't get them into the habit. Thank you and love, Cordelia. P.S. If the children come down next Easter, please don't serve rabbit pie.")

These were the years when my grandparents and Uncle Buck were deeply involved in turning Trinity College into Duke University, and Mother later said she was fascinated to have a ringside seat during many of the developments. She said that back then, there was some local grumbling that the Dukes had stolen little Trinity College with the huge endowment they had promised were the name changed to Duke University. The fact was, though, that my grandfather Ben had been supporting Trinity so substantially, and for so long, that the college might not have survived without him. The endowment Buck set up in their father's memory was responsible for turning the little local college into the world-class university it eventually became. The endowment's stock in the Duke Power Company grew to be worth hundreds of millions of dollars.

Though he himself had had little affinity for secondary school, let alone higher education, Buck threw himself into the planning of the new Duke University. He made an exhaustive study of universities around the world, and took charge of overseeing the architectural design and building of the campus. Ga-Ga, meanwhile, studied plants and trees in order to come up with a landscape design that would make Duke one of the most beautiful campuses in the country.

Though she was famously frugal when it came to personal spending, Ga-Ga spared no expense in bringing in rare shrubs and exotic trees. She hired the best landscape architects and then rejected all their suggestions. She must have been right. The Sarah P. Duke Gardens became the crown jewel of the Duke campus, and the gardens remain famous among horticulturalists and landscape architects throughout the world.

Ga-Ga took Angier and me from New York to Durham for the official opening of the university in 1924, when I was six. We traveled by overnight train, with the three of us sharing a "drawing room." I hoped we could have supper in the dining car, which looked so elegant with its beautifully set tables, but Ga-Ga presented us with sandwiches in our little hotel room on rail. Before our arrival in Durham, she also presented each of us with a gift to mark the occasion, enticingly wrapped in shiny, dark blue paper. Angier received a silver hairbrush with his named engraved on it. I eagerly opened my gift, only to find a bottle labeled "Toilet Water." *Yech.* What could Ga-Ga have been thinking? I poured it into Angier's suitcase. Surprisingly, it didn't smell too bad. But it lasted for months.

Things didn't improve when we arrived in Durham and I climbed into the outfit Ga-Ga provided me for the ceremonies. It featured a stiff and horribly tight collar, an accoutrement to the equally tight Eton suit. "You look like a stuffed owl!" Angier said with a hoot. For some reason his suit fit much better. In the archives at Duke there is a picture of the two of us standing that day in front of Baldwin Auditorium. Angier looks smooth and cool, his hair slicked back—a nine-year-old dandy. I, on the other hand, appear deeply troubled, on the verge of tears. We sat between our grandparents at the ceremony, and I couldn't wait to get back to their house and change. We celebrated our liberation that night by going into the garden and catching a garter snake and a bunch of fireflies, which we presented to Grand-daddy Ben and Ga-Ga in an empty sarsaparilla bottle.

As a graduate himself of Duke's predecessor, Trinity College (and then a member of its board of trustees), my father might have gotten involved in helping develop the university. But he was very much the New Yorker now. And although he was on the board of directors of the tobacco company, my father showed little enthusiasm for getting involved in the family's various business interests. For that, it was Ben and Ga-Ga's son-in-law, my mother's brother Tony, who was seen at that time as a potential heir to the family's business interests. After the war, by which time he was all but retired from the tobacco business, Buck Duke had begun to show Uncle Tony the ropes of the Duke Power Company by taking him on a tour of the its dams and properties in the Carolinas. Knowing nothing about the business, all Tony could do was tag along as they climbed rugged terrain for days. Trying to make himself useful, he offered to take care of travel and lodging arrangements. At one place, he checked in, then presented Buck with his room key.

"What's the other key for?" Buck asked suspiciously.

"That's my key," Tony said. "I'm in the next room."

"You'll get nowhere in business wasting money like that," Buck scolded him, then turned to the desk clerk and said, "Give us that room with the double bed that Ben and I always slept in."

The Dukes installed Tony in a fine suite of offices in New York but he never did show the instincts for business the Dukes had hoped he'd possess. His one venture was taking over the Sonora Electric Phonograph Company, which made phonographs and radios, including some of the first portables. Tony persuaded his brother-in-law to join him, and so in his late thirties my father had the first real job of his life. He began going to the company's headquarters on Varick Street, though I have no idea what he did when he got there.

For mother, life as Angier Duke's wife certainly had its advantages, but things started to turn sour for her when it became evident that my father had a fierce and suffocating jealous streak. Seeing her speak to another man at a party, to cite one example, would make him furious. I must say here that I knew nothing about this until I was a grown man, and even then my mother was uncharacteristically circumspect on the question of her marriage to my father. Her otherwise trenchant and candid book, published in 1955 when I was nearly forty, contained not a word about their married life. It was, to me, a conspicuous and regrettable omission. (Though writing my own memoir has given me an appreciation of the complications involved in relating the details of one's failed marriages.)

My own incomplete memory of my parents' separation starts one day when I was four or five and Mother scooped up Angier and me and fled with our nanny to the Dorset Hotel. I didn't understand what was going on, only that my mother was very angry with my father about something and had to be talked into coming home. The final straw—which my mother related to me only after I hounded her with questions many years later—came one day when we were at the cottage in Sands Point, Long Island, that we were renting for the summer. Mother came home from shopping and received a call from the local telephone operator.

"Is this Cordelia?"

"Yes it is."

"Well, honey, you should watch your step. I don't know what you're up to but your husband pays me five dollars a week to monitor all your telephone calls."

"Oh, my Lord!" cried Mother.

"I've never heard anything that could shake him up, but I thought I should warn you anyway."

For all intents and purposes, that moment marked the end of my parents' marriage. Mother wouldn't allow Daddy back in the house when he came home later that day, and she quickly filed for divorce. She became so emphatic about her decision that when Daddy came to visit she wouldn't let him set foot in the house, because he would invariably use the opportunity to implore her to take him back. A losing battle, to be sure, though he fought it valiantly. Eventually, when he was due for a visit, she would leave the house in advance in order to avoid having to see him. We were left in the care of Miss Mack, our loving but temperamental and somewhat scatterbrained Irish housekeeper who had a fondness for Irish whiskey. On some occasions, when Mother had a place to go, she would allow Dad to spend a weekend with us, and we loved it. I remember one visit when Angier and I had great fun locking Dad out of the house, mimicking our mother. We ran up to our bedroom and hung out the window, laughing uproariously, to which Dad responded by getting the garden hose and gleefully squirting water right up into the room. "I'll fill the whole room with water if you don't let me in, and you'll drown!" he yelled, enjoying the scene as much as we were.

Writing now more than eighty years later, I find my bank of recollections of my father limited to little more than glimpses of him, impressions. Fortunately they are good ones. Most distinct is my memory of the stump where his right hand had been before his hunting accident years earlier. I was amazed at how agile he was with his left hand. Watching him shave was one of my favorite activities. He would keep his shaving soap in a little tube under his left arm while holding the razor in his hand. Then, somehow, he would flip the tube into the air, catch it, squeeze the soap onto his hand and then spread it on his face, which he would then shave, all with his left hand. He also made tennis interesting, especially the games when he was serving. With two balls tucked under his right arm, he would extricate one with his left hand while still holding the racquet, then quickly toss it high in the air and make a very tough over-spin serve. It was fascinating to watch and impossible to imitate. The last time I tried it I fell down and nearly broke my arm.

In the summer of 1924, after my parents' divorce became final, Mother commissioned a well-known artist named Harrington Mann to paint an enormous, life-sized portrait of my brother and me. Mr. Mann was a testy Englishman of about sixty, well-known for his portraits, particularly of children. For half a dozen sessions, three hours each time, I sat on a green chintz couch in the living room at Sands Point while Angier stood beside me, each of us in our portrait uniforms: short pants and shirts made of something called pongee, as I recall. It was a kind of linen I associated with dress-up events, and though I did not ever like to dress up, I minded this pongee suit less because I liked its name. I'd call my brother Pongee Angier.

"Be still," Mr. Mann would say, over and over. I hated it, as any five-year-old boy would. Having to waste a perfectly fine summer afternoon sitting on a couch without moving a muscle for three hours—well, it made me cranky. One would think Mr. Mann would be used to handling fidgety children, but he had little patience with me. "You are a nasty, wiggly little boy," he told me at one point, finally exasperated. I don't often look at the portrait (which hangs now in the apartment of Angier's widow, Robin), but when I do I am invariably reminded of the trauma that coincided with what should have been a moment of celebration—the end of those miserable sittings.

It was Labor Day weekend, and Dad had spent Sunday with us, taking us and some friends out for a day of fishing and swimming in Manhasset Bay. Mother was due back on Monday, and since we were scheduled for our last session with Harrington Mann in the morning, Dad had decided not to stay the night. Instead, he brought us back to the dock in Manhasset, and then he and his friends took the short, diagonal course across Long Island Sound to Greenwich, Connecticut.

The next afternoon, Mr. Mann was putting the final touches on the portrait when the phone rang. I heard Miss Mack answer it in the kitchen. She came in a few moments later, very upset but uncharacteristically unable to speak. She hovered behind Mr. Mann, who made "go away" gestures with his palette. Finally she burst into tears and blurted out: "Mr. Mann, it's terrible for me to tell you in front of the boys, but I just got a call from Connecticut. And, oh dear God, the boys' father has drowned!"

I will never forget that statement; it still echoes in my head. *The boys' father has drowned!*

The artist hastily tied up his brushes with an elastic band and stuffed his easel into his canvas bag. He left without a word and I never saw him again.

I was in a five-year-old's version of shock. Just the day before, Angier and I had had a great time with Daddy on the boat and at the house.

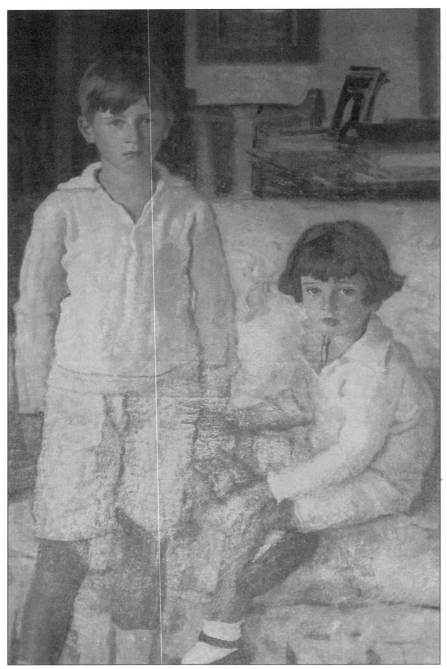

The portrait of Angier and me that Harrington Mann was finishing when we received the terrible news of our father's drowning.

I'd watched him shave, as always, and marveled at his tennis serve. Just five weeks earlier, for my fifth birthday, my father had come out to Sands Point and taken me, Angier, and all my friends out for a day of fishing on a boat staffed by a Filipino steward who made us sandwiches and gave us ice cream. And now he was gone, forever.

Mother came home later that day, and we all cried together. She had been angry and exasperated with him, but I'm sure she did love him in her way, and above all she was sad for Angier and me. The story in the next day's *New York Herald* said that our father, two other men, and three ladies had arrived at the town dock in Greenwich after visiting a yacht club in the area. As the group was boarding a dinghy to return to my father's moored fishing boat, he accidentally stepped on the gunwale of the dinghy, which capsized. In the darkness and confusion, as the others managed to get up on the dock, no one noticed at first that he was missing. When they did realize it, they began a frantic search but couldn't find him. His body was found seven hours later, caught under the floating raft that was secured to the dock. Uncle Tony told us that it seemed our dad had hit his head as he fell, possibly on an oarlock.

Years later, I found myself with Angier near Harrington Mann's portrait of us and asked him, "Do you remember that day?" It was a rhetorical question; *of course* he remembered that day. But Angier said no, he had no memory of it.

"Dammit, Brother," I said. "Don't you remember Miss Mack coming in crying and distraught and telling Harrington Mann, 'The boys' father has drowned'?"

Angier insisted he didn't remember. He must have buried the pain so deeply that he actually could not recall that day. It upset me for years because I needed to talk to him about it, about Daddy. There was nobody else. Mother never seemed to want to talk about him. But once, many years later, during World War II, when he and I got together in London before the Normandy invasion, Angier allowed as how he did barely recall the shock when he first knew Daddy was dead. It was a relief to me.

As we settled into life without a father, my mother would never say anything bad about him other than warning me, whenever I got angry, to be wary of having "your father's temper." The result of this was that I spent a good part of my early years thinking I had some sort of genetic condition with potentially dire consequences. If I got mad at somebody, I'd think: *Uh-oh. Better control yourself. That must have been why Mother threw Father out of the house—and why he was where he was when he drowned.* It wasn't until I became an adult that I realized my temper was no worse than the next guy's, that in fact I was a reasonably even-tempered person, and I could shed this shadow.

Aside from the emotional trauma inflicted by my father's drowning, there was an immediately apparent economic effect. Suddenly we were less well-off—*much* less well-off. It seemed that after their separation, our father had taken Mother out of his will. He provided a modest trust for Angier and me, along with a $250,000 gift to the soon-to-be-renamed Duke University. But most of his half of Grandfather Ben's fortune went to his sister, Mary. He died in the midst of trying to lure Mother back and didn't get the chance to include Angie and me as fully as he probably would have had he lived. We were far from destitute, of course. Grandfather Ben established a separate trust that would put us through boarding school and college. And it appreciated in value over time. But because of the circumstances of my father's untimely death, my personal assets have generally been overvalued by people who see my name and family connection and assume I'm a major heir to the great Duke fortune.

From the house in Manhattan we moved to a small rented home in the community of Cedarhurst, which was on the South Shore of Long Island, just east of what would eventually become Idlewild Field and later Kennedy Airport. Granddaddy Biddle sent his long-time "coachman," Pat Hoban, who had been with him since Mother was a baby, to look after us. We didn't have a car, but Pat one day somehow got his hands on a pony cart, pony included. We all piled in—Pat, my mother, Miss Mack, Angier, with me in the rear—and I proceeded to fall out, which nobody seemed to notice until they were a quarter-mile up the road.

After my father's death, Granddaddy Ben and Ga-Ga made sure we maintained ties to them and to our Carolina roots. On visits Angier and I made to Durham, Granddaddy would tell us the family's long and rich history, knowing, I'm sure, that we couldn't possibly keep all the names straight. Though Buck had made New York the corporate headquarters of American Tobacco, the factories, of course, were still in North Carolina.

Durham was full of cigarette manufacturing plants, and even today when I think of Durham I can almost smell the tobacco.

On one visit when I was eight and Angier eleven, we walked with Granddaddy Ben from his house, Four Acres, to the railroad station down the road, where we boarded his private rail car. Granddaddy signaled the engineer, who waved back with a smile, and we rolled out of town behind the big steam locomotive, its engine hissing and puffing, the train whistle blowing. We chugged along for ten or fifteen miles, arriving at a pond with a small cabin nearby. Grandfather Ben said that was where Jerry, the railroad crossing guard, lived. "When the freight train to Raleigh comes through," he explained, "Jerry pulls the guard rail down 'til it passes." It wasn't exactly a full-time job—the train came through but twice a day—and Jerry, a very old man who'd been born a slave, occupied himself by trapping squirrels, fishing in the pond, raising a few chickens, and growing a patch of corn and some peas and cauliflower out in back of the cabin. An old, white swaybacked horse grazed nearby. He was Jerry's transportation.

We disembarked from the train. Old Jerry produced some beat-up fishing rods and led us to the pond. We fished with reasonable success, catching some pike and pickerel. Then we walked back to Jerry's cabin and sat just outside the door on some broken-down old chairs, around a table made of an orange crate with some boards set on top. Jerry had cooked up the fish and some squirrel stew, and brewed a hot drink he said was "sassafras tea." Angier and I made faces and said something along the lines of "Yuck," but Granddaddy looked sternly at us, held up his hand, and told us to be grateful. The message was very clear: all this was Jerry's gift to us, it was what he had, and we should appreciate it and show respect.

On my next trip south, Grandfather Ben and Ga-Ga arranged for me to go out and spend a night or two in Jerry's cabin. Jerry rode his old swayback to Four Acres and I rode back with him. In the evening we fished for pickerel and skinned and ate a squirrel; I enjoyed it. Jerry told me stories about his father, who'd been a slave long before the War Between the States, and how he himself had worked on the old Duke farm that Washington Duke returned to after the war. It was still light out when I fell asleep on a cot next to the potbellied stove in the cabin, one very happy little boy. Early the next morning, a rooster crowed outside and some chickens hopped onto my cot and walked across my stomach. The sun was streaming in and somehow I felt a lot of warmth and comfort being there. I had a new friend in Jerry, and with it a lesson in respect.

Of course, you didn't have to go to Durham to see Dukes. My cousin Doris, Buck's only child, lived in a grand house on Fifth Avenue. Five years my senior, she looked after me a few times after my father died. One of my earliest memories of Doris was at a party for her twelfth birthday. She was tall, graceful, and pretty, and she was very nice to me. She made sure I had enough sarsaparilla, ice cream, and cake, which I used to decorate one of her mother's best brocaded dining room chairs, as Doris played the harp for her guests.

FROM AS EARLY AS I CAN REMEMBER, Mother's nickname for Angier was "Bunny" and for me it was "Mr. Bones." Though I know it was an extension of the nickname she'd always had for her older brother Tony—"Bones"—I can't say how it was derived. It certainly wasn't a comment on Uncle Tony's physique. He was a big, husky man. But whatever parallels Mother saw between Uncle Tony and me, it was her younger brother, Livingston, who became my first father figure after the death of my own dad. Uncle Livingston had graduated from Princeton and then served in the Army, losing an eye during World War I—not in combat but in the boxing ring. Now he was trying to break into the Manhattan real estate business, and sharing a house at 113 East Sixty-second Street with a couple of college friends. It was a spacious place, so he invited my Mother, Angier, and me to move in with him for a while. Angier and I shared a room on the top floor.

I went to the Beauvais School, a little school nearby headed by an elderly lady named Miss Campbell. I suspect it might have been built on a slight slant. One day in kindergarten I lost a battle to control my bladder, and watched in horror as a narrow stream made its way slowly, slowly between the desks toward the front of the room. Finally it reached the feet of the teacher, Miss Glover, who followed the stream back, eventually arriving at my desk. "Shame on you!" she shrieked. I ran out of the classroom, down three flights of stairs, and hid in a coat closet, inadvertently locking myself in. I starting knocking, hoping someone would come by.

Finally the door opened, and I saw in front of me a chubby boy named Walter McVeigh. The problem here is that Walter and I would go on to become great lifelong friends, which meant the story of our first encounter was to be told over and over and over again: *I rescued Tony Duke from a coat closet after he peed on the floor in first grade.*

I had another friend named Julian Gerard in my class, and he was like a junior entomologist. He was just obsessed with bugs. He had a big board filled with every kind of dead bug pinned to it—ants, moths, spiders. I loved going over to his house to see the bugs. Or so that's what I told Julian. Julian had an older sister. Betty was seventeen, and she was the most beautiful thing I had ever seen. But in order to see her I had to pretend it was the dead bugs that were the most beautiful things I'd ever seen. "Maybe I can come over this afternoon and see some more of your bugs," I'd tell Julian at school, praying that Betty would be there. One day I spent the entire visit with Betty, talking to her as she put on her makeup. Julian was furious. Then the doorbell rang, and it was a college boy named Ned, Betty's boyfriend. I hated him. My beautiful Betty jumped up, gave me a kiss, and then one to Ned, and left. I seethed, and never went back to look at Julian's dead bugs again.

Mother's romantic life was going better than mine. She began seeing a man named Thomas Markoe Robertson. He was of Scottish stock, Yale-educated (Class of '01), and one of New York's leading architects. His firm, Sloan and Robertson, designed the thirty-story Graybar Building adjacent to Grand Central Station, among others. It was the tallest building in New York City when it opened in 1927, and one of the first to use steel in its structural design. Another building, at 895 Park Avenue at Seventy-ninth Street, was considered a prototype of the art deco style. When Mother met him through acquaintances, Tom was involved with Grace Moore, a famous actress and opera star. I remember a lot of plotting going on in my mother's circle about how she was going to get him away from her. "I love Tom," Mother explained to my brother and me, "and I'm going to steal him away from her." And she did.

Among other things in Tom's favor was that, unlike our father, he respected Mother's independence and her love of a good party. But the age gap was even wider than it had been with Dad. Tom was more than twenty years older than Mother. Once again this didn't bother Granddaddy Biddle, who took an immediate liking to Tom after learning that he'd been a champion golfer and an infantry lieutenant in the Great War. "I want you to meet my dear friend, Captain T. Markoe Robertson," he would say to people, giving Tom another promotion with each introduction, until finally, Tom said to Mother, "I don't mind being a major general, but I wish you'd tell him to stop implying that I won the war."

To Angier and me, Tom seemed at first a bit stern and forbidding—nothing like our father. He was tall, had a black moustache, and carried a cane. He seemed so important and worldly that I couldn't imagine that he would understand or even care what went through the mind of a little kid. But when Mother told Tom that she wouldn't marry him without Angier's and my approval, he made a real effort to connect with us. Eventually he won us over by giving us a .22-caliber rifle and teaching us how to shoot, while delighting us with stories of trips he'd taken to Egypt and Africa.

Mother and Tom were married in 1925, when I was seven. They honeymooned in Paris, and then we moved into an apartment at 717 Madison Avenue, in a building owned by my new stepfather's best friend. Actually, we lived in two separate apartments—mother and Tom on the top floor and Angier and I, Miss Mack and Pat a floor below. It was a little complicated, but it only lasted a year, until it was decided that we should live in the country. (That is, in addition to the summer house Tom owned out in Southampton, which was the real country. It had been built by Tom's father, who was also an architect.)

At first we rented a house near the train station in Manhasset with a huge lawn. Tom put on a fireworks show for the Fourth of July, but toward the end a bunch of rockets and Roman candles fell over and caught fire, blasting off every which way. The only injury was to the lawn. There was burned grass all over. As it happened, the house was for sale and the real estate agent was due to come the following day with a client. Mother, ever resourceful, hopped on her bicycle, returning a little while later with two big cans of green paint hanging from the handlebars. She handed out brushes and we all got to work painting the lawn. The real estate agent brought his client the next day at sunset as scheduled. Mother gave them both gin martinis and they remarked on how extremely green the lawn was. Of course a day later the lawn was dead. "The man at the store must have sold me the wrong kind of paint," Mother remarked.

Mother and Tom went looking for a place to buy. They found a property called Guinea Hollow Farm, a big, old farmhouse in Old Westbury that dated to colonial times. The house sat on twenty-five acres and included a stable, a cottage, and a chicken coop. There an Italian man we called Johnny Peanuts lived and tended the land, the chickens, and a pair of cows. (His actual name was something like Pinnucio, or maybe Penezia—whatever, it was Johnny Peanuts to us.) Tom bought four horses for the stable, and Pat took care of them. Nearby were the Whitney and Morgan estates—palaces, really—surrounded by hundreds of acres of farmland.

PROHIBITION WAS IN EFFECT for most of my childhood—from when I was two until I turned fifteen—but I grew up with the impression that it was a kind of minor inconvenience, with guns. Bootleggers in our area were as common as milkmen, and most families had one. Ours was Harry Hurt, a big, ugly man who would drive up in an Oldsmobile sedan and come through the front door carrying a wooden box filled with bottles of gin, whiskey, and wine. Mother and Tom would always greet him warmly, and the three of them would have a drink together. I became aware that Harry was not quite the milkman when I saw something sticking out of his pocket one night and asked him what it was. He casually removed a big revolver and let me hold it. "It's a forty-five," he said.

Mother was fascinated by criminals—not that she considered Harry a criminal, exactly—and she was always peppering him with questions about the life of a bootlegger. When Harry took out the gun she asked him, quite matter-of-factly, how many men he had killed.

"Cordelia . . . " Tom interjected, but Harry just laughed. "Well, I never had to do that," he said. Mother was unconvinced. "I want to know if you killed anybody," she persisted. "And have you ever been shot at?" Tom finally cut her off. "Now, Cordelia," he said, "we don't want to talk about these things with Harry. We want to keep him as our friend"—meaning "our bootlegger." Tom paid him, put in his next order, then saw Harry to the door. We all put the liquor in a cabinet in a big closet between the living room and the dining room.

A day at the races with my
mother and stepfather,
Tom Robertson, at Belmont
Park in 1926

My mother, Tom, and our
beloved friend Pat Hoban
in Old Westbury.

At age eight, with one
of our dogs, a Scotty
named Sandy.

That liquor could be a perilous commodity also became clear when we made our annual trip for the summer out to Southampton. I would help Pat cover up boxes of liquor in the trunks of our two cars. We'd put rugs on top of the boxes, and on top of the rugs we'd put flowerpots with pansies in them. Every time Pat saw a policeman on the drive to Southampton or back to Old Westbury after Labor Day, he would get visibly nervous and slow down, steering with one hand and crossing himself in prayer with the other.

My Biddle grandparents were enthusiastic Prohibition drinkers. By the end of dinner when they visited, Granny was mumbling her words and Granddaddy would claim she had been to the dentist again. He gave her a lot of painkiller, he'd say, so don't ask her too many questions. When they were in New York they often took me to a speakeasy on the West Side called Tony's. Granddaddy would park a few doors down, then escort us to the door (which was of course unmarked), then down a few steps from the sidewalk. He would knock, a light would come through a small hole in the door, and then he'd say something in a low voice that would cause the door to open. Once inside, we followed him into a dimly lit room, where a beautiful girl named Anna would take our coats and give us all kisses. Tony himself would then greet us with great enthusiasm and show us to a table, where Granddaddy and Granny would order cocktails for themselves and a ginger ale for me. Dinner was always delicious, and interesting people would be seated all around us. Once, when my mother came, she pointed to a man at a nearby table and said he was a famous gangster.

Prohibition, of course, was the best thing that ever happened to the mob. Besides keeping the gin flowing, mobsters made life interesting (and often lucrative) for cops and newspapermen. One evening, when I was eleven, I drove with Pat into the village of Westbury, to Bauer's Drugstore, to pick up the newspapers and a prescription for my mother. As we turned off the Jericho Turnpike, I saw a big truck lying on its side on the road ahead. People with guns were running around shooting, and two police cars and several motorcycles were on the scene. Just then, the truck's gas tank exploded with a great boom and burst into flames. A cop Pat knew, Dick Hennessey, came over and told us there had been an attempted hijacking of a bootlegger's truck by a rival gang.

"The driver's dead," he said in an Irish brogue. "Two other fellas got shot, but I'm guessin' they'll make it."

Hennessey was a burly man in the dark blue uniform of the Nassau County Police Department. I was taken by how nonchalant he was about what had just taken place. As I eventually realized, Prohibition was like a little war, and this was just another battle. One day I was riding my pony on the Morgan estate when I discovered a dead body. Scared to death, I raced home and told Pat, who called Hennessey. He rumbled up on his motorcycle and took a look at the bullet in the corpse's head. "Bootlegger," he said. "Got himself shot."

The warfare seemed to follow us everywhere. When we arrived in Southampton one summer, the town was still talking about the big shootout that had taken place over the winter on the beach at Gardiners Bay. A large shipment of liquor had landed on the beach aboard lifeboats off a big ship. Bootleggers met the boats and stacked the crates, but when a big truck backed down the trail to pick up the shipment, a gang of hijackers started shooting from the woods and managed to make off with the booze in their own truck. But that wasn't the end of it. Federal agents, tipped off about the shipment, waited at the head of the trail near the main road and engaged the hijackers in another shootout. All the bootleggers were either killed or arrested, and who knows what happened to the liquor after the government agents hauled it away. Some wild parties in the neighborhood were said to ensue.

In 1932, Tom figured that Prohibition was on its way out and decided to bring our liquor out of the closet. He had a carpenter build a beautiful pinewood bar and surrounded it with paneling, shelving, and lighting. The open display of liquor was a striking change, but it was another three years before Prohibition officially ended. At that point, Tony, our speakeasy proprietor, moved to the East Side and became a legitimate restaurateur, with Anna as his legitimate hostess. Tony's would remain my favorite restaurant until it closed in the 1960s.

Mother and Tom spent a lot of time in Europe, mostly Paris, where Tom was getting an advanced degree at the Beaux Arts school. When they were in New York they stayed most weeknights in their apartment in the building at 895 Park Avenue that Tom had designed. I didn't stay with them in the city all too often, but when I did I invariably found myself among celebrities. I remember meeting Cole Porter, Gary Cooper, Mayor Jimmy Walker, and all sorts of Broadway stars and sports figures. Charlie Chaplin, meanwhile, was a regular at Southampton. He took a liking to me, and for three years—when I was nine, ten, and eleven—he made sure he was out in Southampton for my birthday so he could lead the party. He would tell jokes, direct us in dances, and then—in what became an annual tradition—take thirty of us kids down to the beach for a foot race. After taking the early lead, Charlie would slow down enough for some of us to catch up, then speed ahead to re-establish his lead. He would do this three or four times before a final sprint to the finish line and the inevitable Chaplin victory.

Mother and Tom later became great friends of the Duke and Duchess of Windsor (the former King Edward and the former Wallis Simpson). The duke was widely known as the black sheep of the royal family, having been forced to abdicate the throne after getting a divorce and then marrying a previously married woman. These rules of British royalty meant nothing to Americans, and my mother and Tom often had the duke and duchess as weekend guests in Old Westbury, where they often had lavish Sunday lunch parties.

During one of these parties, Cole Porter was playing the piano and the duke was leaning on it, chin in hand. Mother had a sudden impulse to goose the duke, whom polite Americans still referred to as King Edward. She goosed, he jumped, and the crowded room began to buzz. *Did you see what Cordelia just did? She goosed the king!* Mother took one look at his face and immediately wished she hadn't done it. "I couldn't think of how to apologize," she said later. "How do you apologize for something like that? So I went to Hammacher Schlemmer and bought him a gadget. He loved gadgets. He eventually forgave me, but even though we saw them many times after that, it was never the same." (Just as well, as far as I'm concerned: the Duke of Windsor led many to believe he was not entirely unsympathetic to the Nazis. There's a picture I still find disturbing: a smiling duke and duchess—my parents' friends—visiting Adolf Hitler in Germany in 1937.)

Then there was the time, during the height of the gangster wars, that Mother dragged Tom to the city penitentiary so she could meet Legs Diamond. Diamond was one of the first celebrity gangsters, perhaps best known for his uncanny ability to avoid getting killed. He was said to have survived seventeen attempts to knock him off, prompting his main rival, Dutch Schultz, to ask, "Ain't there nobody what can shoot this guy so he don't bounce back?!"

On this particular day in 1930, Legs had just survived the latest assassination attempt and was in the hospital section of the city jail on Welfare Island, the spit of land below the Fifty-ninth Street Bridge that's since been renamed Roosevelt Island. According to the *Daily News,* the encounter between "the best of New York's best sets and the worst of New York's worst sets" came about after "Cordelia had a sudden craving to look at some prisoners." She showed up at the penitentiary, Tom in tow, and went to the warden's office. There she asked to see Legs Diamond. The warden sent word up to Legs, who sent word down that it was okay by him. Mother and Tom were marched past a file of police officers to Diamond's bedside. He still had four bullets in him.

"How do you feel, Mr. Diamond?" Mother asked.

"Pretty good, kid," said Legs, then winced.

"Oh, it pained you then, didn't it."

"Well, those were no love taps those guys gave me," Legs assured her.

"I do hope you get better soon," Mother said. After a little more chitchat, Mother bid farewell. "Goodbye, Legs, and lots of luck," she said.

"Thanks, kid," Diamond said, "and come again."

Mother turned to Tom as they walked out. "Really, he's such a nice little fellow," she said. Seeing Tom's skepticism, she added, "What I mean is, he's such an intelligent sort of person, isn't he?"

ON THEIR HONEYMOON IN PARIS, Mother and Tom had bought a Voisin, a fancy French town car that was the equivalent of a Packard or a Cadillac, and had it shipped home. The car was designed to be driven by a chauffeur, with the driver's seat separate from the passenger cabin and open to the elements (aside from a pair of leather flaps that could be put up in severe weather). This wasn't the ideal design if the driver happened to be someone who might think about drinking to keep warm. And Pat didn't need a reason to think about drinking. In fact, he didn't think about it at all. It was like breathing.

The Daily News *had great fun with Mother's impromptu visit with Legs Diamond*

A BIDDLE TO YOU— JUST 'KID' TO LEGS

And Society Queen Thinks Racketeer King Is 'Nice.'

Jack (Legs) Diamond, racketeer king, had a visit yesterday from a social queen in the person of none other than the former Cordelia Biddle of the Philadelphia Biddles. And what a chummy little visit it was.

Jack (Legs) Diamond

Cordelia, leader in the best of New York's best sets, was calling Diamond, leader in the worst of New York's worst sets, by his first name when she left him.

"Good-by, Jack, and lots of

(Continued on page 14)

Mrs. Cordelia Biddle Robertson

My mother, around 1930,

Pat had come to America as part of an Irish soccer team when he was nineteen. The team went to Philadelphia to play a local squad, which they thoroughly defeated. After the game, a man came down to the field and started talking to one of the players who had caught his eye. He was more powerful than his teammates, and the man thought he might make a fine boxer. "I need a coachman," the man asked the young Irishman. "How would you like to stay in America?" "Faith and begorra, I would!" he said.

That's how Pat Hoban came to be part of the Biddle, Robertson, and Duke families. My mother had been a baby when my grandfather hired him, and they developed what was to be a lifelong bond. Pat had such cherished memories of those years that when he told me stories about my mother when she was a child, he would invariably shed tears. So it was that when my mother left home and married my father, Pat went with her, stayed with her during her brief time as a divorcee, and came along as part of the package when Tom Robertson married her. When I was little, I was never quite sure where Pat fit into our family. All I knew was that I loved him. He was my friend, he was funny, and he was there for me, come what may.

Now that people had automobiles, Pat, the onetime coachman, was often referred to as a chauffeur, which he did not like. Nor was he fond of being known as a handyman. He didn't like anything people might think of calling him. He was just Pat. He was a member of the family. Mother took to telling people he was her uncle, or her best friend. *That* Pat liked.

Whatever he was, after we moved out to Long Island Pat married an Irish girl named Mary. They lived in a little cottage Tom built for them down the gravel driveway near the entrance to the property. One of Pat's jobs was driving Tom to and from the train station whenever he and my mother were staying out in Old Westbury during the week. He drove the Voisin but couldn't pronounce it. He always called it the *Vah-John*, and my stepfather would get so mad at him. Tom kept trying to get him to say it correctly—*Vwa-san*—but speaking with a French accent was practically a physical impossibility for Pat, whose extraordinary Irish brogue often made him impossible to understand even in English.

Of all the things Pat had trouble learning, not drinking when he was driving was far and away the hardest. I remember one time years later when my best friend, Tommy Phipps, saw Pat driving the wrong way on the Northern State Parkway. Tommy turned around and chased Pat to get him to pull off, which he did, probably saving his life. If it were up to my stepfather, he would have fired Pat on any number of occasions, but Mother wouldn't dream of it. Neither would Angier or I. Pat was part of the family, and we loved him. And after Angier went off to St. Paul's, Pat became my big brother of sorts. When I was eight he gave me a copy of *Paris Nights*, a quite graphic underground magazine, so that I would "know what ladies looked like under their clothes." It was his idea of basic training. (Not quite the introduction to sex that Angier got from our butler. He took Angier to a cathouse in the city.)

I WOULD FOLLOW ANGIER TO ST. PAUL'S when I got to be twelve, but until then I attended the Greenvale School, which was about nine miles from our house. I had a fourth grade teacher there named Miss Hurt, an Englishwoman whose name suited her. If you didn't get your spelling right, she'd get you up before the whole class. "I'll rap your knuckles!" she'd shout, and then proceed to do just what she said, with a ruler. I found it best to squeeze out a tear or two right off the bat rather than have her continue her knuckle-rapping until you really did cry. My teacher the next year, Miss Rice, was the antithesis of Miss Hurt. She was young and pretty and, unlike Miss Hurt, she seemed to actually like children.

On May 19, 1927, Miss Rice asked the class, "Would any of you children care to watch Lindbergh take off tomorrow morning?" Charles Lindbergh, who had been working as a mail pilot a year earlier, was going to attempt the first non-stop flight across the Atlantic, leaving from Roosevelt Field for Paris. My hand shot up immediately. Four of my classmates also said they wanted to go. "I'll pick you up in my station wagon, but it will be very early—five A.M.," Miss Rice said, "so be ready." We gave her directions to each of our homes, and the next morning, she drove around picking us up in the pre-dawn darkness. Only three of us were ready—Freddy Lewis, Marjorie LeBoutillier, and me.

We arrived at Roosevelt Field, where a crowd was already gathered outside one of the hangars. Miss Rice instructed us to cut through the crowd, crawling if we had to, until we got to the front. "When you see Lindy, sit down," she said. "Now scoot!" We headed off and got to within thirty feet of Lindbergh as he stood beside his little monoplane, Spirit of St. Louis, and chatted with reporters. He wore khaki pants, an army shirt, and brown boots. At one point he spotted us, smiled, and gave us a wave and a thumbs-up signal. Shortly before eight o'clock, he got in his plane. A mechanic spun the propeller, and Lindy began to move out onto the dirt runway for takeoff. Minutes later he gunned the engine, and the plane, loaded with 450 gallons of fuel, bounced down the muddy field. Gradually he became airborne, just barely clearing a tractor and then telephone wires at the edge of the field. Lindbergh wasn't to touch ground again for more than thirty-three hours and 3,500 miles. At Roosevelt Field, there were perhaps a thousand spectators. In Paris, there were 100,000. I still think about that day.

At Greenvale, I had a teacher and football coach named Doc Breen who dispensed lessons about life. "What's important to you guys?" he asked a group of us in the locker room one day, as we waited for the Great Neck football team to arrive for a game. We talked for a while, and then he said, "Your names, your possessions, your looks, your image to other people—these things are not important. What *is* important is how you feel about yourselves, and how you're going to feel about yourselves inside as you grow older." This philosophy hit me in the heart and has stuck with me to this day.

Perhaps Doc Breen's influence was heightened by my parents' frequent stays in New York or overseas. My Biddle grandparents sometimes came from Philadelphia to stay with me, and I spent many weekends at the homes of friends from school. But most often it was just Pat and Mary, Miss Mack, and Annie the cook. Each of them had a hand in my upbringing, but it was perhaps inevitable that what I learned best was how to be independent and self-sufficient.

I found it easier to learn from experience than from schoolbooks. I was slow, not in the euphemistic sense, but in the literal one. I knew I wasn't stupid. But it took me longer than the other kids to complete my assignments. I had no trouble reading, but I would have to go over what I'd read two or three times to really get it. I was always up late, finishing my work. In class, if a teacher was describing a situation, I would have to go over it in my head several times, analyzing it. In retrospect, if I was born with what we now would call a learning disability, fortunately I was also born with a certain amount of determination. It was my natural inclination to work hard enough to do what needed to be done.

There was, however, one occasion when no measure of determination could overcome the brick wall I found in front of me. In fifth grade I came home with an assignment to write a poem about nature. I wrestled with my inner poet for several nights, but just couldn't come up with anything. Miss Mack was used to me burning the midnight oil to finish my schoolwork, but she saw that in this case I was stuck, and getting increasingly desperate. Taking pity on me, she told me to go to sleep, and when I awoke she presented me with a rather sweet little poem. I rewrote it in my own hand, and turned it in, knowing I was committing some sort of crime against education but hoping the whole thing would pass quickly without notice.

A few days later, at the weekly assembly in the school gym, the headmaster, Mr. Jackson, announced, "Will the boy who starts his poem, 'Little ice ponds frozen fast, make a path for squirrels at last,' kindly stand up?" I was pretty sure that was mine, or Miss Mack's. Full of fear and shame, I managed to stand as the audience applauded and Miss Mack beamed from the balcony, tossing her head this way and that, smiling proudly to those around her. I managed a weak smile before sitting back down, and thankfully the day passed with punishment no more severe than some snide remarks from classmates who knew something was rotten in Denmark. I tried to forget the whole thing, but that was hard to do after the poem was printed in the school magazine. Miss Mack had it framed and put it on the wall over her bed. Miss Mack's pride was poignant, for it seemed not to be so much for her accomplishment as an anonymous poet, but for her triumph as a surrogate mother.

In my mother's absence, Miss Mack had a little fantasy life going. She would go into Mother's closet and borrow a certain pinkish chiffon dress, which she would wear for the evening. On special nights she would sit at Mother's dressing table and apply a variety of rouges and powders. Then she would start humming and tossing her head. She would make her way to the bar downstairs, which would lead her to being unusually cheerful at supper and positively lenient regarding homework, before completely disappearing. Mother called from New York one night, and after I gave her the day's rundown, she asked to speak to Miss Mack. I looked all around and called out for her, but Miss Mack was nowhere to be found. Even Pat was puzzled. He got on the phone and told Mother not to worry; she'd probably gone out for a breath of fresh air in the moonlight. Mother said goodnight, but I was a little concerned, and kept looking. Finally I went back into Miss Mack's room and, on a whim, opened the closet door. There she was, sitting on a chair, a dim light burning overhead. She was smoking a cigarette and drinking gin, happily tossing her head and humming her favorite Irish melody. I quietly closed the door and went to bed.

Of course nobody found more bliss in a bottle than my pal Pat. One day when I was twelve, and my parents were in Egypt for the spring, I woke up for school, had breakfast, and went outside to the car. It was not the fancy Voisin but an old Buick station wagon that Pat used to drive me to school, or to the bus stop, which was a couple of miles away on Route 25A. Usually I would hear the engine running from inside the house. But on this particular day the car was still in the garage up the hill. I went down to the cottage to look for Pat, but Mary said he wasn't there. "We had an awful fight last night," she said, with no elaboration necessary. I went back to our house and up into the attic, which is where Pat usually ended up after a night of drinking (and the fight with Mary that inevitably ensued). I found him there, snoring, still smelling of the night before. You could tell from the tenor of his snore whether it was worth trying to rouse him, and this time the snore was deep and rumbling.

What to do? Pat had prepared me for this moment, or so I believed. I went down to the garage, fully confident in all those lessons he'd given me on the dirt trails on our property. All I needed was a little height. I sat on my geography book, moved to the edge of the seat to reach the clutch and the footbrake, and backed the Buick out of the garage.

I didn't dare go on the main roads. Luckily, having ridden a horse throughout the countryside countless times, I had a good sense of how to get to school by going through the big pastures that made up most of the eighty-acre and hundred-acre properties that lay between our house and the Greenvale School. Twenty-five years later, the Long Island Expressway would be built right through all these properties, but in those days it was just endless farmland and pastures, one property running into the next. I crossed about half a dozen pastures, drove around the house owned by the Manice family, then went another four or five miles through the Garvin,

Whitney, Phipps, and Morgan estates. The famous old Meadow Brook Hounds club dominated the fox-hunting scene back then, and they had arrangements with many land owners to allow the hunters to track the foxes through their properties. This involved creating special post-and-rail fences over which the horsemen and horsewomen would leap as they followed their hounds. For a boy in a Buick, the fences were an impediment. I had to disassemble them, drive through, stop, then reassemble them. This added quite a bit of time to my commute to school. But I finally made it. I parked in a grove of maple and pine trees across from the school on Route 25A and arrived in my seat about forty minutes late, offering a story about car trouble, which was not entirely false. After school, I disappeared into the pine trees and returned home by the same route.

A little cocky with my success, I made a habit of driving myself to school whenever Pat was unavailable. After school one day, I went behind the bushes to get to the Buick and heard a voice say, "Duke—I gotcha!" I turned around to find one of my classmates beaming with self-satisfaction. The boy had become something of a nemesis. We were both headed for boarding schools the following year, and he lorded over me the fact that he had done better than I on the entrance exam.

"Please don't squeal, Buddy, please," I said, explaining the situation with Pat. "It would be terrible for Pat and not so good for me."

Buddy said he wouldn't tell—if I drove him home. He lived in Huntington, a good ten or twelve miles in the opposite direction of my house, and there was no way I could avoid Route 25A, the main road.

"I'll get caught," I pleaded.

"I don't give a hoot in hell," Buddy said. "If you don't want me to tell, you'd better drive me home."

Weighing my options, I knew this guy wasn't bluffing and had to chance it. I drove east, through Old Brookville, Upper Brookville, Muttontown, Laurel Hollow, and Cold Spring Harbor, and finally made it all the way into the Huntington hills. I dropped Buddy off—the son of an extremely wealthy banker, he lived on a big piece of property—then turned around to go home. A bit heady at having driven all the way to Huntington without getting caught, and a bit concerned that it was beginning to get dark, I decided to drive home on the main road. I was nearly all the way home when I noticed a motorcycle policeman trailing me. I didn't panic; it didn't seem that he was onto me. But when I made a left turn at the Bull's Head light he turned on his siren. I pulled over. Now I was scared.

The cop dismounted and walked over. It was Dick Hennessey. He looked in at me, this puny eleven-year-old sitting at the wheel on his geography book. He recognized me right away.

"You're Patty's boy, aren't you?" he said.

"Yes, sir," I said.

"Is your mother home?"

"No, sir," I said.

"And your stepfather?"

"No, sir. They're in Europe."

"Well, we're going to see Patty about this. Follow me." He returned to his motorcycle, flipped on his siren and flashing lights and led the way. Cars pulled off the road to let us by, and suddenly I felt like Jimmy Walker or President Hoover, some bigwig getting a police escort. The excitement made me forget about the trouble I was in for the moment. I wished someone I knew would see me, especially one of the girls from school—Maggie or Elise or Marjorie. But in a few minutes we arrived home and I was gripped once again by fear—not so much for me, but for Pat. This time, even my mother might have to fire him.

Officer Hennessey knocked on the door of Pat's cottage. Mary came out and told him to check the attic. We went up, and there was Pat, snoring in bed under a sheet with his feet sticking out. Hennessey took his club out and whacked Pat on the bottoms of his feet. Pat jumped out of bed and Hennessey launched into a ferocious tirade, laced with every curse word I'd ever heard and some I hadn't, which caused Pat to break down and weep. All he could say was, "Don't be tellin' the bize mither! Please, Dick, I beg of ya."

"Does Mrs. Robertson know what's happening around here?" Hennessey demanded. "Does she know you let the boy drive that Buick out on the main road?" Pat offered no defense; he just kept pleading for mercy and silence. "In the name of Jesus and Mary and all the saints in heaven, I pray that you'll not be tellin' the bize mither." He turned to me. "Oh, me laddie buck," he said. "Don't be tellin' yer mither." We went down to the kitchen, where Annie the cook made tea and we all sat around the table as Hennessey tried to figure out what to do. "What do you have to say, laddie buck?" he asked me.

"I won't tell Mither either," I said.

"I'd be banished forever," Pat said.

"It would be terrible if my stepfather knew," I agreed.

Finally, Hennessey said he wouldn't tell my parents if Pat and I promised never to let this happen again. And it didn't. I never told my mither—not until the moment thirty-five years later when we stood over Pat's grave in Southampton three days after his last drink and his last breath. When we got back to my mother's house, we drank to him, God rest his soul. Pat was indeed one of my best friends in life, and he will forever have a place in my heart.

LIVING AMONG MORGANS, WHITNEYS, AND GRACES was an education in itself. I went to school with Michael Grace, whose family had a huge place, a kind of castle on a hill with a gatekeeper, an indoor tennis court, and a swimming pool. But their staff of ten or fifteen paled in comparison to the forty or fifty people living on the Morgan estate. There were grooms and stable boys and so many servants that they had ranks: first butler, second butler, third butler. We were not in that league, of course, but we were comfortably well off, especially compared with most Americans. Right on our property, for instance, was Johnny Peanuts, our Italian gardener, who had three kids and lived very poorly in an ancient little house that lacked indoor plumbing. One day my stepfather gave me an envelope with Johnny's pay for the week and asked me to take it over to him. On the way I opened it and was disappointed to find just four dollars. I asked Tom why he paid Johnny so little. He explained that he was providing Johnny with a house and his share of crops, milk, and whatever else our farm produced. Still, I lobbied Tom to give Johnny a raise, which he eventually did. It is one of my earliest memories of perceiving the disparity in the way people lived.

The Great Depression, of course, was the true awakening. The market crashed in 1929, when I was eleven, and I felt the impact immediately. We were fine, but I was surrounded by people who weren't. I had a friend named Freddy whose father was a stockbroker who went home on Black

Friday and blew his brains out. Freddy never came back to school, and he wasn't the only one. Several friends and classmates could no longer afford to attend Greenvale and quietly transferred to the public schools. I was well aware, however, that millions of people suffered fates much worse.

Over the next couple of years, I would sometimes go into the city with my stepfather and notice breadlines on every corner, streams of men waiting on line to pick up the apples the state was providing for them to sell, as their only means of support. Thousands of others shined shoes, while old men who had fought in the Civil War were dying in neglect and misery. Many World War I veterans, meanwhile, traveled the country on freight trains looking for work. I saw signs of catastrophe everywhere from New York to the family homestead in North Carolina. One day my stepfather took me down to the Bowery and we saw all the little "Hoovervilles," clots of people who were homeless. I knew our family was cushioned by its resources, but I couldn't quite come to terms with the disparity. In fact, it worried the hell out of me.

My Grandfather Ben, who was in poor health in much of my memory, was a gentle soul and an understated man, but my grandmother Ga-Ga was anything but. My mother told of the time a building was being erected across the street from my grandparents' house in New York, and the noise caused by the riveters was driving her crazy. She called her real estate agent and instructed him to buy the property. But Mrs. Duke, the man said, it'll cost you a million dollars. "I don't care what it costs," Ga-Ga replied. "Buy it, and get that hideous racket stopped immediately."

Granddaddy Ben died in that house. The funeral service was held in New York. (It was the first time I ever wore long pants.) Then his body was sent to Duke University for his burial alongside his father and his brother Buck, who had died four years earlier. Ga-Ga, who had been married to him for fifty-one years, wrote in her diary that day: "An awful sad day. My best friend and loved one is gone."

In the fall of 1928, a big crowd of family and friends gathered in Durham to celebrate the opening of Duke's new football stadium. On the train down, Ga-Ga sat across from my uncle Livingston Biddle and said, "Tomorrow's a great day for me, Livingston. I very much want everything to go well in my new stadium." That the stadium had been financed by a bond issue sold to alumni and the public in North Carolina was a minor detail that failed to diminish Ga-Ga's proprietary feeling about everything Duke.

It was also a great day for me. Knowing that I had been the quarterback on the Greenvale School's team, my grandparents arranged for me to be the Duke team's mascot for the day. They gave me a full uniform with the leather helmet. They had me run out onto the field with the Blue Devils and lead them in pre-game calisthenics. I was in my glory. The only problem was that it quickly became obvious that the Duke team was hopelessly out of its league in its contest against the University of Pittsburgh, which had four all-Americans, and which would go on to an undefeated season before losing to Southern California in the Rose Bowl. In the stands, my grandparents watched the shellacking with horror. "That awful man!" Ga-Ga would shout as Pitt's all-American halfback, Toby Uansa, cut through Duke's defense time and again. "Why don't our boys stop him?!"

"They're doing their best," Uncle Liv told her, "but I'm afraid they're outclassed."

"*Our* boys outclassed!" cried Ga-Ga. "I've built them this beautiful stadium, and now they do this to me!"

"You've bought them the stadium," Livingston replied, "and now you have to buy them a team."

"Can I do that?" Ga-Ga asked, suddenly brightening.

I watched from the Blue Devils' bench, and when we came into the locker room at halftime, well on the way to a 52–7 slaughter, the players were bloody and beaten, cursing with words I'd never heard.

"Whadya think of football now, sonny?" one of them asked.

"Well, I think it's keen!" I said, which set the entire team to booing, hissing, groaning, and introducing me to more new words.

THREE

A Real Education

M Y GRANDFATHER BIDDLE liked to take long walks carrying in each hand a suitcase filled with bricks, to build his muscles. I would sometimes join him, without the suitcases of bricks, however. One time he told me to avoid, at all costs, stepping on the cracks in the sidewalk. "If you step on a crack you might be one of those people who disappears," he warned. I looked at him quizzically. "That's right," he continued, hopping over a crack. "There are some people who step on the cracks and a black hole appears and down they go and nobody ever sees them again. I don't want that to happen to you." And to this day, I try not to step on the cracks. To do so, I feel, would be taking an unnecessary risk.

That was the kind of effect Granddaddy had on me. After he taught me to box, I graduated to fencing, which he himself had learned from a famous French swordsman. "Parry! Thrust!" he would yell as we danced around the floor. "Parry! Thrust!"

One summer day in our house in Southampton, I was upstairs changing my clothes when I felt the whole house shaking. I heard all kinds of grunts and groans coming from the porch, and when I got there, I found Granddad in fierce broad-sword battle with our neighbor, William von Roth. Mother had recently made Mr. von Roth's acquaintance, which meant that he was informed before too long of her father's prowess in the various personal-defense arts, including all forms of sword fighting. Mr. von Roth had fought in the German army during World War I and then married an American lady with a large house in Southampton. He had been a dueling champion in Europe, and apparently Cordelia's bragging got him so agitated that he all but demanded a duel. "Ve shall zee just how goot he is," said Mr. von Roth about my grandfather.

Mr. von Roth was a bit younger than Granddaddy, who was taken by surprise not only by the German's skill, but by his fury—von Roth was clearly out to destroy him. When I got there, they were chasing each other around the porch and blood was on the floor. Granddaddy's ear was cut and von Roth looked like a sweaty, enraged bull. Finally Mother interceded. "You two fellows are overdoing it," she said, then turned to Mr. von Roth. "I didn't invite you over here to kill my father!"

"He can't kill me!" Granddaddy shouted indignantly. "I'll kill him first!"

Somehow, perhaps inevitably, Granddaddy and von Roth went on to become friends.

When I was accepted to attend St. Paul's school, Granddaddy drove up from Philadelphia, apparently to get me ready. He came in a green Packard touring car, arriving in a fierce rainstorm with the top down. "Granddaddy, you ought to put the top up," I said, a futile thing to say because, generally speaking, Granddaddy was not a man open to suggestions. "No, no," he said, "I like it this way." Okay, I said, then offered the opinion that I thought he was nuts. "Nuts?" he said. "We're going to put the gloves on, and then we'll see who's nuts." He opened the door of the Packard and gallons of water poured out.

We went inside, and Granddaddy took two pairs of boxing gloves from his suitcase. In the living room he marked off an imaginary ring, warning me, "Don't step out of the ring. We'll do two-minute rounds." I did all right because I was fast, and I had learned by now how to duck under his left hand and whack him in his stomach. Staying away from him was key: When he hit me, he hit me pretty hard.

After six rounds, Granddaddy said, "Now that you're going up to St. Paul's, I'm going to teach you how to protect yourself. I'm going to teach you ten ways to kill a man with your bare hands."

I thought: What's with St. Paul's that I have to know ten ways to kill a man with my bare hands? I cannot now recite all ten ways, but

I do remember they involved a lot of choking, hitting in the temple, and breaking of particular bones. "Do you know the thinnest bone in a man's body?" Granddaddy asked. I had no idea. He pointed to his instep and said, "It's the bone right here. If you're confronted by somebody who's going to hurt you, you usually have between half a second and two seconds to figure out how you're going to defend yourself. This is the easiest bone to break, and if you stomp him there it'll put the man at a disadvantage, but you've got to have a pair of good leather shoes on—sneakers won't do. He will lean over in pain. Then you can grab him by his hair—or by the ears if he's bald—and pull his head down on your left knee and break his nose. Now, if you can't do that, you can put your thumbs through his eyeballs . . ." At each step he demonstrated the moves and had me simulate them— gently—on him. ". . . Or you clap the man's ears so hard with your hands cupped that you break his eardrums. I used this one in Shanghai once. And if you hit a man with the back of your hand at this part of the nose here, hit him hard, it drives his bones up into his brain."

And so off I went to boarding school, ready to defend myself. From what, I couldn't imagine.

MOTHER AND I TOOK THE TRAIN up to New Hampshire, and a great big Pierce Arrow taxicab took us from the Concord rail station to the school. We drove up in front of the rectory where the headmaster, Dr. Samuel Smith Drury, lived with his wife. It was a lovely New England house in the center of the campus. Mother rang the bell. When Dr. Drury answered she practically jumped into his arms and gave him a big kiss.

"Why, Cordelia, I haven't seen you in such a long time!" he said.

We went inside. Mother and Dr. Drury had a fine time talking about her brothers, my Uncle Tony and Uncle Livingston, who had gone to the school a couple of decades earlier. "You ought to go over to the library this afternoon and you'll find great big scrapbooks about each class," Dr. Drury told me. "If you look in the class of 1914 book you'll find a lot of wonderful information about your Uncle Tony—president of his class, captain of the football team, captain of crew." Uncle Livingston had followed Tony there, and now my brother Angier was at the school. He was a brilliant and serious fellow, much more of a scholar than I was. Clearly I had a lot of family to live up to.

After Mother left, I felt a bit sad and lost—even though I was well-accustomed to being away from her, and even though my brother was up there. The first thing I did was take a walk through the woods and around the school pond. About halfway around, another boy came from the opposite direction and stopped to say hello. "My n-n-name is Lllllarrry . . ." he said. I had never encountered a stutterer before. ". . . D-d-d-rake." Larry Drake became my first friend at St. Paul's, and my best friend. After that first encounter, he rarely stuttered with me. (He later became a distinguished architect.)

Like almost all private prep schools at that time, St. Paul's was exclusive, in the truest sense of the word. There were few Jewish students, no African-Americans, and of course no girls. It was a church-oriented school, with Episcopalians like me a solid majority. We started every day in chapel, all four hundred students and masters gathering for a hymn, a psalm, and a few prayers. I don't remember that many of my schoolmates considered the services a chore; most of us liked the ritual. Once a week we had Sunday Evensong, which my good friend Paul Moore later described beautifully in his own autobiography:

"Sitting in a long, wood-paneled chapel with the afternoon sun throwing colored patterns through the stained glass after an afternoon of exercise, a shower, and some tea and cake at a master's house, I felt warm inside. The choir proceeded in, and the rector strode down the long chancel in his flowing robes, looking very much like God. We would begin with a gentle hymn, such as 'Now the day is over, Night is drawing nigh, Shadows of the evening, Steal across the sky.' Then the rector in his melodious bass voice would commence the Evening Office: 'Let my prayer be set forth in thy sight as the incense, and let the lifting up of my hands be an evening sacrifice.' It was a time when one felt at ease, at peace with the world. It was a time for beautiful thoughts and fantasies. It was a time to think of home, of memories, of hopes for the future. It was a time to think about the school and how much it meant to us."

As was the case in my family and many others, going to SPS was a rite of passage for Paul. He and his older brother Bill, who was captain of the hockey team when we arrived, followed their father to St. Paul's. Mr. Moore the elder was a generous donor to the school. At their home in New Jersey he had a "St. Paul's garden" outside his library, with the school's shield on its iron gate and its symbol, a pelican, over the fountain. (The pelican mother plucking her own breast to supply blood for her young is a classic Christian symbol).

St. Paul's, like the other preparatory schools scattered across New England, was modeled on the so-called "public schools" of England that were regarded as training grounds for future leaders. Indeed, American prep schools of the first half of the twentieth century produced a large number of the nation's political leaders, from Franklin D. Roosevelt to John F. Kennedy, as well as many of the pillars of Wall Street.

St. Paul's followed the British system of designating each year a "form." A seventh-grader would be in the first form; a senior would be in the sixth. The social order of the school ran on a system of clubs that competed against one another academically, athletically, and in more subtle ways. There were the Delphians, the Isthmians, and the Old Hundreds. My uncle and my brother were Delphians; therefore so was I. In my time, our group was known as the rougher element at school— "dirty Delphs," they called us—but of course everything is relative. This was still an exclusive boarding school.

Attending a school like St. Paul's led to lifelong friendships, such as the ones I had with Paul Moore, Larry Drake, and Bobby Fowler; others were ephemeral but interesting nonetheless. The summer after my fifth-form year at St. Paul's, I was in Southampton when I got a call from Jim McCall, a classmate who lived in Massachusetts, who said he was going to sail down from Cape Cod with a couple of friends. One was a friend of ours named Tom Murray, who lived in Southampton, and the other was a friend of Jim's. Tom would be getting off the boat at Southampton, Jim said, and he and his friend would need another hand for the sail back up to Cape Cod. He asked if I wanted to go, and I agreed.

I boarded the boat, greeted Jim with a hearty handshake and met his friend, a pleasant fellow named Jack. We departed Southampton from

Peconic Bay, heading east for the open sea past Montauk. We sailed northeast, eventually passing Martha's Vineyard to starboard, and headed toward Cape Cod, where we'd dock at Jack's family's summer house. Jack was eighteen, a year older than Jim and me. A freshly minted alumnus of Choate who was headed up to Harvard in the fall, he was a lot of fun and a hell of a sailor. When we reached his family's homestead at Hyannisport he invited Jim and me to stay for dinner.

Jack's father turned out to be a famous and wealthy man: Joseph P. Kennedy. A year earlier, President Roosevelt had appointed him the first chairman of the Securities and Exchange Commission (and would, three years later, send him to London to be our ambassador to the Court of St. James at a crucial moment in history) As I later learned, Jack's father had made a fortune in banking, shipbuilding, investment banking, and movie distribution, and with uncanny pre-science he had pulled out of the stock market in 1928, a year before the crash. That same year he bought the fourteen-room clapboard house on a 4.7-acre oceanfront property. Hyannisport was a lovely part of the world, not unlike Southampton in those days, scented by saltwater, wild roses, honey locust, quahogs, and pine. Jack was eleven when his father bought the summer house, and he and his brothers and sisters had spent their summers there ever since, play-ing on the beach and sailing, and walking over to Turner's on Route 28 for ice cream.

We sat down to dinner around a large table, with Mr. Kennedy presiding. "I want you all to tell me what you did today and whether any of it made any sense," he announced. There was clearly a peck-ing order. With Jack's older brother, Joe Jr., off at Harvard, Jack went first. "Well, I figured from the last trip that I ought to study up on my coastal piloting," he told his father. "I bought some charts and I fig-ure I'm a better navigator than I was yesterday. Next time we sail we'll be more efficient."

Around the table he went—Kick, Eunice, Pat, then little Bobby. The ten-year-old boasted about doing well in a basketball game. Finally, Mr. Kennedy turned to me. "And what about you, young man?" he asked. "Tell us what you did today." Caught off guard, I confessed that I'd done nothing of note. I didn't think enjoying a day at sea counted as much of an accomplishment. "That's too bad," Mr. Kennedy said. "You missed a day."

I saw Jack Kennedy again three years later when I went up to Harvard to visit friends of mine and we went to a swim meet. Kennedy was on the team, and we all went out to dinner afterward. I didn't see him again until after the war. By then he was a congressman, just beginning the quest to which his father assigned him after the wartime death of his older brother.

I became President myself—of the St. Paul's student body—when I reached my sixth-form year. I came to the job somewhat accidentally when a boy I'll refrain from naming (for reasons that will become clear) persuaded me to run. A fellow Delphian, he was motivated less by a belief in me than by his disregard for another candidate, a boy who was one of the best scholars in our class but whom my backer judged an intellectual snob at that time. He hoped enough dirty Delphs would vote for me to block him.

Election Day at St. Paul's was a big tradition. Each spring, on the first Saturday of June, the entire fifth-form class would gather at the rectory to elect the next year's officers. I was only moderately interested in the job and felt no compulsion to campaign. But the boy who nominated me was a diligent promoter, and his electioneering got me elected. My opponent was elected vice president (and his father later became the secretary of state in the last year of the Eisenhower administration).

Now that I had the job, I took my responsibilities seriously. I virtually memorized the school's constitution and oversaw the weekly student council meetings with a fair hand and an open mind about issues of concern. There were perks, of course. I got to sit in a special pew in chapel, from which I could look out at my classmates and the entire student body. But the part of the job I didn't like, in fact detested, was the requirement to report serious transgressions of school rules. As it happened, it was my election patron himself who caused me heartache over this obligation. He was a fine person and excellent athlete, but had a terrible time obeying all the school rules. I tried to keep it between us at first, but warned him that if he didn't straighten up and I didn't report him, I would be in violation of school rules myself. Eventually he left St. Paul's of his own volition, saving both of us the pain of a formal proceeding, but only after the episode caused me many sleepless nights. The experience was so unsettling that after I graduated and was at college, I wrote to Dr. Drury, expressing my strong belief that it was both unfair and unwise to place such a burden on boys in that position. (Though my friend went on to graduate from another school, years later our class voted to invite him to join our St. Paul's alumni association, which he did.)

The seriousness with which St. Paul's took itself was reflected in the demeanor of the man who presided over it. Dr. Drury was the most dignified, austere, and forbidding of all school headmasters. Which is why I thoroughly enjoyed my mother's annual visits. Everyone was in awe of the great man and always on their best behavior in his presence, but it was Mother alone who seemed to be able to humanize him. Dr. Drury would host teas for groups of students and their parents, and Mother would break up these invariably stiff gatherings by doing something outrageous. On one occasion, she advanced on Dr. Drury, tweaked him by his prominent nose, and asked, "How is my beautiful, wonderful lover boy these days?" The bystanders were at first shocked and appalled, and a hush even more stifling than the one already present took over the room. Then it was as if something magical happened. Dr. Drury brightened, and even his wife seemed to enjoy the moment. The atmosphere of the whole room changed.

BY THE TIME I WAS IN MY LAST YEAR at St. Paul's, I had an awareness of the world outside school and family that had been evolving for some time. If I had to pick one moment when I began to grasp how world events were unfolding, it would be a night during the summer of 1932. I was fourteen, and Mother and Tom were taking Angier and me to Europe for the first time, aboard a German liner named Europa that had broken the trans-Atlantic speed record. It was the height of the Depression, and I was well aware what a privilege it was to be crossing the Atlantic on a luxurious ship bound for England. For Tom it was something of a busman's holiday; his main interest was inspecting ancient and medieval churches and buildings, always with his analytical architect's eye. We traveled through Britain in a Daimler touring car before taking a ferry to France, where we viewed several more cathedrals and the great museums. A lot of it was tiresome to me, but Angier was more intellectually prepared for a trip like this, and he enjoyed himself more than I did.

From Paris we went to Berlin and then Munich. It was there that Mother and Tom had arranged to join a man they'd met on the deck of the ship coming over. He introduced himself as Ernst Hanfstaengl but said his friends called him "Putzi." He was a publisher from Munich whose father was German and mother was American. He'd lived in both countries after graduating from Harvard. Putzi was charming, funny, worldly, and played the piano beautifully. When Tom told him we would be going to Munich, Putzi gave him a list of places to go, including the opera house on a particular night when there would be a performance of Wagner. Putzi said he would leave tickets for all of us at the box office.

We went to the opera house on the appointed night and found that Putzi had gotten us excellent seats, about ten rows from the stage. As the performance began, fifteen or twenty seats in the two rows directly in front of us were conspicuously empty. Tom said the seats must be reserved for some important people—judging by the large number, perhaps they were for President Hindenburg and his staff. The seats remained empty through the first act. Then, early in the second act, there were murmurings in the back of the opera house. The music suddenly stopped and the lights came up as a contingent of men in brown uniforms with swastikas on their arms marched down the aisle. I noticed that Putzi, the man from the ship who had arranged for us to be here, was among them. Then a spotlight was shone on one of the men, who turned to the crowd as the uniformed men with him extended their arms and shouted, *Sieg heil!* "God almighty," Tom whispered. "It's Adolf Hitler."

At fourteen, I wasn't up on European politics. I'd barely heard of Hitler and had never seen a swastika before. My brother was more informed and well-read, and from the look on his face and the tone of his voice I knew something important and troubling was going on. Now Hitler extended his own right arm, returning the salute. I looked at

Hitler's shortish figure and little brush-cut mustache and felt the tension around me as half of the well-dressed Bavarian audience stood up and saluted back, shouting their allegiance with a hearty *Heil Hitler!* The other half remained seated, silently and nervously. Mother and Tom were stunned and told Angier and me to stay seated.

Then Hitler and his entourage took their seats—with Hitler settling into the seat directly in front of me. For the rest of the performance, my eyes kept wandering to the back of his neck. Though none of us knew the extent of what was to come, I became aware that night that Hitler was on his way to seizing power in Germany. Scarcely six months later he completed his personal conquest of the Rhineland, forcing President Hindenburg to appoint him chancellor and taking over altogether two months later. For years to come, all through my future military service in the Second World War and many years beyond, I never stopped thinking about my close encounter with one of the greatest villains in human history. And to this day, I am haunted by the memory of the back of his neck in my mind's eye, just a few feet in front of me, just a few months before he took full control as Germany's murderous dictator. So many times I would play out a fantastic scenario in my mind: what if I had reached out and used my lessons from Granddaddy Biddle to kill Hitler with my bare hands?

And who was Ernst Hanfstaengl, the charming, Harvard-educated "Putzi" who was part of Hitler's entourage? It turned out that he had been one of Hitler's earliest and closest supporters. After returning to Germany with his American-born wife in 1921, Hanfstaengl heard Hitler speak at a Munich beer hall, and within a couple of years he became one of the earliest financial supporters of the Nazi Party. Hanfstaengl joined Hitler in the failed Munich Beer Hall Putsch, an uprising that put many Nazis in jail. While Hanfstaengl fled to Austria, his American wife offered Hitler refuge in their home, where she (unfortunately) prevented him from committing suicide by wresting a revolver from his hands. Hitler was eventually arrested and imprisoned, but after his release he reunited with Hanfstaengl, who remained a loyal supporter and functionary during Hitler's fourteen-year march to power. In 1931, the year before we met him during our trip to Europe, Hitler appointed him the Nazi Party's foreign press chief, and over the next two years Hanfstaengl tried to use his contacts to improve Hitler's image outside Germany. But Hanfstaengl was not to last much longer as a member of Hitler's inner circle. Within a year of that night in Munich, he began to become disillusioned with his Fuhrer's plans to take over Europe, and he opposed close Hitler aides such as the propagandist Josef Goebbels. By 1937 Hanfstaengl was himself marked for death. But he managed to escape to Switzerland, then emigrated to England. He wound up spending most of World War II in Washington, where, under the code name S-Project, he advised the United States as a political and psychological expert on Hitler.

I returned to St. Paul's in the fall of 1932, a little wiser and more worldly, though still only casually interested in the conditions in Europe that were paving the way for Hitler's rise to power. I was more concerned about the troubles in my own country. The Depression was at its worst that winter, with millions of Americans suffering and on the move in desperation: Okies fleeing the Midwest dustbowl for California, Southern blacks flocking to the cities of the north, and World War I vets who were demanding their full military pensions being evicted from Washington by the U.S. Army. I paid close attention to how members of my family felt about what should be done to restore the nation to prosperity. Of all my close relatives, it was my Uncle Tony Biddle whose political point of view interested me most.

THAT UNCLE TONY SHOULD BE my mentor on world affairs would have been highly unlikely only a few years earlier. As a young man, the one-time St. Paul's football star had a reputation as a not-too-serious socialite and *bon vivant* who was often confused with his father, the famously eccentric martial arts expert and bible-teaching boxing enthusiast of the same name. Perhaps to distinguish himself from Granddaddy, who favored military uniforms and boxing trunks, Uncle Tony maintained a large collection of handmade double-breasted suits. He was perennially chosen by the national tailors' association as one of the best-dressed men in America. His manner, meanwhile, was smooth as silk and genuinely solicitous. No matter a person's station in life, Uncle Tony seemed overjoyed to make his or her acquaintance.

In the years following his marriage to my father's sister, Mary Duke, in 1915, Uncle Tony had no particular career in mind. He dabbled as a prize-fight manager and restaurateur. Uncle Buck's attempt to groom Tony for the Duke family business didn't pan out, and before long neither did Tony's membership in the Duke family itself. After they had two children (whom Mary and Tony named Mary and Tony) their marriage imploded during a croquet game with my parents in Hot Springs, Virginia. The two couples had decided to trade partners for the last match, with one set of siblings competing against the other: the Biddles versus the Dukes. It was while they were playing on opposite teams that Uncle Tony and Aunt Mary got into a fight that Uncle Tony later confessed to my mother was only the latest in a series.

Tony and Mary were divorced, and the following year my uncle married Margaret Thompson Schulze, an heiress to a diamond mining fortune. Margaret was a lady of great substance, with an awareness of the world that had a noticeable effect on my uncle. He seemed to become a much more serious man after he married Margaret. In 1932, they contributed $30,000 to Franklin D. Roosevelt's campaign for President, which expanded Uncle Tony's circle to include men of national influence. He and Margaret also traveled regularly to Europe, mixing pleasure with government service. At the request of J. Edgar Hoover, the director of the FBI, Uncle Tony traveled around Europe interviewing officials in various countries about the practices of their secret police forces. (It's unclear why Hoover was so interested in this subject or how he came to ask my uncle to research it, but it's hard not to wonder whether it played a role in the notorious domestic spying tactics Hoover himself put into practice in the United States three decades later.) Uncle Tony never had trouble finding ways to keep his life adventurous. While in Europe on his fact-finding mission, he found time to hunt wild boar and chamois, a variety of mountain goat with curved, black horns, in the Austrian Alps. He also competed in a series of international court tennis matches, winning the French singles championship.

In the summer of 1934, Uncle Tony and Margaret leased a *schloss* (German for castle) owned by a wealthy Austrian banker. It was near a village called Rottenman, tucked into a region of the Alps about three thousand feet above sea level and known for chamois hunting. Uncle Tony invited me to spend the summer there, and I eagerly accepted. I slept in a cabin and worked as a "dräger" for a professional hunter, carrying his equipment and helping him find bucks. All day long we climbed up and down the mountains—excellent preseason training for football at St. Paul's.

In late July, just before my sixteenth birthday, my mother, stepfather, and brother arrived in Vienna by train from Paris and then drove the two hundred miles of winding mountain road up to the schloss. Uncle Tony and Margaret came up, along with Margaret's sixteen-year-old son Ted, and a twenty-three-year-old cousin of ours from England, Chris Maidstone, whose father was the Earl of Winchelsea. With his charming ways Uncle Tony made friends everywhere he went, and he had invited an array of them to join us. There was Gilbert Miller, a famous Broadway producer and theater owner, and there was Spain's King Alfonso XIII, who had fled his country amid the tumult that would eventually lead to the Spanish Civil War. The exiled king was accompanied by his aide de camp, who was introduced as Count Del Merito, and the count's wife. But the most interesting guest would be the chancellor of Austria, Englebert Dollfuss, who was to join us later in the week.

Austria in that year had been a republic for only eighteen years. With its continuing economic crises, Hitler and Germany's Nazi Party had been gaining influence in the country, fueling anti-Jewish sentiment and rioting. Dollfuss opposed the Nazis, and after he became chancellor in 1932 he outlawed discrimination against Jews in housing and jobs. But his position became tougher after Hitler gained complete control of Germany in June of 1933 and began pushing for his goal—first stated in *Mein Kampf*—of re-annexing Austria. Dollfuss soon outlawed the Austrian Nazi Party, but it continued to operate illegally. The Austrian government had put down a brief Nazi uprising in February. But no one believed that would be the last one.

Uncle Tony had invited King Alfonso to visit after the king mentioned to him that he had once hunted chamois in the region, and that he'd enjoyed it immensely. The visit was timed to coincide with an annual drive. But as it turned out, chamois wasn't the only thing the king was interested in pursuing. In his hasty exit from Spain he'd left his wife behind. He was now carrying on with the wife of his sidekick, the count. And within seconds of our arrival, Alfonso became immediately and obviously infatuated with my mother. He seemed completely unconcerned that she was accompanied by her husband and two teenaged sons.

I always knew when Mother was being a little too coy for her own good, innocently giving a man the wrong idea. In this case I saw it happening at dinner, when the king sat next to Mother, took her hand, and wouldn't give it back. At one point I noticed he said something to her under his breath. After dinner, Mother took me aside and said, "You've got to help me. He wants to come to my room at one o'clock in the morning. First he wanted me to come to his room. I said no, so he said he's coming to mine. I don't know what to do. I don't dare tell Tom."

Not that Tom was oblivious. He was plainly seething at the king's attentions to Mother. This constituted a serious diplomatic dilemma for my well-mannered stepfather: How would he defend his wife's honor, not to mention his own, without offending the king and creating a scene? Of course, had he known that the king had actually propositioned Mother, I'm sure there would have been an international incident right then and there. I wondered if perhaps things worked differently in Spain; maybe it wasn't considered poor manners to pursue a man's wife in his presence. More likely, once a king, always a king. Even in exile, he was probably accustomed to getting whatever he wanted.

I felt honored that Mother, who had never had trouble taking care of herself, was coming to me for help. "Why didn't you just say no?" I asked her.

"He didn't give me a chance—he wouldn't listen to me," she said. "He's so insistent. I just know we're going to have trouble."

I told Angier what was going on and we came up with a plan to defend my mother's borders. "Tonight, we just don't go to bed," I said. "We'll guard the room."

I got a large chair from the living room and parked myself in front of my parents' room. Sure enough, the king came out of his room at one in the morning. Apparently, he was planning to go right in—with Tom

Our group at the Austrian hunting schloss prior to the assassination of the anti-Nazi chancellor in 1933. The exiled king of Spain is seated front center. Uncle Tony is far left in the middle row. Angier is third from left in the top row. To his right is my stepfather, Tom Robertson, and seated just below Tom is Mother. I'm off to the right, in front of the stair railing. In the foreground are the day's quarry of chamois.

right there. He must have been accustomed to having his way no matter what. Maybe he was going to declare his love and beseech Tom to step aside—or outside. In that case, who knows what might have happened? There were too many rifles on the premises for comfort.

The king stepped up to me as if it were the most natural thing in the world for a sixteen-year-old boy to be sitting on a chair outside his parents' bedroom in the middle of the night. "I have something to speak to your mother and your stepfather about," he said, in the manner of a messenger addressing a sentry at the palace gate. "It's very important. Kindly let me enter."

"I'm sorry, Your Majesty, but my parents are asleep," I said. "You'll have to see them in the morning."

The king nodded angrily and returned to his room. But I doubted that would be his last attempt. Around three, Angier took over guard duty. Sure enough, he told me in the morning, "He came down again at five! Can you believe it?" I could.

The king at that point had to turn his attentions to the chamois. It was time for the big hunt. Rifles were distributed, and we made our way to a spot where a forester explained the strict rules governing the hunt. Should an animal fall from where he's been shot, he explained in German, a hunter is honor bound to retrieve him, no matter how far away or how difficult it is to reach. The annual hunt was a major local event. Several dozen people from the village went out and banged on pots and pans to herd the chamois to an area where the hunters could view them and get within their range.

Upon our return to the house, the tone of our visit changed suddenly and drastically when a flash came through on the radio saying that there was trouble at the federal chancellery in Vienna. The information was sketchy, but it appeared that there was some kind of Nazi attack underway. My uncle and his friends listened to the reports and pondered the situation all day. Around midnight, the rest of us went to bed but my uncle stayed up. When we came down for breakfast at seven the next morning, he gathered the men—and in this he included Angier, Ted, and me—and said, "I don't want my wife and your mothers to hear what I'm about to say. Chancellor Dollfuss is dead. He's been assassinated by the Nazis. This means huge trouble."

As we later learned, Dollfus had been told that he could remain as chancellor, but only if he turned Austria over to Hitler. When he refused, the Nazis acted on their threat. According to the radio, Nazi SS men dressed in Austrian army uniforms had broken into the chancellery and shot Dollfuss in the throat.

The news sparked uprisings by Nazi sympathizers in many parts of the country. But by nightfall the Austrian government was reported to have succeeded in putting down the unrest. Meanwhile, funeral plans were announced. "This is history in the making," Uncle Tony declared. "We should go!"

But was it safe? My mother and stepfather were very concerned and wanted all of us to stay put. But Uncle Tony was confident that as long as we had our American passports we would reach Vienna safely. He suggested that Chris, Ted, Angier, and I leave at daybreak in Chris's car. He and my parents would follow later. We would meet in the evening at the Hotel Bristol, across the street from the state opera house in Vienna. Angier and I were eager to go, excited that Uncle Tony was treating us as adults. We departed the schloss at six the next morning and began the long drive to Vienna with a small American flag Uncle Tony gave us flying from the radio antenna.

We had an uneventful drive across the beautiful summer countryside of Austria in Chris's beat-up MG Roadster. Passing village after village, all seemed well. We had a radio in the car and heard about the funeral plans for the next day. After a couple of hours, we saw a sign for the town of Leoben. According to the map, we were about halfway to Vienna. "We're going to be fine," Chris said.

And then, suddenly everything changed. As we approached a bridge, we saw some men in long military coats up ahead. As we got closer we could see they had swastika armbands and that they were carrying rifles. We heard a shot and a bullet smashed through our windshield—right between Angier and me. Chris slammed on the brakes, and we were immediately surrounded by a group of men—boys, really, no older than my brother—all carrying rifles and wearing swastika armbands on their coats. One of them forced his way into the tiny MG and nervously ordered Chris to drive on. With the two years of German I'd taken at school, I understood his directions.

In a couple of minutes I realized we had given him a lift to where the rest of his unit was.

Now we were surrounded by a dozen more young Austrian Nazis, who pointed their rifles and bayonets at us and shouted, "*Heraus! Heraus!*" (Get out!). They were agitated and nervous. One of them smashed our car windows with the butt of his rifle, while another fired shots in the air and into the ground, for no apparent reason. The leader shouted in German—the only word I caught was "Juden." Chris, a student at Oxford who spoke German best among us, nervously translated. "They want to know if we're Jewish," he told us—the clear implication being that we might well be shot on the spot if we were. Then he addressed the Nazis, explaining that we weren't Jewish, that we were three Americans and a Brit. The man demanded our passports, looked at them, then said, "*Nein, nicht Juden.*" ("No, they're not Jewish.")

We realized now that we had driven straight into a siege, or what was left of one. These men were part of a larger force that had taken over the town and were trying to evade the Austrian nationalist army troops, *Heimwehr* as they were known. Chris explained that we were driving to Vienna, and tried to persuade the leader to let us go. "Nein!" the man shouted. But it seemed he really didn't know what to do with us. They herded us across the street and pushed us into a bakery where they had tied up the owner and his family. They put the four of us down in the cellar and locked the door. We were scared, of course, our hearts practically beating out of our chests, our minds racing: Why were they holding us? What's going to happen next? There was a wooden crate, and by standing on it we could peer through a small ground-level window to see what was happening. Just outside the window, sitting on a stool, was a young man who appeared to be about my brother's age. He was puffing away on a cigarette that dangled from his mouth.

"The radio said the uprisings have been put down," Angier said.

"Well, this must be one little pocket of Nazi sympathizers they didn't catch up with yet," Chris said.

"Why do you think they're keeping us here?" I asked. "What are they going to do with us?"

"I'm not so sure they know," Chris said.

One of the men brought us water, which I saw as a good sign, and I decided to use my rudimentary German to see if I could find out what was going on. I asked him if he could tell us how long he thought we would have to stay here. But he just looked at me blankly and then turned around and went back up the stairs. Chris, who had a lieutenant's commission in the British army, told me to keep quiet. "Don't talk, don't get into any conversations," he said. "Just do what they say."

Outside I could hear the Nazis talking excitedly, arguing. It seemed they were just a bunch of young zealots who had no idea what they were doing. "The worst thing we can do is cause them trouble," Chris said, looking at me. "We're definitely a problem for them at this point."

"I think we are seeing the beginning of a second World War," Angier said, words I will never forget. It was just 1934 when he uttered them.

After an hour or so, we heard the rumbling of approaching trucks. Angier got up on the crate and looked out. "They're packed with troops," he said. "They're Heimwehr!"

The lead truck came to an abrupt stop about sixty yards from where we were, and a dozen or so soldiers jumped out and started shooting at our captors. The first one hit was the man sitting on the chair outside our ground-level window. The impact of the bullets sent his body crashing through the window. Blood-stained glass crashed into the cellar, and then his body lay wedged there, blood dripping from a mortal head wound. Now dozens more Austrians jumped off the trucks and opened fire on the squad of Nazis by the bridge. "Get down!" Angier shouted, knowing that the men guarding us would be fired upon any second. And they were. The one closest to us suddenly flew backward, his head seeming to explode as it crashed through the window, splattering blood into the cellar. *So this is war,* I thought.

Finally the shooting stopped. Still unsure if we were really safe, we stayed still for a few moments. Then we began shouting to the Austrians to let them know we were in the cellar. They came down the stairs and shot the door open—almost hitting Chris—and we explained who we were and what had happened. An older man, a captain who spoke decent English, told us that most of the Nazi uprisings had been put down within twelve hours of the assassination, but that two pockets of resistance had remained. This was one of them. "You young men are lucky," the captain said. "An awful lot of innocent people have been killed in this business. You're very fortunate that they took you prisoner."

Angier asked if it would be safe to resume our trip to Vienna.

"We don't think there's going to be further trouble," the captain said. "All the main cities have reported in that the uprisings are finished." So much had happened this day—it all felt so unreal.

We decided to press on in our bullet-riddled MG, and eventually made our way to Vienna, where we were reunited with my parents and uncle later that night. When Mother saw us at the hotel, she ran to us. "We're all right," we assured her. "We're fine."

At dinner that night, Uncle Tony said, "I've been studying the Nazis. I've read *Mein Kampf*. But not until today did I realize how bad it is going to be." Upon his return to the United States, Uncle Tony went to Washington to tell President Roosevelt how serious a threat he believed Hitler and the Nazis to be.

A few weeks after we returned from Europe, Mother and Tom were at a Labor Day weekend party in Southampton. Tom's account of our ordeal was the talk of the party, and when a reporter for *The New York Times* showed up to cover the event, she found a much better story than the usual Hamptons society fare. The following day the *Times* ran a full-column story under the headline:

AMERICANS RODE PAST NAZI-FIGHT

Guest of Anthony J. Drexel Biddle Jr. Tells of Trip Under Flag of Truce in Austria.

DUKE BROTHERS ARRESTED

The experience in Austria ignited my interest in world affairs, especially anything related to Adolf Hitler. Uncle Tony sent me an English translation of *Mein Kampf*, which I read with a mix of fascination and dread. Though the Austrians survived the revolt in those couple of days in July, there was never a doubt in my mind but that Hitler would continue his hateful aggression, and that we Americans would have to take him on some day. As fate would have it, our British allies would take him on first. It was at Dunkirk, in 1940, that my cousin Chris Maidstone became the first person we knew to die in the fight against Hitler. He'd been such a friend to Angier and me, and his death was a shock.

In those years, some St. Paul's men from the classes ahead of mine had volunteered to fight in the Spanish Civil War—some supporting the Socialists and Communists who wanted Spain to be a republic, and others joining General Francisco Franco's nationalist forces. I wasn't interested enough to pick a side—until I read that Hitler was backing Franco. I immediately declared myself a supporter of Republican Spain. It was a simple decision. I knew—before my classmates and indeed before most Americans—how dangerous Hitler was. So whatever side he was on, I was for the other one.

It hardly counted as opposing Hitler in any real way, any more than sitting in the basement of that bakery and awaiting our fate could be considered fighting back. But in a few years, I'd get my chance. I knew deep inside that eventually the United States would have to confront Hitler, and that my brother and I—and our entire generation—would be of age to join the fight.

Back at school in New Hampshire that fall, it all seemed so distant and unreal. The memory of those few days in Austria stayed with me, but I was with my friends and classmates now, getting ready for the football season. I tried to share my experience with them, but it was impossible.

FOUR

The First Boys

THE INCIDENT IN AUSTRIA gave me a unique perspective of world events, to say the least. Back home, however, I was like any other young person, trying to figure out what I believed in. At this difficult point in history, at the height of the Great Depression, there were choices. I read publications of all political views, though I found myself most in line with such left-leaning magazines as *The New Republic* and *The Nation*. At St. Paul's, reading such titles was enough to get you branded a communist by some of your classmates. But I had read enough about Stalin's purges not to fall into that orbit. Still, I had uneasy feelings about the disparity between the life I was leading and the one being lived by so many other Americans in these years. I had been born into a comfortable life, and my mother's choice in husbands assured that I would not be wanting. We had a lovely home in Old Westbury, another in Southampton, and an apartment in Manhattan. We traveled to Europe and stayed in the best places, and we had people who attended to our needs. I went to a private boarding school with other well-heeled children (though a number of others came from less privileged backgrounds and were on scholarship).

All this came into sharper focus during the summer after my fourth-form year at St. Paul's. I had spent recent summers in Southampton and traveling to Europe. I'd had a lot of fun (aside from those harrowing few hours in Austria), but the last year or two the country club life had lost its allure. I enjoyed tennis and swimming, but how much sit-

St. Paul's football squad my senior year, fall of 1937.
I'm in the top row, fourth from left..

Climbing Ben Nevis
in Scotland, the high-
est mountain
in the United King-
dom, with Angier in
1936.

ting around the Southampton Beach Club could a person do? Fortunately, St. Paul's offered an interesting alternative.

Dr. Drury, the school's revered rector, had been a missionary in China, and he tried to imbue us boys with a sense of obligation to try to improve the lives of those less fortunate. It was in this spirit that he had established a club at school called the Missionary Society, along with a summer camp that took disadvantaged kids from New York and Boston. The head of the Missionary Society, Mr. Flint, arranged for some of us to sleep one night in a shelter in downtown New York to see how "hobos" lived. It was at once depressing and impressive, a real education. Members of the Missionary Society who had finished their fourth-form year (tenth grade) could apply to be counselors at the camp. I decided to put an application in. It was different, and I figured it might be a good way to get in shape for the football season. The school master, who was also the director of the summer camp, said I could come up for two weeks. If I did well and I enjoyed it, I might be able to stay longer.

The camp was a simple, rustic retreat set on a lake in the wild country near Danbury, New Hampshire. The campers, all boys, were either underprivileged or had gotten into minor trouble with the law and been labeled "delinquent." In those days, stealing an apple from the corner market, or getting into one too many fights at school, was enough to get that tag. Many were children of immigrants—Irish, Italian, Russian, Polish, German, Swedish—who sold apples on the street to make a living. The boys from New York came from the streets of the Lower East Side, Hell's Kitchen, and the Bronx, where they ran around unattended and undisciplined with more than enough idle time on their hands to get in trouble. Some were picked up by youth organizations such as the New York Boys Club and Big Brothers, and the lucky ones were those taken off the streets and sent to camp for the summer.

The St. Paul's camp was run on a philosophy of mutual respect, with a certain underlying religious tone that my grandfather would have appreciated (or tried to turn up a few degrees). It was Dr. Drury's thinking that all the boys—the underprivileged campers and the often overprivileged counselors—could benefit. And he was right. For the St. Paul's boys, at the very least, it gave us a chance to see what it was like to work. We slept in tents or cabins and got the kids up at six each morning. We'd go outside for calisthenics, teach the boys swimming in the lake, and then spend most of the day coaching whatever we were good at. I coached football, baseball, swimming, and, of course, boxing.

The boys came to camp and brought the streets with them. Breaking up fights was one of a counselor's many responsibilities, and this proved to be one of my better skills. I was so good at it, in fact, that I once inadvertently broke a kid's leg in the process. He was a big, blond boy named Harry. He outweighed me by twenty pounds at least, and he decided to test me by jumping on me from behind. Instead of trying to get him off, which might have been impossible, I threw myself on my back, with him under me. His leg snapped and he screamed. On the way to the hospital, I was about to apologize when he beat me to the punch. "I shouldna' jumped ya'," he said. "Jeez, Mr. Duke, you were really good at that." Harry and I became friends.

Teaching boxing to these boys reminded me of a lesson I had learned when I was younger—that there were two ways to fight. There was the proper boxing method with Marquis of Queensbury rules. And then there was *fightin.'* When I was ten, I won a club championship in Southampton, and the instructor, Mr. Monahan, who had been a sparring partner for Gene Tunney and knew my grandfather, wanted me to fight a boy who had won a tournament in town. He was the son of Tony Machione, a local plumber. At the start of the fight I came to the center of the ring to shake hands, and young Machione came at me swinging, putting me flat on my back. I got up but the kid hit me and hit me again before I could get into my formal boxing stance. I was reduced to tears, and Mr. Monahan apologized, but I was determined to learn that other way of boxing so I'd never be a sucker again. I changed my whole style, became more aggressive, and asked Granddaddy Biddle to teach me some tricks, which he was only too happy to do. His favorite was the "Fitzsimmons Shift," in which you started with a few left jabs, then followed with a right cross while simultaneously putting your right foot behind your opponent's left foot and making him fall over. It was eventually outlawed (except in the World Wrestling Federation.) In the rematch, I fought Machione to a draw. So when I started teaching boxing at camp, I knew what I was dealing with.

The camp opened a whole new world to me. I really enjoyed getting to know these kids whose backgrounds couldn't have been more different from mine. From an almost anthropological view, I was fascinated by the different ways they talked, curious about what their lives were like. I wanted to know how they did in school, and I appreciated their individual skills and talents. (Some were better athletes than us counselors, especially in basketball, though their game didn't seem to have many rules.) I could see all kinds of potential in most of these boys. They were a little wild but by no means incorrigible. What they needed, it seemed to me, was some discipline, and for people to care about them. "Look," I said after a few days of trying to get them to respect the basic rules, "it would be better if we cooperated with each other. That way I don't have to be yelling at you all the time, and we can become friends. I appreciate the fact that you're out of the city, and maybe you're feeling freedom you never had before, but I'm here to do a job and you've got to understand that. If we respect each other we can have a much better time." By the end of the summer I had a very good cabin; we won an award for cleanliness. And we were friends.

At the end of the summer I gave a couple of boys a ride home to the city. They were brothers, Russian immigrants, who lived in a tenement on the Lower East Side, a world I'd only heard about. I parked, then walked them to their tenement building. We climbed four flights of narrow, sagging stairs. The hallways were dimly lit and smelled of stale food and urine. Finally we reached their apartment, where we were greeted by the boys' mother. Actually, to say we were greeted would be a slight exaggeration. The mother was the picture of weariness. It was the height of the Depression, her husband had abandoned her, and she was raising four kids on her own. The apartment was cramped and drab, such a contrast to the open space and fresh air of camp. I had never been in a home so utterly depressing, and as I descended the stairs, knowing I was heading back to my life of privilege and comfort, I felt unsettled. I sat in my car, watching swarms of kids playing in the street and thinking of those boys upstairs. I wondered if I would ever see them again.

I did see them again the following summer, after a school year in which I could hardly wait to return to camp. By the middle of that second summer, it was dawning on me that we St. Paul's boys could probably help these city kids in more ways than by just showing them a good time. It seemed to me that a lot of them were capable of doing better in school, and doing more with their lives than they expected. One day I made up a couple of tests, one in math and another in reading, and asked one of the boys in my cabin if he would give them a try. He gave me a strange look but agreed. I was no expert in education, but from what I could see he was brighter than his marks in school indicated, and I thought he had a lot of potential. So for the rest of the summer I worked with him. And I encouraged my fellow counselors to follow my lead. "If you're good at something," I suggested, "share what you know. Whether it's math or history or grammar, why don't we try to give these kids a hand? Getting away from the city is great, but what happens when they go back?"

I worked with some of my best school pals at camp. There was Larry Drake, who was my first friend at St. Paul's and later my roommate. He came from the Virginia horse country. There was Paul Moore, whose family had huge houses in New Jersey and Palm Beach and whose father entered him in St. Paul's the day after he was born. And Walter McVeigh—Quigg, as we called him, for reasons unknown. He was one of my first friends, the boy who rescued me from the closet at the Beauvais School after I'd peed in class during the first grade. I didn't see him after we moved out to Long Island, and then one day six years later he showed up at St. Paul's. His father was the head of an important law firm in New York.

My friends from Southampton would ask why I spent my summers up at that camp for poor kids, rather than enjoying the country club life on Long Island. All I could tell them was the truth: I liked it more. It wasn't any more complicated than that. Some didn't get it— especially my girlfriend, Catherine, who was furious at me for leaving. "Don't you love me?" she would ask. I didn't know if I loved her; I liked kissing her. But I must have loved camp more.

After a couple of summers I developed strong bonds with many of the boys, and made a point of visiting them in their homes during school vacations. I wanted to keep track of them, and I wanted to see what their real lives were like. It was a shock to see how desperately poor many of them were, living with parents who spoke no English, who were unemployed, who were so hopeless and depressed themselves that it was hard to imagine how they could raise children. It was these experiences that started me thinking about the failings of our great democracy. If we were all created equal, why did we live so unequally? It was ludicrous to think that everyone in America had the same opportunity. The playing field certainly was not level. From my travels in Europe, I had no doubt that we were the greatest country on earth. We had unprecedented rights and freedoms—and yet, I found myself asking, how free were people who had no real chance to join the mainstream? In those years, some young people were flirting with communism. I read the manifesto, listened to some speeches, and got interested in what the trade unions were doing. But I never felt a different political system was the answer. Instead, what had to change were educational opportunities. Even from my limited experience at camp, I could see how properly injecting a dose of academics brought measurable results.

I worked one last summer at camp, after graduating from St. Paul's in 1937, and with camp ending in early August, I volunteered to take some of the older boys and two counselors back home to New York. These were boys I had worked with for three years. They were fourteen and fifteen now, only three or four years younger than me. Most had reached the unofficial age limit for the St. Paul's camp, and with the three of us counselors having now graduated, we all knew this was the end of a great thing in our lives. It made for a bittersweet trip home. I looked back at the dozen boys in the pickup truck as we rattled along the highway. They were all sons of immigrants heading back to their city tenements, back to the reality of their precarious lives. They were Dead End Kids.

I drove the truck down through New Hampshire, Massachusetts, and Connecticut, and we crossed Long Island Sound on the old Orient Point ferry from New London, a little steamer in those days. The talk was all about next summer. "What're we gonna do?" someone said. "There ain't no more camp."

"Well, there could be—maybe we can start our own camp," I said impulsively.

I heard a chorus of hoorays and hot damns from the back.

"If I can just get my hands on some land. But you boys will have to build the tent platforms with me." The idea excited the boys, though my more realistic and practical fellow counselors from St. Paul's regarded me skeptically.

We arrived in the city at midday. It was a searing day, and the heat radiated up from the streets as we headed for our first stop, a dingy building on the Lower East Side where a boy named Tom Alongi lived. I was surprised and troubled that no one was home to greet him, and the look on Tom's face was heartbreaking. I told him to get back in the truck, then turned around and headed back for the Brooklyn Bridge.

"Where're we goin'?" one of the boys asked.

"Back out to Long Island," I said. "Camp isn't over yet." If I was serious about starting a camp for next summer, why not get a head start now?

We arrived in Southampton a few hours later, and my mother was astonished at the sight of me pulling up with a truckload of boys. But she trusted me and said we could set up a temporary camp in the two-room pool house out back. It was a little cabin that my stepfather had originally built on the beach. When someone bought the land, we took the cabin apart and hauled it on a big truck to our property on Main Street, where it was reassembled next to the pool.

Our little post-camp camp lasted a few weeks, during which time I told Mother my idea about starting a real camp the following summer. What we needed was some land. "Why don't you talk to Mr. Tilton?" she suggested. It was a good idea. Newell Tilton, a retired financier, owned about eight hundred acres on a part of Peconic Bay known as Jessup's Neck. Maybe he'd lend us a few. I knew the land very well; ever since I was twelve or so, my friends and I would go on little adventures with a little eight-foot motorboat I had. We'd find a spot and pitch a tent, and often as not it was on Mr. Tilton's land there on Peconic Bay. Of course, if we wanted to pitch some tents and build some cabins for an actual camp, we'd probably have to ask first. So I loaded the boys on the pickup truck and headed over to pay him a visit. "Wait here," I told them, then went around the back to talk to Mr. Tilton. He was about seventy, sunning beside his swimming pool.

I explained what I had in mind, and Mr. Tilton said he only used the land on Jessup's Neck in the fall and winter. He had a little hunting club with a beautiful old wooden lodge. I was about to pop the question—Could we use it for the camp?—when my gaggle of city kids came around looking for me. The truth was I didn't want him to see them just yet. I wasn't sure what he'd make of them. And he did look a little nervous, sprawled out on a chaise lounge, wearing nothing but bathing trunks and tanning oil, looking up at these tough-sounding, rough-around-the-edges tenement boys.

"I was just discussing with Mr. Tilton here whether we might use a small piece of his land for our camp," I told the boys.

"What'd he say?" one of the boys asked excitedly, as they others leaned forward to hear the answer.

"Well, he really hasn't given me his answer yet.".

Finally Mr. Tilton sat up. "Tell me really what you're talking about," he said. "What would you do?"

"If we found a place, we'd make a clearing and set up some tents, and I would create a program out there for these kids and others. We could use the old wooden lodge as a mess hall and space for counselors."

"How old are you, son? he asked me.

"Eighteen," I said.

"Well, if you get someone older to join you, someone who would understand the legal aspects of this deal that you're asking me to make with you, I'll think about it."

I was about to thank him when one of the boys blurted out, "Why don't you think about it *now?*" I cringed, but Mr. Tilton smiled. "I guess if you're really serious about this, you go ahead," he said. At that point, Tilton became a hero to my boys. They picked up the president of the Southampton Beach Club and carried him around his lawn, yelling, "Two, four, six, eight, who do we appreciate! Mr. T! Mr. T! Mr. T!"

I was relieved to see that Mr. T found the surprise attack amusing. When they put him down, he said, "We'll make a deal but I want to make it legal. So bring a lawyer with you next time. And one more thing. You'll have to persuade my wife that this is a good idea." He looked around at the boys. "I'd come alone if I were you."

Mrs. Tilton couldn't have been nicer when I went back that night. She was a naturalist, and her only concern was that we respect the land. She even offered us the use of the hunting lodge. "You can use that as your kitchen and mess hall, and you'll have a place for counselors who aren't in the cabins."

I told my parents the news, and my stepfather said, "He's right, you know. You should have a lawyer. We'll get John Jackson"—the twenty-three-year-old son of the head of the firm that represented Tom. "He's just graduated from Columbia Law School. This will be his first job." For a fee of ten dollars, the newly minted attorney arranged a rent-free lease of the land, the only provision being that since I wasn't twenty-one, my parents would accept responsibility for any damage. Thus was planted the seed that would eventually become Boys (and Girls) Harbor.

I went off to Princeton that fall. I'd been advised by my St. Paul's football coach that he knew the freshman coach, and he encouraged me to try out for the team. I made the squad, and some of the boys from camp came down to see me play. Of course they couldn't afford the train fare, so they proudly told me how they'd gone to Penn Station and just climbed along the side of the train like spiders and held on. They showed up at my dormitory room in Holder Hall and talked excitedly about going to camp the following summer on Long Island. What I didn't tell them was that I wanted something more than a typical sports-oriented camp. I wanted to recruit counselors who could teach the kids—English, history, ethics, whatever they wanted. You can't just play all the time, it seemed to me, if you're really trying to make a difference in these kids' lives.

One of the first to volunteer to be a counselor was my friend Claiborne Pell. One weekend, he and I went up to our fledgling, as-yet unnamed camp with some of the boys I'd had at the St. Paul's camp. At one point some ducks flew in and landed right in front of us.

"Look at the boyds," one of the campers said.

"Not *boyds*," Claiborne corrected him.

"Well, they look like boyds."

"*Birds,*" Claiborne said.

"That's what I said. What kind of boyds are they?"

"Ducks," Claiborne said.

From that moment on, the camp became known as Duck Island. It was actually a peninsula, but Duck Peninsula didn't have quite the same ring. Now that the camp had a name, I started what was to become a lifetime of fundraising. I went around Southampton telling people about my fledgling camp and asking for donations. My plan was to recruit sixty kids, thirty in July and thirty in August, along with ten or so counselors. We'd need to build four decent-sized platforms for tents. Most people thought I was some kind of lunatic, that my mother and stepfather were crazy for letting me do it. "What are you going to do, live out there in the woods with a bunch of kids?" they'd ask. But somehow I raised enough money to buy lumber for the tent platforms, and a local carpenter was kind and generous enough to build them without charge. At one point I talked to my cousin Doris Duke about my plans and asked if she might help me with a small financial contribution. Doris, who had inherited the majority of the Duke tobacco fortune, thought it was a worthy cause and gave me a hand.

In early spring I began to recruit counselors, asking friends and putting up notices around campus. I signed up my cousin Nick Biddle and friends such as Quigg McVeigh, Paul Moore, Lonsdale Stowell, and Cord Meyer. I also went up to St. Paul's one weekend when the Missionary Society invited me to come and talk about my camp. A few of the more adventurous St. Paul's boys decided to volunteer to work at my experimental little camp rather than at the St. Paul's camp. One of these was a fine boy named John Lindsay, a fifth-former who revealed something of his future aspirations that summer. He told me he was interested in running for school president, and asked how I'd gotten elected two years earlier. John wound up winning, the first of many election campaigns for him. Nearly thirty years later, he would become the mayor of New York City and then make a bid for a Presidential nomination.

I went up to the city to find kids, which would probably get me arrested were I to do it today. Some of the boys who had gone to the

On the beach at Duck Island: The top photo shows me with the boys from the St. Paul's camp at the end of the summer of 1937. Kneeling in front are Teddy Vavoulis and Lester Pike. Beside me are George Vavoulis, John Meyer, and Tom Ball. The bottom photo was taken during the first full summer the following year. Flanking me are Bob Gehres (a medical student who served as camp doctor), and counselors Nick Biddle, Walter "Quigg" McVeigh, David Challinor, and Newton McVeigh.

St. Paul's camp belonged to the Big Brothers movement or the New York Boys Club. So I started there, asking the people who ran the clubs to recommend deserving kids. We wound up with a combination of poor kids with great potential and some who had gotten into minor scrapes, but who I thought should not be written off. These boys were commonly referred to as juvenile delinquents, or JDs, but I found that their worst crimes, if you could call them that, were things like fighting in school or stealing food from a grocery store. Remember that these were often desperately poor kids trying to survive the Depression. Even the "good" kids were growing up on mean streets and could wind up going down dangerous paths.

Typical of these first kids were two teenagers from East Harlem, Tony Albarello and Fred Cicerelli. Tony's mother had died when he was four, leaving his father to raise ten kids on East 111th Street. "It was like a paradise, that camp," Tony recalls. "I'd never been out to the country, away from the hot streets of New York. It was like a whole new world, Peconic Bay, with all the trees and the grass. We went on boats and canoes, we went to movies in Southampton, we played games. I never wanted to come home. If I didn't go to that camp who knows what would have happened, because a lot of bad stuff came out of that neighborhood."

"East Harlem was mostly Italian and Irish in those days, and the Mafia ruled the neighborhood," Fred Cicerelli agreed. "If you came from there, you wound up either a priest or a gangster. You could go one way or the other." Fred's parents, like Tony's, were Italian immigrants. His father was a shoe repairman, and to help the family Fred shined shoes on the streets. "I was picked to go to the camp because I had just gotten out of the hospital with pleurisy. I looked miserable and Miss Romaine from the Boys Club felt sorry for me. The camp was unbelievable. There was a super chef out there, and I think our favorite activities were breakfast, lunch, and dinner. It's something when you think that this wasn't supported by the city, or the Boys Club, or anyone but these boys in college."

Based on my experience at the St. Paul's camp, I made a point of having rules that the boys would find easy to follow, rather than being so strict that I'd defeat my own purpose. Most of all, I wanted to imbue the kids with a sense of respect and responsibility they'd never known—and I wanted them to feel respected and free in return. In an interview with *Town & Country* in 1986, Fred Cicerelli recalled how the adjustments he made in just the first few days at camp formed the basis of the principals he would live by the rest of his life:

"We were grateful to these people for driving us to the country in their cars and feeding us, but we'd steal food from the kitchen anyway, get into knife fights, swipe their cars when they weren't around. One day I took a car, raced it around and crashed into a tree. I was sure I'd get beat up, because that's what I was used to. Instead, they sat down and talked to me. 'Do you know what this will cost?' they said. 'Can you pay for the repairs? Do you know you could have been killed and made your family miserable? We trusted you,' they said, 'and you broke our trust.' They were teaching me responsibility and consequences. But the way they disciplined me was something else. Maybe I had no dessert and movies for a week, or got put on K.P., but the big thing was they cold-shouldered me for a while, to let the seriousness sink in. That was the most painful punishment of my life, because I loved those guys and wanted to be with them no matter what."

Just as camp was revealing to us St. Paul's boys, introducing us to a culture of tough, street-smart kids and a way of life we knew nothing about, many of the boys from the tenements looked upon us with wonderment. "The way they walked and talked, were clean and orderly and said 'thank you' all the time—it was like a fantasy world," Fred said. "The effect on me was as if I were a train going a hundred miles an hour and had run into a stone wall. Suddenly I was ashamed to act like a hoodlum around these gentlemen. We all tried to emulate them, and it stuck."

I tried to find out as much as I could about the boys, and then give each one the latitude to make his own choices about what he wanted to do at camp. I also wanted them all to learn a thing or two. "Everybody here has talent, from the campers to the counselors," I said when I gathered everyone together on the first day. "And those of us who are a little older would like to share some of our skills and talents with you younger guys." In effect, we set aside time each day for individual tutoring. Counselors were matched with boys according to their strengths and weaknesses. A counselor who was strong in history, for instance, would take on a boy who had trouble in that area.

The kids hated it at first. "We didn't come out here to go to school!" they'd complain. But you did come out here to learn *something*, I'd reply. They got over it soon enough. In fact, many became eager. I vividly remember a boy named Steve poignantly asking why it was that we knew so much. "How come you learned all this mathematics and science and English?" he asked me. "And how come Mr. Stowell speaks French? How come Mr. McVeigh knows so much about religion?" I explained that we were fortunate enough to go to good schools and that we understood the importance of education from an early age. "Let's see if we can share what we know with you," I said.

Quigg McVeigh proved to be one of the more provocative teacher-counselors. He would gather the kids and talk about all their different religions, and it provided for some pretty wild talks. The idea was to offer a forum for discussion, for saying what you believed in and then listening to what other people believed. The message was respect for those who might be different. This began what was to become a Sunday tradition: a weekly meeting of the whole camp—kids, counselors, and staff—with me in the middle. Anyone who wanted to say anything or display a talent could do so. Singers would sing, actors would act, dancers would dance, and then we'd have a discussion about how things were going in the camp and how they related to what was going on in the city and the world. I came to love those discussions because people felt comfortable and secure enough to come right at you.

Of course, nobody came at you more forcefully than Granddaddy Biddle, who became a fixture at Duck Island. He thought of the camp as an extension of his Athletic Christianity movement and tried to get me to require the boys to wear uniforms. But that didn't feel right to me. "The kids can come as they are," I told Granddaddy. "As long as their clothes are clean, that's good enough for me." Eventually, we adopted a uniform of sorts: khaki pants or blue jeans, plain white t-shirts, and of course, sneakers.

Granddaddy was in his mid-sixties by then, but he spent a good deal of time at the camp and threw himself into all the activities. He boxed with the boys, some of whom were bigger than he was, and he always insisted that I take him on for the main event. The match was always the same. I would try to take it easy on old Granddaddy, which only made him burn. As I laid back, he would lunge at me, furiously shouting, "You white-livered sissy! Fight or die!" One day he caught me with a right and I landed in a heap. "By gum!" he crowed to the boys. "That was a good one, eh?"

I appreciated and loved Granddaddy's involvement in camp, but I was always leery of what he might do next. When he announced his intention to get rifles and bayonets from the Marines Corps, I quickly vetoed the idea. Instead, he brought in wooden display rifles and told the boys to come after him. "Kill me!" he wailed. "Kill me, you cowards!" I could only imagine what the boys thought of this, but they obligingly took their best shots—only to find the old man would easily foil them. At the end, Granddaddy would pick out the biggest boy, stick out his neck and taunt, "Choke me! Come on, choke me to death!" One after another they tried, egged on by their pals, but I knew from personal experience that my grandfather's neck was like iron and none of these so-called delinquents would get anywhere. One night after one such demonstration, I was walking by a tent when I overheard some of the boys discussing Granddaddy's neck.

"Why, you couldn't even hang that old sucker," one said. "You'd have to give him the chair."

The boys didn't quite know what to make of Granddaddy, especially when he followed one of his hand-to-hand combat demonstrations with morning prayers, which he led by falling to his knees and imploring God to protect these "helpless infants" and then likening us counselors to Christ. One time, I was out on the water in a sailboat with a couple of counselors when the boat turned over. We were close to shore and all of us were good swimmers, so it wasn't a perilous situation. But Granddaddy jumped into a canoe and directed the rescue. "Granddaddy, you nearly killed yourself in that canoe," I said when we were all on shore. "How dare you!" he shot back, then made us all kneel on the beach in prayer. For nearly an hour he had a personal talk out loud with God, thanking Him for saving us and asking for more brains on our behalf so that we could avoid future incidents of this sort. According to Granddaddy, the message from God was that we had been spared for the sole purpose of carrying on the camp for these boys. It was a testament to my grandfather's powers of religiosity that we were convinced.

My mother also made herself a presence at the camp. "She loved being with us, bantering with the boys," Fred Cicerelli remembered. "She opened her home in Southampton to us." Fred reminded me of the day during his second summer at camp when he came home with me and found my mother entertaining Errol Flynn. "You introduced me as if I was just as important as he was," Fred said. "You said, 'Errol Flynn, this is Fred Cicerelli.' And he said, 'Hello, young fellow, I'm pleased to meet you. Are you having a good time at camp?' "

My mother loved Fred and many of the other boys. One day, she told him, "Fred, you're a monster!" Fred wasn't sure what to make of it until I explained that this was my mother's favorite term of endearment. If she called you a monster, it meant you'd arrived. You were in her circle.

The director of Big Brothers was a man named Joe McCoy, and when he learned that seven or eight of the kids from his organization were going to a camp on Long Island run by eighteen- and nineteen-year-olds, he came to check us out. He later said he came loaded for bear, but was taken by surprise by what he saw. "This is the most interesting and constructive camp I've ever seen," he told me. "You fellas are doing something that I've never really seen done. There's a feeling here I don't see in other places, the way the boys and the counselors get along and respect one another." With Mr. McCoy's stamp of approval, we were able to go to the city Juvenile Court the following year and ask them to recommend kids who might benefit from a month out of the city with some college men who could serve as role models. The Boys Club, meanwhile, had a big camp with nearly three hundred boys in nearby Mattituck, and one day the director and two assistants drove up unannounced in a station wagon. "I heard about you from Joe McCoy," the director said, "but I didn't believe him. I couldn't imagine kids running a kids' camp." He spent the day with us and also gave us high marks. "Any time you want to bring your boys over to our camp to go swimming or play ball, you're more than welcome," he said. And we did.

Mr. Tilton had a caretaker on the property named Fred Overton. Fred was a jack of all trades: house builder, painter, plumber, electrician, and, mostly, a real fisherman. Incredibly strong, he would carry a boat on his back, dump it into the bay and then row for miles to ply his trade. He thought Mr. Tilton was crazy for renting this great place to a bunch of kids like us. But he admired our initiative and helped us in many ways.

ONE DAY THAT FIRST SUMMER I gathered all the boys and told them we had gotten some interesting news: A bunch of circus animals had escaped from a rail car at Cedar Point. The forestry service and the police had found all of them except for two gorillas. "Maybe we can help get them back," I said nonchalantly. "So keep your eyes open." The boys looked at each other, not knowing what to think. None of them knew they were being set up for what was to become a camp legend.

Back in the city a week later, I went to Eve's Costumers, a famous store used by theater people, and rented a very real-looking gorilla suit. When I put it on, I really felt like a gorilla. When I got back to camp, I brought the counselors together to plan a mischievous escapade. Each evening, the whole camp would go up to Jessup's Neck and walk along the beach as the sun was going down. The boys would pick up shells and stones for their growing collections. The walks took us beneath a hundred-fifty-foot bluff. I said to Claiborne Pell, "Somehow you've got to get them to look up onto the top of the cliff. I'll be up there but whatever you do, don't give me away."

That night, I disappeared with my gorilla suit and went up to the bluff. As the kids were approaching below, I made some wild gorilla sounds and got their attention. I saw through the bushes that they were all looking up. Then I appeared, and that got them all excited. Most looked terrified and some screamed, but one brave boy started climbing up toward me with a rock in his hand. When he got within about fifty feet, I came out, roaring and beating my chest. The boy turned and ran, screaming all the way down.

I disappeared into the bushes, then took off the gorilla suit and hid it. I had to get back down to camp by the time the boys returned so they could tell me all about it. When they saw me, they ran up with the news.

"Tony, we seen a gorilla!"

"Yeah, he was up on the cliff!"

"He was so big and scary!"

"How about that," I said. "Well, you know there are two of them on the loose and that must have been one of them. We should call the police tomorrow. If you guys would lead the way we might be able to capture him."

The next morning, I went to the police department in Sag Harbor, where I knew a young motorcycle cop. I told him about my prank and asked if he'd come up to the camp that evening and bring his forty-five revolver with blanks in it. He was game, so to speak, and even volunteered to bring another police officer with a rifle. "Make sure they're blanks," I reminded him. "I'd like to survive this plan."

From there the scheme got even more elaborate. I planned to play dead after I was shot, then the counselors would have the kids bury me. "Bring a straw or something so you can breathe," Claiborne Pell suggested. Good idea, I said.

That night, the camp was in a high state of excitement. The policemen showed up with their weapons and a powerful searchlight. I feigned the flu, said I'd be spending the night in Southampton, and wished the boys luck. With Claiborne, Paul, Quigg, and the other counselors leading the posse, the boys set off on the gorilla hunt. As soon as they were gone I made a dash for the spot on the bluff where I'd left the suit and got it on quickly. A few minutes later I saw the group, and they were clearly emboldened by their armed escort. I looked down from the bluff and saw the entire mob striding up toward me, gathering rocks to throw at the gorilla. The sight of this made me a little nervous. They could kill me with those things. Apparently Quigg thought the same thing, and called everyone back. "There may be more gorillas up there," he warned.

Now I made my appearance, complete with chest-beating and grunting. A boy named Dickey Lebeck fainted.

"We have to kill this beast!" I heard my cop friend yell. "Before he kills somebody."

"Kill him!" the boys yelled. "Kill him!"

He and the other cop shone the searchlight and began firing their

*The gorilla
unmasked.*

When Claiborne Pell visited Boys Harbor as a United States senator in the
1960s, I gave him the section of plaster ceiling he'd put his head through
when he was a counselor thirty years earlier. He took it back to Washington
and proudly displayed it in his Senate office.

blanks. I came out of the shadows after pushing a pouch of ketchup through a hole I'd poked in the suit with an ice pick earlier. I fell dramatically down the bluff. Unfortunately, at this point, the boys tried to finish the job by pelting me with rocks, which my buddies couldn't stop before I got quite a few bruises.

"Put another bullet in him," Quigg told the cops.

The boys stood back as my friend shot his forty-five at the gorilla's head. I could hear gasps from the boys, whose excitement was bubbling over. They came and lifted me into the bed of my pickup truck, and on the way down to the camp they were singing like maniacs. They had killed a gorilla!

They arrived at the place I'd designated for burial, a spot near the mess hall where the earth was soft. Shorty Mercer, Tony Albarello, and a couple of other boys dug a nice hole, then the counselors put me in it. They stuck a pipe in the ground—my breathing tube—to which they attached an American flag. Finally, Fred Overton came to my rescue. He helped me out of my grave and filled it in when no one was around. Then he drove me to his house, where his wife, May, rather unsympathetically put witch hazel on my cuts and bruises.

"Tony Duke, you deserve every bruise you have on your body," she said. "You're out there scaring those kids."

"Well, yeah," I said, "But Mrs. Overton, they're never going to forget this."

"Well, you better not do it again. Who knows what kind of accident could happen."

The camp didn't calm down all night, and when I returned in the morning I was surrounded by boys screaming out their versions of the episode. They dragged me over to the grave by the mess hall, the pipe with the flag still standing where I'd left it after rising from the dead the night before.

The hoax was such a success that, despite Mrs. Overton's reservations, we repeated it for the boys who came in August and again the following summer. This time, we had *two* policemen coming out, and not just with pistols but with shotguns. Joe McCoy, the head of Big Brothers, loved the performance but thought we ought to call a halt to it. "Some people might get the wrong idea if they heard about it," he said. "They might think you're running a camp so you can scare children."

If you ask Fred Cicerelli or Tony Albarella about those first two years at Duck Island, it won't be long before they tell the gorilla story with big smiles across their faces. Among his many successes in life, Tony Albarello was an agent and manager for entertainers who played the Catskills circuit. But he says he never saw a better show than the night they killed the gorilla on Duck Island.

It was a memorable summer for all of us counselors as well. On the last night of camp, we got together in the little cabin I used as an office. We were all in a celebratory mood, proud of ourselves for the successful summer we'd had with the kids, and to be honest, just a bit relieved it was over. At one point, Claiborne Pell leaped into the air, shouting, "Hooray—the kids are gone!" He leaped so high and with such force, in fact, that he went right through the plaster ceiling and actually got his head stuck. We all looked in disbelief at the sight of our friend hanging there from the ceiling from about the nose down. I grabbed a chair and managed to get him down, but he really could have broken his neck. After the rescue, we all stared up in awe at the hole Claiborne had made with his exuberant self-launching. I cut out the section of ceiling plaster and saved it for posterity, and eventually gave it, framed, to Claiborne. During a visit with him years later I was pleased to see it prominently displayed in his office, which was by then in the Senate Office Building in Washington. Claiborne, a Democrat from Rhode Island, was first elected to the Senate in 1960 and would serve until 1997. His seven elections to the Senate would be the most in U.S. history.

THAT FALL, I RETURNED TO PRINCETON for my second year of college. I was most interested in history and sociology, least interested in things like math and physics. I played football and rugby, and rowed on the 150-pound crew. As for how I envisioned my life unfolding, it was my summer experiences that influenced my true ambitions.

Though I knew I had to earn a living, I hoped that eventually, some-how, I could make enough money in business to subsidize my inter-est in helping disadvantaged kids.

It wasn't just an idealistic desire to improve the world, though that was part of it. On a more personal and gut level, I cherished the relationships I formed with the kids, many of whom would remain part of my life for decades to come. It wasn't out of any sense of pity or superiority. The director of the St. Paul's camp routinely used the word "delinquent" to describe the boys who came up to New Hamp-shire. They were "slum kids" or "ghetto boys." Though he and oth-ers who used these terms meant no harm, it seemed to me that the words carried a negative connotation. I tried to put myself in the shoes of these boys and quickly realized that such labels *were* harm-ful. They were insulting and judgmental. The boys deserved respect, and I vowed to excise these commonly accepted but fundamentally demeaning terms from my own vocabulary.

From that summer on, I had a different feeling about the boys I had worked with. They weren't "bad" kids. They were just kids who needed some help, and that with it they, too, could truly partake in the Amer-ican dream. The boys that summer might have thought they taught me a lot, but over time they taught me more.

Princeton crew, 150-pound class. I'm at the far right.

Celebrating my twenty-first birthday at the Racquet Club, July 1939.

With Angier and our cousin Nick Biddle at Angier's wedding in 1937.

FIVE

To Sea on the 530

IN THE SPRING OF 1939, the Princeton rugby team went to the international collegiate championships in Bermuda. Our team won the trophy, and I won the heart of a beautiful girl named Alice Rutgers. Allie was on vacation with her friends from the boarding school they attended in Connecticut. She was in the stands for one of our matches against Yale, when I got banged up went to the sideline with a cut over my eye. Apparently seeing something that interested her, Allie decided to come down to the field and assist the medic who was tending to me. She accompanied me to the hospital, and then, at my request, to dinner.

Allie came from a fine New Jersey family. Like me, she was a descendant of a founder of a great university. In her case it was Colonel Henry Rutgers, for whom Rutgers University was named in 1824. We returned north from Bermuda, me to Princeton, Allie to Farmington, and kept up a lively correspondence, including one letter in which I asked her to visit me at camp on Long Island during the coming summer. Thus, Allie became the first female counselor at Duck Island. At the end of the summer I proposed to her, and she said yes.

We were married in September of 1939. That would have been the start of my junior year at Princeton had I not decided to interrupt my education to enter the service. On some level, enlisting was probably a decision I had made years earlier, not long after my Austrian scare in 1934 made me a serious observer of world affairs. In the five years since then it had become increasingly obvious to me that war with Hitler was inevitable. At the end of my sophomore year I felt that getting involved in that coming battle was more important than going back to school. I could always finish my education after the war.

The only question was which branch of the armed forces I would join. At first I considered the Marine Corps because of my Grandfather Biddle's deep involvement. He was still an active reservist in his sixties. When I talked to him about it, he was thrilled—he immediately began making phone calls to various departments in the Corps. It sounded to me as if he was trying to get me in as a general, and that he would go with me. I reconsidered and decided I'd be better off in the Navy.

I applied to Officer Candidates School, and during the entry interview I was asked what I'd like to do once I was commissioned. I didn't have to think about it. I wanted to go to sea, preferably on a destroyer. But the chances of that were nearly nil, I was informed, for the simple reason that there weren't enough ships yet. At that point the Navy was looking for men with at least two years of college who would be trained to go abroad and serve as intelligence officers. What the United States sorely needed at this early point, it seemed, was information—information to help understand and forecast events in Europe, and to plan for the ever-more-likely possibility that the United States would enter the war. With that kind of experience under my belt, I would have much more opportunity to go to sea later on.

Two months after Allie and I were married, I went to Washington to begin my schooling at the Office of Naval Intelligence, where I learned code-breaking and other techniques of espionage. It wasn't what I had in mind when I joined the service, but they made it sound exciting, and I figured I'd get on a ship before too long. Indeed, the ONI school turned out to be a fascinating education in rudimentary espionage and information-gathering. After finishing the course I was told to go home and wait to be called to active duty.

It turned out to be a long wait, more than a year, but I put the time to good use. At first I worked as a credit investigator for the Colonial Trust Company, a small bank on William Street in Manhattan. Then, on a whim, I did something that probably didn't make a lot of sense for a young man expecting to be called to active military duty at any moment. I bought a three-thousand-acre beef cattle ranch in Dutchess County, north of New York City, with a lake and a mountain on the property. It came with a herd of top-grade Aberdeen Angus cattle, seven high-quality bulls, a few dairy cows, and a cattleman who had lived on the ranch for twenty years. The idea was partly to earn a living in the short term, but I also had a long-range plan in mind. The property had a lake, and eventually, I thought, it could make a good site for a summer camp. We moved upstate, and Allie gamely lived the cattle ranch life until my call-up finally came from the Office of Naval Intelligence in April of 1941.

My assignment was to be an assistant naval attaché in Argentina, doing undercover intelligence work while attached to the U.S. embassy in Buenos Aires. I'd be assigned to the ambassador's staff, and since I would be working with civilian members of the State Department, Allie was permitted to come with me to enhance my cover. It was a wonderful perk. A few months after our arrival, I had not only a wife but a son. We named him Anthony Drexel Duke Jr.

Argentina had a large German population, and Hitler's government had many agents and supporters there, as well as in Brazil and Chile. Though the country was officially neutral, it was a hotbed of pro-Nazi activity. The clearest evidence of this was that Allied merchant ships, on their way to Europe, were being sunk by German submarines at an alarming clip as they sailed up the Atlantic Coast. It turned out that Nazi agents were finding out the ship's secret schedules, and then putting out coded radio signals to German subs.

Upon arriving in Buenos Aires, my primary job was to help shut down the sabotage operations, which were continually sinking British and Norwegian ships—and eventually, after Pearl Harbor, American ones. I would spend hours at the embassy decoding signals. Then I'd try to find out where they were coming from so we could shut down the transmitters. I worked with an English fellow who was an expert. We drove a truck containing a radio direction finder, tracking the signals until we could isolate them to a house or other site. Because both the United States and Argentina were officially neutral at this point, we had to turn the matter over to the local police. We'd inform them that an internationally hostile act was being carried out in their jurisdiction, and ask them to shut down the transmission. If they were uncooperative, we'd simply resort to bribery. For a hundred dollars, sometimes two hundred, they'd go into the house or shop from which signals were coming, seize the radio transmitter, and bring it out to us.

My other job involved frequenting an Argentine officers' club called the Circulo de Armas to try to identify those who were pro-Nazi. I'd go in my American uniform and get into conversations and arguments about the war, invariably returning to the embassy with a list of Argentine military officers who were pro-Nazi and a report of what their thoughts were. The idea was to keep the ambassador in tune with what was in the air in military circles, though I can't say it had much effect.

A few months after I arrived in Argentina, Pearl Harbor was attacked. With the United States' inevitable entry into the war now coming to pass, I wanted to get out of South America and into action. I immediately applied for sea duty, but my boss, Captain William D. Brereton, rejected my request. He said my work in Buenos Aires was more important than ever, now that we were at war and our ships were at peril, not just the Brits'. My frustration grew as I began to hear of classmates from St. Paul's who had already been killed in action. I felt it was wrong to virtually sit out the war, decoding transmissions in the snugness of an embassy in a neutral country. To me it was all about actively opposing Hitler, ever since my experience in Austria nearly a decade earlier. And my feelings had only intensified after meeting a man named Gustave Glück soon after I arrived in Buenos Aires.

I was at the embassy one day when the captain of a Norwegian ship made a call to us. He said he had a stowaway on board whom we might want to talk to. "He's got quite a story to tell," this captain said. "Can you send someone down to talk to him?" Captain Brereton told me to go to where the ship was docked and interview the stowaway.

Within a few minutes of meeting Gustave Glück, I knew two things: that he was a delightful and sympathetic character and that he needed a shower, a decent meal, and a friend. I took him back to our apartment, where Allie got him cleaned up and we listened to his story. He was from Berlin, a Jewish man in his late thirties who worked for Deutsche Bank until the day he was warned not to go home. Nazi soldiers had arrested his parents, he was told, and he would be seized as well if he went home. It was the first time I'd heard of this happening. Gus said that he made his way on foot to Norway and stowed away on an ocean liner in Oslo. He slept the whole way in a lifeboat. Gus told me that the Nazis had been rounding up Jews all over Germany for a couple of years and sending them to concentration camps. He said he only knew about the concentration camps because he spoke to two men who had escaped.

I brought Gus to the embassy to tell his story to the naval attaché and then to the U.S. ambassador. "You really uncovered a lot of heavy stuff here," Captain Brereton said. I wrote a lengthy report of what Gus told me and asked the captain to send it up the line to officials in Washington. "I will," he said, "but I can tell you it's not going to get results. We don't have the ships or the men to declare war on Germany." At least not yet.

Gus remained in Buenos Aires, and he I became good friends. His story opened my eyes to what was really happening in Europe, and it put a human face on the tyranny and brutality of Nazi Germany. I feared greatly for Gus's parents, and in his anguished face I saw the pain Hitler was inflicting across Europe. It made my assignment in South America—my confinement, as I saw it—all the more frustrating.

WHILE I WAS GETTING BITS AND PIECES of what was going on in Europe from my remote outpost in South America, my Uncle Tony Biddle was right in the middle of it. In the years since Hitler's rise to power had plunged Europe into war, Uncle Tony had transformed himself from a carefree young man adept at marrying and living well into a serious and highly respected American diplomat. The turning point for him was the episode that occurred during my family's visit to the hunting schloss in the Austrian Alps in the summer of 1935.

The assassination of Austria's chancellor by the Nazis had an immense impact on Uncle Tony, and the informed and incisive report about the Nazi threat he personally delivered to President Roosevelt had a significant impact on FDR. A few months later, Roosevelt asked Uncle Tony to return to Europe as chief of the United States mission to Norway. With Uncle Tony arguably having little more qualification than his and Margaret's hefty contribution to Roosevelt's 1932 campaign, it was generally viewed as a standard political appointment. But Uncle Tony, thirty-nine when he went to Oslo, quickly proved himself to be an important asset to our government. At a time when information from Europe was valuable currency, Uncle Tony's way with people helped him cultivate contacts and harvest critical intelligence. A decade later, the legendary reporter A.J. Liebling wrote a three-part profile of Uncle Tony for *The New Yorker* and observed that he would have made a marvelous journalist. Ambassador Biddle's reports from Oslo so impressed State Department professionals that President Roosevelt soon promoted him to the key post of ambassador to Poland.

It was in Warsaw that Uncle Tony truly took to the world stage, and where he established himself as a trusted adviser to FDR. While Norway was on the fringe of the unfolding events, Poland was in the thick of them. The Poles knew it was only a matter of time before they were attacked—the only question was whether by Germany or Russia. Arriving in Warsaw, Tony and Margaret rented for the American embassy and residence the home of Poland's minister of foreign affairs, Colonel Jozef Beck. It was an eighteenth-century palace whose previous occupants included Napoleon. They also rented a villa eight miles outside Warsaw and a country estate owned by the Polish ambassador to the United States. Tony explained that spending time in the country was the best way to get to know the Polish people. He and Margaret would ride around the country roads on his motorcycle. The trappings might have suggested a pleasant, even carefree life if not for the darkness that they saw descending on Poland and Europe. In fact, Ambassador Biddle was so alert to the growing Nazi menace that Holocaust historians have cited his reports to Washington as evidence that President Roosevelt was well aware of the plight of European Jews but failed to take action soon enough.

On the nights of November 9 and 10, 1938, roaming gangs of Nazi youths and SS troops carried out a nationwide pogrom against Germany's Jews. In a campaign of terror that was to become known as *Kristallnacht* (Night of Broken Glass), more than a hundred synagogues and thousands of Jewish businesses were destroyed and

26,000 Jews were arrested and sent to concentration camps. On the second night of attacks, Tony wrote to President Roosevelt that "the plight of the Jewish populations as a whole in Europe is steadily becoming . . . untenable."

Roosevelt himself acknowledged Uncle Tony's vital reporting from Poland. In one letter to him, FDR wrote: ". . . We cannot stop the spread of Fascism unless world opinion realizes its ultimate dangers. I am awfully glad to have you and Margaret in Warsaw where you are literally on the firing line."

This became literally true on September 1, 1939. At five o'clock that morning, Uncle Tony was awakened by a call from the Polish foreign ministry informing him that German planes were on the way. He scrambled to government offices in the middle of the city to see what was going on, and to inform Washington. An American correspondent later told A.J. Liebling, "I knew something historic had happened because his hair was ruffled." When Uncle Tony's calls failed to go through to Washington, he tried to reach our ambassador in France, William Bullitt. The call was routed through Lithuania, Latvia, Estonia, Finland, Sweden, Denmark, Holland, and Belgium before finally reaching Bullitt in Paris. Shortly before three in the morning, Bullitt reached the White House with Uncle Tony's momentous report: the war in Europe was on.

In the days and weeks that followed. A German plane bombed Uncle Tony's summer residence when he, Margaret, and Margaret's teenaged daughter Peggy were there. Miraculously the bomb didn't detonate—unlike the one that destroyed the villa next door. It wasn't long before the Polish government felt it had to abandon Warsaw. Uncle Tony decided the American contingent should leave as well— members of the embassy, expatriates, reporters, everyone. He personally went around looking for Americans, and at one point went to the house of a favorite reporter and shouted his name from the street until he was sure the man wasn't there. Then he returned to the embassy, where he, Margaret, Margaret's children, and the entire staff, including the Polish house workers, crammed into eight cars on whose roofs they painted "USA" in large letters. This turned out to be not such a good idea: German planes spotted them and chased them with

machine-gun fire. So much for neutrality. Two years before we officially entered the war, the Nazis served notice that they already considered us an ally of the countries they intended to conquer.

The exodus from Warsaw turned out to be the beginning of a harrowing, two-week flight across Poland, with embassy staff members
doing the driving. One of them was Uncle Tony's chief administrative assistant, Eugenia (Genie) McQuatters, who was accompanied
in one car by four other women who were members of the staff. She
stayed at the wheel all night because she was the only one who knew
how to drive. The others sang and shouted to keep her awake.

As it happens, I learned in 2005 that Genie was alive and well, at
age 102, and living in New York. One afternoon, my cousin Tony
Biddle, Uncle Tony's youngest son, and I had the great fortune to
meet Genie in the apartment of Robin Duke, my brother's widow.
Genie's memory for sixty-year-old details was remarkable. (Particularly impressive was her instant recall and perfect pronunciation of
the most unmanageable Polish names.) One thing she had no trouble remembering, though, was how more than once during their
escape from Poland, the embassy staff had to stop and dive into
ditches along the roadside. This was in spite of traveling a route that
was designed to avoid places the Germans had reached, a round-
about path that tripled the time it took to get out of Poland.

Somehow they all survived to the border and the caravan made its
way into Rumania, then Hungary, then Italy, all still neutral at the
time. Finally they crossed into France, where the Polish government
was being set up in exile. Upon his arrival Uncle Tony was surrounded by correspondents. His account of the fall of Poland was
given a lot of space in newspapers both in Europe and America, but
the French—being the French—acted as if he were overreacting.
Their military leaders said the German offensive might have been
impressive to a civilian such as Ambassador Biddle—or to the
Poles—but that no such tactics could succeed against a "real army."

The United States refused to recognize Germany's occupation of
Poland, so the State Department instructed Uncle Tony to remain in
France and establish an embassy-in-exile to go with the Poles'
government-in-exile. The provisional government was set up in

Angers, a serene city in western France, where Tony and Margaret occupied a Renaissance chateau while waiting for the Germans to invade France, which they did soon enough. In May of 1940, as the Nazis drew closer to Paris, it seemed only a matter of time before the French government would do as the Poles had and flee their own capital. Secretary of State Cordell Hull approved Bullitt's request to stay in Paris even if the government didn't, but insisted the United States have a representative to the French government wherever it went. Uncle Tony spoke French and had distinguished himself in Poland, so he was the logical choice. He was appointed Envoy Extraordinary to the government of France, and when the government inevitably abandoned Paris on June 10, Uncle Tony followed the next day. "In five years," Liebling later wrote, "he had evolved from a society man playing at diplomacy to the agent of the United States in one of the most tragic and delicate situations in history."

Serving now as the American representative to not one but two displaced European governments, Uncle Tony's next stop was the city of Tours, where the French regrouped for four days, long enough to confirm that Paris would fall. And then the retreat continued to Bordeaux, where he found the French premier, Paul Reynaud, in despair at the rapidly declining resolve of his colleagues to defend their country. Reynaud's hope to move the government to North Africa to continue the fight seemed increasingly futile without outside help—from the United States.

Upon his arrival, Uncle Tony also found an American consulate jammed with jittery American expatriates clamoring for exit visas and steamship reservations. He couldn't even get up the wide stairway leading from the entrance hall to the consular offices on the second floor. When he tried, people asked him who he thought he was. He considered a straight answer but thought better of it. Instead he put his years of athletic training to work, climbing on the outside of the banister—"kind of a human fly," he said—and hopped over when he got to the top. Few of these hundreds of Americans had a place to stay in Bordeaux, so at night the streets of the city were filled with people, some walking around, others sitting on curbs and talking. There was a man who spent days on end at a table on the terrace of a café, his head cradled in his arms. He was the piano player from Harry's New York Bar in Paris. It was up to Uncle Tony and his coterie to get all these Americans out of France. Spain, the nearest country, was being uncooperative, but after a lot of scheming with the American ambassador in Madrid, Uncle Tony's staff managed to get the great majority of refugees across the border and eventually onto ships headed for the U.S.

During these tense and grim days, Uncle Tony darted around Bordeaux for eighteen or twenty hours a day, gathering intelligence and keeping Washington abreast of the rapidly unfolding events. Meanwhile, he tried to give solace to Reynaud, whose grip on the country was slipping away by the hour. Solace was just about all he could offer, for he knew that the United States was not about to enter the war. Still, for what it was worth, he tried to leave the impression that France wasn't completely alone. He made sure to be seen going to meet Reynaud, and he later said that the two of them would sit in Reynaud's office for ten minutes so that people would think they were actually discussing something.

On June 16, two days after the fall of Paris, Reynaud sent for Uncle Tony. The premier had decided he would have no choice but to turn the government over to those who would capitulate to the Nazis. But he wanted one last crack at trying to convince his closest colleagues to continue to resist. When Tony arrived at Reynaud's quarters at six in the evening, the premier asked him to help him buy some time. Return at midnight, he asked Tony. That would give him six hours to try one last time to persuade his allies to go to Africa. After Tony left, Reynaud beseeched his colleagues to delay their final decision until midnight. Tony Biddle is expecting a message from Washington, he told them, implying the Americans might be coming to France's rescue.

Over the next few hours, word circulated that Ambassador Biddle was awaiting word from his government, and by the time he headed back to the premier's quarters at midnight, the city was abuzz. Liebling described the scene: "As the Ambassador's car made its way through the Place de la Comédie on its way to the rendezvous, the crowd packed so closely about it that the chauffeur had to stop for a moment. The people began to cheer. Somebody had started a rumor that the

United States had entered the war on the side of the Allies and that that was why Monsieur Biddle was on his way to see Reynaud in the middle of the night." Recalling the moment for Liebling two years later, Uncle Tony said, "I sat there in that car and I had a lump in my throat. Because I knew that we weren't going to do a damn thing."

Reynaud that night turned the government of France over to Henri Philippe Pétain. Marshal Pétain had been France's greatest hero during the first World War, but turned out to be its greatest traitor in the second. Pétain immediately sought an armistice with Germany, and within weeks the new political order of France was established. Germany ruled the occupied lands and approved Pétain's institution of a government in Vichy to govern the unoccupied territory. Taking on the title chief of state, Pétain became a notorious collaborator with the Nazis. His fascist-oriented Vichy government was marked by repression and anti-Semitism, ultimately following Hitler's darkest path into evil, deporting Jews to German concentration camps.

Uncle Tony, meanwhile, went home to America. He reported to President Roosevelt, then went around campaigning for him in the fall election. What he talked about most on these campaign stops was what he had witnessed in Europe. By early 1941, he felt the need to return to Europe. And surely there was a need for him. After Poland and then France, three more countries had fallen to the Nazis—Norway, Belgium, and Holland—and all of them had followed Poland's lead, reconstituting their governments to continue to fight Germany from outside their homelands. Though the United States had encouraged and now recognized the growing list of governments-in-exile, we had no ambassadors to them. All our envoys had come home, rather than accompanying the governments to their provisional bases in London. Uncle Tony himself had left the Polish government without an American ambassador on the scene after it fled France along with everyone else. The Poles, too, had found refuge in London—if you could call a place that was being bombed regularly a refuge.

With all these vacancies in the diplomatic corps and few takers—in fact, there were none—President Roosevelt appointed Uncle Tony to them all. Thus, in addition to being ambassador to Poland he was made ambassador to Belgium, Norway, and the Netherlands, and minister to Czechoslovakia, Yugoslavia, Greece, and Luxembourg. The multi-armed job was of course unprecedented, and friends couldn't imagine why Tony and Margaret would want it. "They said, 'What are you making—a collection?'" Margaret told A.J. Liebling. The only country Uncle Tony wouldn't be assigned to in Britain was Britain.

They flew to London in March of 1941, taking along their trusted right hand, Genie McQuatters, and the largest collection of baggage ever carried by a Pan American Clipper. At first they set up at the Ritz, taking the same suite they had occupied during their honeymoon ten years earlier. Uncle Tony would talk to the foreign minister from one country in one of the living rooms while another foreign minister waited in the other; two others would sit in the bedroom waiting their turns. Each country's representative seemed to have a different view of events, and they would talk to Tony in whispers for fear of the others hearing the conversation.

Eventually, Tony found a suitable headquarters for the multiple-embassy in a large apartment on Berkeley Square, marked by a wooden shield with an American eagle on it in the window. From there he would dart about in his trademark sartorial fineness—black overcoat, Homburg hat, striped trousers, and long, square-toed pumps—often sprinting to Grosvenor Square, site of the permanent American embassy, where he would jump into a cab for a visit to the ersatz headquarters of one displaced government or another. As Liebling reported: "The Ambassador's job is largely reportorial, and American newspaper correspondents in London, some of whom are old police reporters and should know, say that he is the best leg man they ever saw. Each of the eight exiled governments receives a steady stream of intelligence from its German-occupied territory. Each has its special needs for aid from the United States government and its individual projects for the European settlement to be reached after the war. Biddle must keep the State Department informed of the news, the pleas, and the programs, and must at the same time do what he can to keep the little Allies reasonably happy. After sound legs, the next essential to a good reporter is the knack of stimulating people to talk freely. A third essential is the ability to remember exactly what they say. Biddle happens to have all three, while a great many grave, profound, and dyspeptic diplomats have had none of them. His Majesty's Government maintains a full-time envoy to each of the exiled regimes, but Biddle outfoots the pack."

Uncle Tony would speak of "my governments" as I might speak of "my boys" at camp. He was so sympathetic to their plight and considerate of their needs that sometimes it was hard to tell whether he represented the United States to them or vice versa. People were always calling on him for help—a minister of health in need of an X-ray machine for a Belgian field hospital, say, or a Norwegian seaman's union chief wanting help in getting a shipment of Christmas packages through an Allied blockade. "Biddle is happy if he is able to do what the caller wants," Liebling wrote. "If he can't, he looks so sad that the disappointed caller feels sorry for him."

In his office, on top of a bookcase, there was a wooden flower holder with the flags of his governments stuck into it. It had a few empty holes in case he got any more countries. The exiled governments—each of which had its own intelligence service in London—were wary of one another and jealous when it came to Uncle Tony's attentions. Genie McQuatters, when I met her recently, told of the time a freelance spy who was working simultaneously for two of the governments turned up dead. Genie, in addition to being Uncle Tony's all-around aide, played a crucial role as a courier of top secret messages he sent to his contacts around London. She had an extraordinary ability to commit to memory an entire memorandum, word-for-word, and then deliver it orally and in person to the recipient.

NINE MONTHS AFTER UNCLE TONY'S ARRIVAL in London, Pearl Harbor was attacked and we finally entered the war. President Roosevelt's stirring declaration of war made me increasingly impatient, nearly desperate, to leave Argentina and join the war effort in a real way. But it would be another six months before I got the chance. Early in the summer of 1942, the Navy put out a notice that seemed just the ticket: "Ensigns and Lieutenants (junior grade) under 33 years of age who are physically and psychologically qualified and who have 50 hours' solo flying and a pilot's certificate may now become naval aviators . . . Upon successful completion of a civilian pilot training instructor's course, these officers will be transferred to naval flight training centers for refresher courses leading to the designation of naval aviator . . ."

The Navy was building thousands of fighter planes and needed men to fly them. If I couldn't go to sea, maybe I could take to the air. I took the idea to Captain Brereton. "Forget it," he said. "With your job here, it'll take you five years to get all that training and solo time."

"Well, what if I don't want to forget it?" I said defiantly.

"I can't stop you from learning to fly on your off time," he said, "but you'll need those hours to get out of here."

I showed the notice to Don McNeil, a good friend of mine who was also a lieutenant junior grade. Don was a national tennis champion who had defeated Bobby Riggs for the U.S. Open title at Forest Hills in 1940. He was game. But where were we going to learn to fly? We asked around and heard that there was an American colonel named Cloyce Tippett—"Tip," to his friends—who was teaching Argentinean Air Force flyers about modern aerial tactics at a nearby flight school. We went to him and asked if he'd teach us. He said he'd do what he could to squeeze us in. "If you're willing to get up at five in the morning," he told us, "I'll give you as many hours as I can."

Over the next year I flew every chance I got, and before long, Navy men were coming to *me* to teach them how to fly. The flight school had a World War I-era Fleet biplane with two seats, one behind the other, each with a joystick.

A friend of mine, another lieutenant junior grade named Jim Casey, had the same job as me in Uruguay, and he, too, saw flight training as a way out of South America. He would come over from Montevideo each week and meet me at the airport, where I'd take him aloft and teach him to fly. But after a couple of lessons, the manager of the flight school was onto me. He removed one of the joysticks to discourage me from doing any unauthorized teaching.

But I wasn't discouraged. Hell, I told Jim, I'll get the plane in the air, then give you the joystick. All I had to do was unscrew it from its metal fitting and hand it over to him. He would put the joystick into the fitting in front of him, fly the plane, then give it back to me when we were ready to land. We took off and the plan worked fine until we got to the last part. He tried to unscrew the joystick to give it back to me for the landing, but he couldn't get it out. He had screwed it in too tight. He turned around and looked at me with panic. Flying at 120 miles an hour, we couldn't hear each other, so I motioned to him to keep trying. For a good ten minutes, he strained and pulled. I realized I'd made a big mistake and started to think it might get us killed. Finally, Jim was able to loosen the joystick and hand it back to me without dropping it. We landed safely, but that was the last lesson I gave him or anyone else.

It took me a little more than a year, until the fall of 1943, but after two hundred hours of flight time I finally got my fifty solo hours, my navigation certificate—and my exit from Argentina. My friends—fellow Navy officers, embassy staff, and various cohorts of assorted nationalities—gave me a grand send-off, and Allie and I headed home to the United States with eighteen-month-old Tony Jr. First stop: Jacksonville, Florida, where I happily presented my flight-training credentials, only to face a crushing bit of military bureaucracy.

"You're not eligible," I was told by an officer.

"Sure I am," I insisted. "I've got my hours. Here's my certification."

"No, that's not the problem," the officer said. "The eligibility is for ensigns and lieutenant jg's only."

"Right," I said. "I'm a lieutenant jg."

"No, you're a full lieutenant."

"No, I'm not," I corrected him. "I'm a jg."

"No, you're a full lieutenant," he insisted me. "Says right here." He showed me a directive dated a few days earlier that all jg's who were approved by their commanding officers were promoted to full lieutenant, retroactive to a month earlier. "You're on the list," he said. "I guess your mail hasn't caught up with you. Congratulations!"

He was right. I'd been promoted and didn't even know it, and it meant that I no longer qualified for the flight-training program. I was incredulous, furious—all that flight time for nothing. I tried every argument and angle, including offering to decline the promotion. But there was no fighting the Navy. When I finally cooled down, I went down to the Navy headquarters in Miami to see what my options were. With the air blocked, I set my sights back on my original plan, to go to sea.

My first choice was to qualify for a PT boat training, but the training school was full. The next possibility, I was told, was to join the amphibious forces, an innovative and increasingly critical branch whose performance would later come to be seen as one of the key differences between victory and defeat for the Allied forces. In order to land men and equipment for assaults from the sea on enemy territories, the Navy was designing all kinds of new vessels. The one that appealed to me was a football-field-sized ship called an LST, the brainchild of Winston Churchill himself.

With the 1940 British evacuation of Dunkirk in mind, Churchill had pressed President Roosevelt on the need for a ship that could transport large numbers of battle tanks, heavy rolling equipment, and men directly onto the beachheads of forward battle areas. Roosevelt and his war planners agreed, and made the project a priority. In three separate acts between February 1942 and December 1943 Congress authorized the construction of more than a thousand landing ships for tanks, dubbed LSTs, along with destroyer escorts and assorted landing craft. These amphibious forces would spearhead the eventual Allied invasions of Europe and the Pacific.

The LST was a 327-foot, 10,000-ton amphibious vessel with two decks. It was designed to carry up to a thousand men and dozens of tanks, plus a 110-foot landing craft, called an LCT (for Landing Craft-Tank), that would eventually carry tanks and infantrymen to the beachheads. In addition, the LSTs would have six 36-foot troop carriers called LCVPs (Landing Craft Vehicle-Personnel). Commanding an LST sounded challenging and good to me. But I would have to prove myself worthy of such great responsibility.

After some basic training at Fort Schuyler, New York, I was dispatched in December of 1943 with a group of other prospective commanding officers to the Navy's amphibious training program at Solomons, Maryland, on the Chesapeake Bay. There we went out on LSTs with a senior captain, a four-striper who showed us the ropes during a series of arduous maneuvers and mock landings that made clear how much we needed to know before we would even be considered as commanding officers. At that point we didn't know where in the world we'd end up—with invasions of both Europe and Asia likely, we could be sent to the Atlantic, the Pacific, or the Mediterranean—and so our trainers tried to simulate landings on different kinds of beaches. It was Normandy and Guadalcanal on the Chesapeake. Often they wouldn't tell us where we were going when we left port. Then they'd throw little surprises at us to see how we reacted. "Lieutenant Duke, get up on deck and take over deck watch," I would hear. Then: "There's a fire in the starboard forty-millimeter magazine!" At first, I must admit, I didn't know what the hell I was doing. But I learned, and by the end of the month I demonstrated that I could react quickly and correctly to just about every possible situation that might present itself. I quickly learned how to make the ungainly LST do what I wanted it to do. And I felt I had the leadership qualities to get men to do what I wanted them to do.

Pronounced fit for duty as an LST captain at the age of twenty-five, I was presented with the first members of what was to be the nucleus crew of LST 530—a ship that had not yet been built. There were seventeen of us, and we were a young and pretty green bunch. George Ragle, a schoolmaster from Texas in his late twenties, would be my executive officer. Charlie Pierce, a fellow New Yorker who was a graduate of Fordham, would be the ship's deck officer. Charlie was gregarious, funny, extremely hard-working—and modest. It would be a full year before we would find out that before the war he had been one of the "Seven Blocks of Granite," the fearsome line of the Fordham football team that included Vince Lombardi and played in the Rose Bowl. To get an idea of just how sturdy Charlie was, consider that he played both offense and defense and never missed a single minute of play for two full seasons.

With one exception, none of my men had ever set foot on a ship or boat before. The exception was Roy Black, an ensign who would be my engineering officer. Roy was to become my closest friend and adviser. He was about ten years older than me and had been in the Navy since he was sixteen. A funny, wise, somewhat cynical man, he gave me advice that got me through my early days as a novice ship captain headed for perilous waters. Though it was my nature to be affable and accommodating—and I was determined to have a "happy ship" after reading books that described grim ones—Roy advised me to come on rather stone-faced with my nucleus crew. "When everyone asks, 'When do we get leave?' don't be too easy," he told me. "Wait and see how they do their jobs and how they behave before doing any favors. You want to know who you can depend on later when the chips are down. You can loosen up a bit later on, but if you're too easy on them right away, you might not know till it's too late." (As Roy foresaw, I was frequently put to the test later on as we went from port to port before shipping out for Europe. I must have had sixty men ask for leave so they could get married. Some actually were getting married—all I had to do was decide which ones.)

Roy's advice felt right, even from my limited experience in leadership positions at St. Paul's and at Duck Island. I'd learned that it was crucial to make clear that expectations for performance were high, and that the best way to get people to strive to do their best was to put some barriers in front of them. The other piece, which I haven't stopped emphasizing to this day, was the importance of creating an atmosphere in which everyone respected one another, no matter his rank or status. Of course the Navy was no summer camp. Presumably the nucleus crew of LST 530, and the rest of what would eventually be its crew of more than one hundred, would understand what was at stake. But the principles were the same. "Every one of us must know our specific job and do it the very best we can," I told them. "When things get rough, our very survival will depend on all of us using our maximum abilities and, above all, working together."

After training at Solomons, we went our separate ways for a few days of leave, then met in Chicago for anti-aircraft training. From there we regrouped in Jeffersonville, Indiana, a town on the Ohio River directly across from Louisville, where our ship was being readied for action by the Jeffersonville Boat & Machine Company. After the last bolts were tightened, I toured my brand-new ship. I couldn't help but be impressed with the captain's quarters. It was bigger than I expected—about the size of my dorm room at Princeton—with a desk and a filing cabinet that would be staffed by a yeoman who would be my administrative assistant. Behind it was my sleeping quarters.

The 530's maiden voyage was down the Mississippi, destined for New Orleans. It was there, on March 6, 1944, that the ship was officially commissioned to the reverberating sounds of the Star Spangled Banner being played on the dock next to where we were moored. In New Orleans, a giant hoist swung the 110-foot LCT directly onto the 530's main deck, where heavy cables were used to secure her for the voyage across the Atlantic. The six LCVPs, meanwhile, were secured to the 530 on davits—steel braces with pulleys—that could be raised and lowered. There were three on each side of the LST, and in addition to carrying troops and tanks to battle they could also be used as lifeboats if need be. Three weeks later we were declared ready for combat and ordered up to New York City. We crossed the Gulf of Mexico, rounded the southern tip of Florida, and sailed up the Eastern Seaboard, stopping in Norfolk and other ports. All along the route we picked up more crew members. We had about 125 by the time we were ready to leave New York as part of a large convoy bound for Britain. When Ensign Cliff Sinnett introduced himself in New York, I thought of the Mack Sennett comedies, and informed him that from here on he would be known as Mack. Mack and his pal, Ensign Geoffrey Bromfield, spent the next few days hunting down guns, rockets, and other equipment around the Brooklyn Navy Yard—"cumshaw," as we referred to gear that was scrounged, swapped for, and often liberated without requisition (if nobody was looking).

Before our ship was sealed—nobody on or off—I kept three-year-old Tony Jr. aboard with me one night, and he woke up the next morning to the blare of the ship's horn. Hoping for a last, memorable goodbye, I ignored the loose-lips-sink-ships dictum and told Allie to take a ferry over to Staten Island and stand with Tony Jr. at a certain spot at a certain time and look for the 530 in the convoy of ships headed past the Statue of Liberty on its way out to sea. The next day, I stood on the bridge peering through my binoculars as we sailed near the designated place. I spotted Allie and Tony waving wildly, and I waved back with a big smile. Hoping but not knowing, of course, that I would come home to them safely.

WE WERE PART OF A HUNDRED-SHIP CONVOY starting out on what would be a twelve-day voyage to Europe. It was an eventful voyage that included a four-day storm that kept most of the crew in their bunks, stomachs turning mercilessly. At one point Mack and I were the only officers on deck; we ran the ship ourselves for an entire watch. More treacherous, though, were the encounters with German submarines that we were told to be prepared for. With German agents certainly reporting the departure of such a large convoy—something I knew about from my time in Argentina—we would have to sail on a zigzag course and observe a total blackout at night. Not even a cigarette could be lit. I saw a man on gunnery watch on another LST light one up; that ship was later torpedoed, and lives were lost. Two or three of our ships were attacked by submarines, and one of my men swore he saw a torpedo pass in front of our bow at one point. I felt myself literally moving steadily toward a war that up to now had seemed remote and almost unthreatening.

Meanwhile, the members of my crew were still getting to know one another. Among them were four black men, including one whose obvious intelligence some of his white shipmates seemed to take as a threat—especially when I assigned the man to more responsible duties. I knew I had to take immediate action. "I'm just not going to tolerate that," I told the men. "We are all Americans on this ship and I'm going to insist that every man be recognized and respected for who they are." If that wasn't direct enough, I warned that if I heard any of them use racist language on my ship they'd be looking at two days in the brig. I'm not going to say I eliminated racism from the minds of my men, but I can say that on the surface, at least, it was rarely an issue again.

We arrived safely in Milford Haven, Wales on May 5, and from there we headed for the Thames River, south of London, to join the British Amphibious Command. To get there we had to make a hazardous trip through the English Channel, slipping through the Dover Straits under cover of night to avoid the German U-boats infesting the waters. By late May we knew we would be involved in an invasion on a grand scale, but exactly where and when was, of course, information well beyond my pay grade. Rumors were rampant—they had been since our Atlantic crossing—but there was no point in believing any of them. My own feeling had been that we'd pick up troops and tanks and invade France as soon as we reached Britain. But for six or seven weeks all we

The officers of the 530.

Returning to Plymouth, England, after D-Day, we received orders that all ships' crews were to be photographed on deck. This is about two-thirds of ours; the rest had jobs to do.

did was move around a lot, partly to avoid giving any hints to the Germans but also to continue training for the invasion.

The men got a fair amount of liberty during those weeks, sampling the fish 'n chips, the pubs, and the girls of the English countryside. Meanwhile, I tried to reach my Uncle Tony Biddle, whom I knew was in London—and in uniform. I had received a letter from Mother saying Uncle Tony had resigned his diplomatic positions and been commissioned a lieutenant colonel in the army, stationed at the Allied Central Command headquarters in London. It struck me as an odd development, but Mother's letter offered no clarification. Not surprisingly, Uncle Tony knew that I was headed for England, and he gave Mother a special code number I could use to reach him once I arrived. He was very happy to hear from me, and we made plans to meet at a time when my ship would be tied up in Southampton for a few days.

I took the train up to London, and Uncle Tony met me with a great hug. He cut a dashing figure in his colonel's uniform. He took me to lunch at White's Club, where we drank martinis—my first taste of alcohol in well over a year—and talked about everything but what his job was. I knew it had to be important, based on his history. And he did seem to know a lot about the coming invasion, though he shared very little.

After lunch, Uncle Tony's sergeant major took the wheel of his jeep and began driving us through the streets of London. I reminded my uncle I had a train to catch, but he said not to worry, we had plenty of time. "Come on back to my office," he said. "I'll show you around and you can meet my boss."

"Who's your boss?" I asked.

"I think you might recognize him," he said coyly.

We arrived at a beautiful old house on Grosvenor Square and went in a back entrance, past a sentry with a rifle who greeted my uncle respectfully. "Good afternoon, Colonel Biddle." We boarded a small elevator, and went up a couple of floors. We walked down a long, narrow hallway, and Uncle Tony knocked on the last door on the left. A colonel opened it and let us in. And there, sitting at a desk framed by the flags of the United States and Britain, was General Dwight D. Eisenhower. Ike in the flesh. He stood up, and locked eyes with me.

"Captain Duke—you've arrived," he said, soberly. "We can now proceed with the invasion plans."

I was too stunned (and a bit light-headed from the martinis) to utter a word in response. Ike turned to the colonel and said, "Captain Duke has come from the United States with part of the invasion force. I'd like to have the staff come in and meet him." The door opened and half a dozen high-ranking officers entered the room and saluted me. Was I dreaming this? I managed to return the salute without passing out. The room was silent for a moment, and then Uncle Tony began to laugh. The others joined him, Ike included, and then the whole room erupted in an explosion of chuckles.

After the laughter subsided, Eisenhower told me, "Your uncle's told me all about you. I understand you had a camp for underprivileged boys before the war."

"Yes, sir," I said.

"Well, with God's help you'll get back to it."

"I hope so, sir."

Ike asked me a few questions: what convoy my ship had come over with, how long my men and I had trained, how well-equipped we were. Then he pulled down a map of Europe and slapped it with a pointer. "We're going to invade sometime in the next twelve months," he said. "I know all about your type of ship, and I hope you realize how important it is. You do know that you will be going over on D-Day."

"I do, sir," I said.

He extended his hand and said, "I hope to see you again."

Returning to my ship later that day, I called everyone together and told them, "I've just been to London and I bring the greetings of our Supreme Allied Commander." I told them the story, but no one believed me.

It wasn't until after the war that I learned the full story behind Uncle Tony's decision to trade his high-profile and influential ambassadorial posts—a job he loved and thrived on—for a military position of uncertain significance. He had the impossible title Liaison Officer of the Supreme Allied Commander for Relationships with the Allied Governments, which suggested that he was doing basically the same work as before, the major difference being his wardrobe. As I later learned, it was essentially the result of a falling out he had had with President Roosevelt.

Late in 1943, Roosevelt, Winston Churchill, and Josef Stalin met for the first time, in Teheran, Iran. Though maybe less famous than their later meetings in Yalta and Potsdam, the Teheran summit is considered by many historians to have been the most important "Big Three" conference of the war because it was here that D-Day was firmly set in motion. Among other issues, it was agreed that a "supreme commander" for the Allied invasion of Europe would be appointed. Because the United States had become the dominant military force among the Allies, there was no disagreement that the supreme commander should be an American. Roosevelt and Churchill first thought of Army Chief of Staff George C. Marshall, who had played the principal role in coordinating the overall American military effort. But Roosevelt decided Marshall was more valuable in Washington. He suggested General Dwight D. Eisenhower, commander of Allied forces in North Africa and the Mediterranean. Churchill and Stalin agreed.

Besides the Allied invasion of Europe, there was discussion in Teheran of the continent's post-war geography, particularly of Poland. In a deal that he kept to himself, Roosevelt informally agreed to Stalin's insistence on pushing Poland's borders west, expanding the Soviet frontier. Roosevelt was in a mood to pacify Stalin because he wanted the Russians to join the war in the Pacific as soon as Germany was defeated. But it would be an abandonment of the pledge Uncle Tony had made to Poland's exiled government, and by extension to all his other governments in London. There were many reasons for Roosevelt to keep this secret, but the one he cited to Stalin was that there were nearly seven million Americans of Polish extraction and he didn't want to lose their votes in the 1944 election. Roosevelt was so secretive, in fact, that he kept even Secretary of State Cordell Hull in the dark. Ambassador Bullitt later said that Hull complained to him a few months later that he still didn't know what had happened in Teheran.

But through his own channels, Uncle Tony found out. And he was furious. He wrote to FDR, warning that if the President went ahead with his plans, not only would it mean breaking a solemn pledge we had made to Poland and the other governments, but it would be creating a new problem after the war. How astute he was.

When Tony's sources in the Polish intelligence service told him that Roosevelt planned to abandon the other central European countries as well, Tony asked to come home and have a personal conversation with Roosevelt at the White House. "I know what you're going to do," he told the President. "You can't know what I'm going to do," FDR replied. When Tony told the President what he'd heard from his Polish intelligence sources, Roosevelt said, "Those goddamn Poles."

Uncle Tony, of course, failed to change Roosevelt's mind. Having made pledges that he now knew would not be kept, he felt he had no choice but to resign his ambassadorships. But by no means did he want to leave Europe, or even London. And he didn't have to. General Eisenhower immediately hired him, commissioning him a lieutenant colonel and promoting him to brigadier general a few months later.

EISENHOWER HAD TOLD ME we'd be invading Europe "within the year," but I knew he was being overly vague, implying for security reasons that D-Day wasn't imminent. But it *was* imminent. Our orders came less than three weeks later.

We were sent first to Plymouth, where I saw a man named Larry Snell, whom I'd known from the Racquet Club in New York. He told me a harrowing story about a tragedy that had befallen the LST squadron that included several ships whose crews I had trained with in the Chesapeake Bay. "This is very secret stuff," Snell said. "I'll only tell you if you promise never to divulge it."

I agreed, though I can tell the story now because it has since become open history. Larry told me that just a few weeks earlier, in late April, the U.S. Command had staged a rehearsal for the coming invasion, landing assault forces of the 4th Infantry Division on a stretch of beach along the south coast of England, near Lyme Bay. The spot, known as Slapton Sands, had been chosen because it resembled a beach on the French coast of Normandy code-named Utah. The practice assault was known as Exercise Tiger, Snell said, and commanders had considered it so vital that they'd ordered the use of live artillery fire by the amphibious forces involved in the exercise. (Three thousand British civilians had been relocated from the region.) A flotilla of eight LSTs, including the group I'd been with, was sent out to transport a follow-up force of tanks, jeeps, and a thousand troops. In all 30,000 men were involved in the exercise.

About a quarter-mile out, the LSTs divided into two columns and began to fan out for their landings on the beach. They had just begun this maneuver when, out of the darkness, German torpedo boats suddenly appeared. (It was later determined that they had been on routine patrol out of the French port of Cherbourg and learned of heavy radio traffic in Lyme Bay.) The Germans sped right down the line of LSTs, firing 40-millimeter shells and hitting three ships. One keeled over and sank within minutes; another burst into flames, with gasoline from the vehicles aboard feeding the fire. Trapped below decks, hundreds of soldiers and sailors went down with the ships. A total of 749 men were lost, by far the most costly training incident of the war. Orders were put out for strict secrecy about the incident. Most worrisome for the military command was the possibility that ten officers who had been closely involved in the planning of the invasion—and could not be accounted for—might have been taken prisoner by the Germans. But the bodies of all ten soon washed ashore.

The story of Exercise Tiger was a burden to know, adding to the tension that was mounting as we got closer to the invasion. On the first of June, we were ordered to proceed from Plymouth up the Thames River to an inland British naval base at Deptford. Assigned to the British fleet, we would load up with about twenty Churchill tanks, along with trucks, ammunition, and eight hundred men. Because we would be serving as a medical ship after the initial landing, we would also take on three doctors and large quantities of medical supplies.

At Deptford, I encountered my first attack—not by any German torpedo boat but by a British colonel who became furious when the low tide caused my ship to get stuck on the concrete that came down the bank of the river. We had gone in at high tide but by the time we were all loaded up, the tide level had dropped, running us aground.

The British colonel came aboard, screaming. "Get this bloody fucking ship out of here! You're going to break its back!"

"I was ordered in here, and we're now loaded up and we'll just have to wait for high tide to withdraw," I said.

He continued to rant and rave, finally becoming so hysterical that I had to get two of my men to remove him. I'll never forget the sight of them walking up to this full colonel of the British army, lifting him into the air, and carrying him off the ship. Nerves were frayed, indeed. Sometimes the waiting is the hardest part.

On Sunday, June 3, I received orders to report with my executive officer to a large tent adjacent to the shipyard. We would be there for four hours, the order said, and when we returned our ship would be sealed. This seemed strong evidence that the invasion was imminent. I got in a small boat with George Ragle, my executive officer, and Mack Sinnett brought us to shore. We made our way to the tent, which was set up with three hundred folding chairs facing a stage that resembled a boxing ring. When the place was full, I saw that the great majority of men were British; I could see only about half a dozen American uniforms sprinkled around the room.

Suddenly there was a hush, a shuffling of feet, chairs squeaking over the floor as everyone rose to a standing position. A British major general and his aide preceded a tall, graying admiral to the platform. They were followed by a dozen men carrying individual packages and charts. The blackout curtains were drawn, and the only light came from a single, bare bulb suspended over the platform.

The admiral was Sir Bertram Ramsay. He had spearheaded the evacuation of Dunkirk in 1940, and was now in charge of the Allied Naval Expeditionary Force for the invasion of France. "Good evening, gentlemen. Please be seated," he said in a calm but booming voice.

"Gentlemen, this is what you have been training for, and I wish you all well and Godspeed," the admiral began, words I will never forget. He turned and pulled down a large rolled map behind the platform. It showed the area in France where the invasion was to take place. It was between LeHavre and Cherbourg, a stretch of some one hundred miles in the region known as Normandy. "For you who are assembled here today, your particular sector for landing is here." He pointed to the western extremity of the long series of beachheads. "For you naval captains, there are detailed charts, instructions, and battle plans contained in these packages. You will take them back aboard your ships now and together with the military commanders study them carefully and commit them to memory. Be prepared to get underway within twelve hours." I couldn't believe what I was hearing. Twelve hours? Clearly they weren't taking any chances of word getting out.

We commanding officers returned to the boat landing escorted by members of the Royal Marines who had Thompson submachine guns slung over their shoulders. Back onboard, I opened my orders and read that the 530 was to join a circle of ships off the Isle of Wight and proceed to an area off the Normandy coast designated Juno Beach. From west to east, it was the second of the five landing areas for the invasion. We were to remain six miles off the coast until the ships ahead of us had landed and discharged their personnel. The orders spelled out very specifically where we were supposed to be and what we would be doing at every hour. I was overwhelmed with the amount of information I had to study and keep in my head. I realized that even one or two ships going the wrong way at the wrong time could have disastrous consequences.

All that day, the 530 loaded up with men, trucks, tanks, jeeps, and virtually every kind of military weapon in the Allied arsenal. Hundreds of British soldiers marched, walked, drove, or rode aboard through the ship's immense, open bow doors as she sat tied up at the loading ramp at Tillbury, on the Thames estuary. We were secured by port and starboard cables leading forward and by an anchor dropped off the stern from about four hundred feet offshore. It was a neat trick: The anchor not only kept the ship perpendicular to the shoreline, but when it came time to back off it also helped the ship reverse in a fairly straight line, a tricky maneuver with rows of LSTs landing close together.

The pressure I felt in this moment was enormous; I had to work hard to mask my queasiness. I'd never had so many men aboard before, and I was well aware that more than a few of them outranked me. At the same time, I felt pride at seeing these fully-seasoned British troops pour aboard my ship. At the captains' meeting the day before, I'd learned that I would be transporting units of the famed 8th Army Desert Rat

SUPREME HEADQUARTERS
ALLIED EXPEDITIONARY FORCE

Encouraging words from General Eisenhower prior to D-Day.

Soldiers, Sailors and Airmen of the Allied Expeditionary Force!

You are about to embark upon the Great Crusade, toward which we have striven these many months. The eyes of the world are upon you. The hopes and prayers of liberty-loving people everywhere march with you. In company with our brave Allies and brothers-in-arms on other Fronts, you will bring about the destruction of the German war machine, the elimination of Nazi tyranny over the oppressed peoples of Europe, and security for ourselves in a free world.

Your task will not be an easy one. Your enemy is well trained, well equipped and battle-hardened. He will fight savagely.

But this is the year 1944 ! Much has happened since the Nazi triumphs of 1940-41. The United Nations have inflicted upon the Germans great defeats, in open battle, man-to-man. Our air offensive has seriously reduced their strength in the air and their capacity to wage war on the ground. Our Home Fronts have given us an overwhelming superiority in weapons and munitions of war, and placed at our disposal great reserves of trained fighting men. The tide has turned ! The free men of the world are marching together to Victory !

I have full confidence in your courage, devotion to duty and skill in battle. We will accept nothing less than full Victory !

Good Luck ! And let us all beseech the blessing of Almighty God upon this great and noble undertaking.

Dwight D Eisenhower

One of our landings on Normandy after D-Day in the summer of 1944.

battalion, veterans of the battles that drove German Field Marshal Erwin Rommel and his army out of North Africa. Their commander was a forty-six-year-old brigadier general named Gibbons who had led a squadron of Churchill tanks in Africa and had seen action in France. He, his officers, and most of the men he brought aboard the 530 had the kind of military experience that made my crew seem like schoolchildren in comparison. Yet there was no hint of arrogance in their attitude. They were friendly and respectful.

On Monday, June 4, 1944, General Eisenhower received what was to become the world's most famous weather report. He decided to delay the invasion by a day, requiring some ships already at sea to be recalled. The next morning, assured of a break in the weather, Ike said the famous words, "Okay. We'll go." Within hours, an armada of 3,000 landing craft, including LST 530, would be on its way to Normandy. When we got the word, I assembled everyone—my crew as well as the hundreds of British soldiers we would be delivering to the beaches of Normandy. General Gibbons had asked me to say a brief word to his men before sailing. I'd seen my share of Gary Cooper movies, and I was ready with a stirring speech. But General Gibbons took me aside and said, "Listen, chap, my men have been in Dunkirk, and among them are Desert Rats who've fought Rommel. They're very experienced and cynical, so don't get too fancy."

"Yes, sir," I said, then turned to the assembled troops. "Good luck, men," I said. "Dismissed!"

The only other thing I told them was that the ship was now "sealed," meaning we had gotten our orders and no one was to get on or off—under penalty of death. This was to be the biggest invasion in the history of warfare, and the military command was justifiably obsessive about secrecy. There were known to be German spies all over England, and the military command feared that once crew members were let in on the plan they could be susceptible to being captured and tortured for information. So nobody could get on or off the ship. So serious was the military command that we were told that once we were officially sealed, anyone seen outside the ship would be shot.

That night, a young sailor named Sizemore came to my quarters, looking ashen. "Captain, I'm getting off the ship," he said in a Tennessee drawl. "I heard what you said, but I'm still getting off."

"Why, Sizemore?" I asked, figuring that was the best way to start what was obviously going to be a very difficult conversation.

"I'm scared shitless," he said.

"Well, I'm sure everyone is," I said. "We're all scared."

"But I'm only fifteen," he said. "I don't have to be here."

"Fifteen?" I asked.

He nodded, almost trembling.

"Sizemore, that's fascinating," I said. "How did you get in the Navy?"

"Well, my brother's nineteen and I borrowed his motorcycle license. It got me in and that's why I'm here. I went to boot training in upstate New York, then they sent me down to Solomons, and now I'm here. Please, Captain."

I looked closely and saw that Sizemore wasn't shaving yet. Now he began to cry.

"Sizemore, I'm going to make this easy for you. I'm going to let you in on a secret. I'm probably more scared than you are. So I'm going to give you a job. Tomorrow morning I'm going to keep you near me and if you see me sniveling and crying, doing what you're doing now, you go see the executive officer right away, but quick. And you tell him to have me arrested by armed guards and put in the brig with you. And we will remain in the brig until this invasion is over, and if the ship sinks we will remain in the brig under water for what remains of our lives."

Sizemore's eyes got wider and wider as I spun these ridiculous instructions.

"You got that?" I asked.

"Now, uh . . . what am I supposed to do?"

"If you want, you can write it down," I said. I handed him a pad and pencil and repeated the instructions, embellishing as I went. "You'll tell the exec, 'Mr. Ragle, the captain's going crazy, he's crying and he doesn't want to be the captain anymore. And you have to arrest him.'"

With that, young Mr. Sizemore, now more baffled than frightened, returned to his shipmates. The next morning I would keep him close to me, trying to keep him out of harm's way while showing him that men can be scared as hell and still do what they have to do.

I ORDERED THE OFFICER OF THE DECK to get both engines started, and the signal to do so was passed to the engine room deep inside the hull, forty feet below. A few seconds later a slight vibration told the thousand men aboard LST 530 that we were about to be under way. "Cast off bow cables, prepare to winch in stern anchor," went the call. "Both engines back one-third." The ship shuddered and strained, as if refusing to budge. General Gibbons glanced at me. It was his first time aboard an LST. "Sometimes these tubs give us a hard time," I assured him, "but if you anticipate what they want to do, they behave."

"You enjoy this part of it, don't you?" he asked.

"Yes, I do," I said, keeping my eyes fixed on a point ashore to determine the slightest beginning of movement. Just then, the 530 belched diesel fumes and smoke and shook all over. Then she moved.

Sailing across the channel in a line of LSTs, we saw ships of every description around us: destroyers, minesweepers, even a battleship. Sporadic attacks by German planes and torpedo boats kept all hands at general quarters, but we made it across without casualties. Unfortunately, we witnessed a different fate for one of our sister LSTs, the 682. She struck a mine, exploded, and sank. Hoping our charmed life would continue, we stood off Juno Beach for twelve hours through the night, waiting for six LCVP landing crafts ahead of us to deliver their troops to the beach amid sporadic air attacks by single German planes. Finally, as evening fell, we eased our way through sunken ships, gunfire, and general noise and confusion. We could see the flash of long-range gunfire coming from German forces in the hills behind the town, and bodies sprinkled on the beach. When I saw mines sink two ships ahead of me, I decided to break off ten degrees to port. It would mean hitting Gold Beach rather than Juno, but it was better than hitting no beach at all.

"You're breaking the column!" I heard over the radio from a battleship laying a mile offshore. "Get back in line!"

Under the circumstances, there was no point in arguing. "You're breaking up," I said. "We're going off the air."

We were under fire all the way in but managed to hit the beach in relative safety to off-load our men, tanks, and trucks. Then we pulled out, anchored half a mile offshore, and flew a huge Red Cross flag to turn ourselves into a hospital ship. On D-Day night, our wardroom was converted into an operating room. We took on dozens of wounded, and the doctors worked on them as we headed back to England. Many of the most gravely wounded died as we crossed the Channel. Among the casualties were some of the very men we had transported to the beach earlier in the day. General Gibbons himself lost his right leg. But my crew of 125 survived virtually unscathed. We lost only one crew member, the ship's cook, and it was under unusual circumstances. Prior to our departure he had been tremendously afraid, shaking and crying with fear. Then, while we were under fire he disappeared from his watch position. We found him later in his bed, unconscious. We got him to the hospital when we hit England but he died of an apparent heart attack. It seemed he had literally been scared to death. But I didn't want his family to know that, so I wrote to his wife simply saying he had been killed in action.

D-DAY WAS JUST THE BEGINNING of our European adventure. Over the next six months, we were to make thirty-six round-trips across the Channel. We would transport fresh troops to France, and in one instance made an emergency run to Brittany—under the noses of the Germans holding the Channel Islands—to deliver ammunition and fuel for General Patton's fast-moving army. On our trips back across the Channel to England, we carried many wounded and dead Americans, along with German prisoners of war.

On one memorable trip, we placed eight hundred POWs on the tank deck under guard by my men joined by six British guards with machine guns. At one point, a German captain started to get the POWs riled up and we feared they might try to take over the ship. There was a rumor that one of them had a gun. Finally, I told one of my German-speaking men to get on the loudspeaker: "Tell them if they don't quiet down the captain is going to turn the ship around, drop them on the beach, and let the infantry take care of them." I ordered the ship turned completely around, the big LST shaking and rolling. Unable to see anything from the tank deck, of course, the POWs didn't know we'd come 360 degrees and were still headed for England. That quieted them down.

Returning to Plymouth, we delivered the POWs to a fleet of prison-bound trucks and turned over another seventy-five or so wounded to the Red Cross. We also had the sad duty to transport a large number of flag-draped coffins for burial in England. Anchored off the French coast the night before, we had used our officers' wardroom as a makeshift hospital, and some of the severely wounded men had died before we could get them back to England.

The battles on the European front were so intense in those months that as soon as we and other LSTs arrived back in England we had to take on troops and equipment and turn back around. It wasn't uncommon to go days without sleep. The routine was repeated over and over: Docked next to the city pier in Plymouth, keeping the ship perpendicular to the shore to allow her to rise with the morning tide, we opened the bow doors leading onto the tank deck. "Load ship," I would command from way up on the flying bridge. First would come the weaponry; then the soldiers. I would watch them march aboard through my 7x30 binoculars, wondering what was to become of them.

The LSTs performed their function exceedingly well but the lumbering behemoths took on a reputation as vessels only their crews could love. LST came to stand for "Large Slow Target." And one of my crew members, Tom Tegeder, came up with this endearing sonnet:

Ode to an LST

I think that I shall never see
A worse ship than an LST;
A ship with graceful lines resemblin'
A mud scow fashioned by a gremlin;
A ship whose paint disintegrates
From salt and lesser phosphates;
A ship whose steering engine works
With grunts and groans and nervous jerks;
A ship that doesn't run, but trots;
That labors doing seven knots.
Most any ship will try to please,
But only God loves LSTs.

God and Winston Churchill. After the war, the prime minister stood in Parliament and said that the war would not have been won without the LSTs. All of us who served on the ships loved that unexpected tribute, because for a long time we were considered a lesser part of the Navy than the destroyers, the battleships, or cruisers. That was the spit-and-polish Navy, and to them we were the "dirty Navy," just a big fleet of troop barges whose captains were little better than bus drivers. That began to change after the first few invasions, when people began to realize how vital we were—putting ashore tens of thousands of men, taking care of casualties, and performing heroically enough to win medals. One of the medal-winners was Seaman Second Class Sizemore, my underage crew member who tried to jump ship before Normandy. After performing bravely in the invasion, he wrote to base headquarters asking that his request for a transfer home be disregarded. He was awarded the Bronze Star for bravery under fire. That boy became a man before my eyes.

Because I was so fully aware of the evils of Hitler and his Third Reich well before most Americans—from my personal experience in Austria as a teenager and later from my intelligence work in Argentina before Pearl Harbor—I took particular pride in our role in his defeat. I sometimes fantasized about how history might have been changed had I leaned forward and cut Hitler's throat one night at the opera in Munich in 1932. And throughout the buildup to the invasion, I thought often of my friend Gus Glück and bleakly wondered what had become of his parents. When Gus called me after the war to tell me that they had survived, I thanked God for this miracle. Gus told me it was only because his father was a well-known artist. The Nazis kept him alive for the sole purpose of having him paint portraits of Hitler and his top generals. For this he and his wife were spared the fate of millions of their fellow Jews. (After the war, when thousands of German and European Jews settled in Israel, the United States, and South America, Gus took a different path. He returned to Germany, where he lived the rest of his life and returned to his old job as an officer of Deutsche Bank.)

WHILE I WAS COMMANDING THE 530, my older brother Angier was serving in the Air Force. For Angier, the war was a maturing experience. Though he had always been the more studious of the two of us when we were younger, he had admittedly not been a very serious fellow before the war. He had dropped out of Yale after two years and gotten a job as the skiing editor of a sports magazine. He got married in 1937, took an around-the-world honeymoon, and divorced three years later. When the war came my brother, at twenty-eight, enlisted in the Air Force. He had an administrative position in North Africa and Europe, arranging transportation for generals, diplomats, and, in one case, Winston Churchill. Returning to England after one of my runs across the Channel to France, I received a message from Navy headquarters that Angier was in London. We met at the Savoy Hotel for a three-hour lunch, a wonderful reunion—other than the close call that came five minutes after we said our goodbyes. A buzz bomb landed near the cab I was sharing with another officer, blowing its windows out and turning it over. I limped over to where the cabbie lay stunned but otherwise okay. "How much do we owe you?" I asked. I paid him, then hailed another cab to Victoria Station.

Even Granddaddy Biddle found a place in the war. Because of his renown as an expert in hand-to-hand combat, shortly after Pearl Harbor the Marines called him out of retirement—at age sixty-seven—and put him in charge of training recruits in the martial arts. Granddaddy considered this the greatest honor of his life and dove into it headlong, the way he had always attacked everything. Angier accompanied Granddaddy to Quantico, Virginia, for his first appearance before three hundred young marines who greeted him with audible snickers. They couldn't believe they could learn a thing about hand-to-hand fighting from this bald, heavyset, old man. But then he got down on the ground and arched himself on his head and legs and had his assistant jump up and down on his chest. Granddaddy showed no signs of distress, and the recruits were instantly won over. Then he picked out three of the biggest and toughest-looking men and took them on, one at a time, with his repertoire of judo holds.

"He tossed them around like rubber balls," Angier related with relish. The camp newspaper, the *Quantico Sentry*, reported: "For three hours, the Colonel worked with his classes and never once did he show the least trace of fatigue. He showed a complete mastery of the bayonet by having members of his class stab at him with an open blade. Colonel Biddle, completely unarmed, proved that he could not only block this attack, but disarm and seriously injure his opponent. Upon the close of the last class, Colonel Biddle devoted about fifteen minutes to the arts of defendu and jujitsu and savate. Not one instructor in a hundred has even heard of, let alone mastered, the movements which he teaches." A picture with the story showed Granddaddy lying on the ground, kicking a surprised young marine in the ankle.

On Granddaddy's many subsequent trips to Quantico, Grandmother rode down with him and would sit in the parked car, knitting and talking to people who walked by while Granddaddy would spend hours on the drill field, goading the recruits and thoroughly enjoying the workouts. "That old geezer knows more ways to kill you with his bare hands than any man alive," she overheard someone say. Indeed, Granddaddy was later recognized for training Americans to use against the Japanese their own techniques, which gave our men an advantage in jungle fighting in the Pacific. After the Battle of Tarawa in late 1943—one of the bloodiest in Marine Corps history—General Julian Smith wrote to Granddaddy: "You are as much responsible for the triumph as if you had been in the battle yourself." He also got a letter of commendation from the Secretary of the Navy. But it was the scrawled letters from men he had trained that my grandfather valued most. They came after every battle, often from officers who thanked him for saving the lives of many of their men. I wonder if they knew that this man who taught them the finer points of homicide was also a bible teacher.

Granddaddy took great pride in the service of his sons and grandsons. His letters to me were pricelessly over-the-top. "Beloved Tony," began one, handwritten on stationary from the Bellevue-Stratford, the Philadelphia hotel where he and my grandmother were living at the time. "It is an honor and a privilege to respond to the most glorious letter from your wonderful self. Granny and I re-read this letter many times and rejoice in the honor of being Grandfather of such a superb

Granddaddy was called out of retirement—ate age sixty-seven—to train marines in hand-to-hand combat. The Marines claimed he knew more ways to kill a man than anyone in history.

young American as your famed self. We have many accounts of your fine leadership for our beloved Nation's welfare, in these trying days. As fellow citizens, we thank our valiant grand-son. Your precious Mother is especially happy in the great leadership of her brilliant sons, both leaders for their nation's needs. All our love to you. Your son is glorious and his mother is superb. Your own darling mother is superbly wonderful." And another, on the stationary of the Seaview Country Club in Absecon, New Jersey: "Beloved Grand-son. Of course, we knew that you were one of the greatest men in American History. In your modest way, you have proved this. Our government cites it. Your ship is internationally famous as you have made it as the Commanding Officer."

From writing such as this one might be led to think that I was the only one fighting the war, or at least the war couldn't have been won without me. But of course we were all in this together—my entire generation. The war dispersed all my friends, ripping us from the carefree lives we'd shared. Quigg McVeigh served on a cruiser and then saw a lot of action in the Pacific aboard the aircraft carrier Belleau Wood. Claiborne Pell served on a Coast Guard LST. George Vietor commanded a Navy transport ship. Paul Moore was to be awarded a Navy Cross after miraculously surviving a shot to the heart at Guadalcanal. And Bob Fowler would be decorated with a Silver Star for gallantry. As his ship went down after being hit by a sub, he managed to drag himself to the stern and fire directly at the bridge of the sub and sink it. Cord Meyer was a decorated Marine who lost an eye during an engagement early in the Pacific campaign (and later would go on to a very colorful and complicated career in the CIA). And even Roger Schafer—a conscientious objector—saw action. He was permitted to serve in the Red Cross, for which he drove a truck on the front in France.

On a few occasions I even ran into someone I knew purely by happenstance, a highly unlikely occurrence given that the United States had ten million men under arms throughout the world. One day not long after D-Day, I was peering through my binoculars as a battalion of men marched onto the 530 for transport across the channel to the front in France. In my line of vision was a tall, fine-looking officer walking slightly ahead of his men, keeping them bunched together and in order. I know that man, I thought, and as he got closer, I realized who it was.

I grabbed Charlie Pierce. "Take over, Chas," I said. "A cousin of mine just stepped aboard down on the tank deck. I'm going to see him."

"I'll bet," Chas said. He still didn't believe I'd met General Eisenhower. Now I was saying that of all the men in the armed forces, we happened to be transporting my cousin to battle. But it was true. Hard as it was to believe, my cousin Nick Biddle—whose father was Granddaddy Biddle's older brother—was down below, organizing his men for a night at sea.

"Tony!" Nick said as he saw me approach in full stride.

"Nick!" I said.

After a hearty hello, I hastily offered Nick my CO quarters. God only knew what he would soon be facing, and I felt that was about the only thing I could do for him. But Nick said he couldn't—one of the other officers coming aboard was a full colonel and he wouldn't feel right about it. A fine soldier, athlete and gentleman, my cousin. I felt honored to be his transporter to Europe—but also worried. Thank God he did survive some of the bloodiest battles of the war.

Not only wasn't that the only time I had a chance encounter with someone I knew, it wasn't even the only one *that day*. That same morning I'd seen Paul Corrigan, an old friend from Southampton, when I'd briefly gone ashore after receiving orders for a quick turnaround back to France. Paul appeared out of nowhere and whacked me on my back as I was boarding a small boat to return to the 530. We had a quick reunion over coffee in the wardroom. (Years later, Paul's two sons, Rory and Peter, would become two of my best counselors at camp.)

IN DECEMBER OF 1944 we got orders to bring the 530 home. We were to sail back across the Atlantic to the Brooklyn Navy Yard. After some welcome leave time we would go back to war—this time in the Pacific, the last front. The men celebrated news of our upcoming vacation with a costume ball on the tank deck as we sat in Plymouth Harbor. Then we set sail for the States, part of a slow convoy of ships dodging German subs and the usual raging waters of the Atlantic in winter. We

A wartime family reunion in Mother and Tom's apartment in New York. I'm at the far left with my cousin Nick Biddle, a paratrooper; Nick's father and my uncle, Ambassador Tony Biddle; and my brother Angier, a major in the Air Force.

Prior to D-Day, Uncle Tony left the diplomatic corps and joined General Eisenhower's staff. He remained in uniform after the war. Here he is getting his brigadier star from Eisenhower and General Alfred M. Fruenther in Paris in 1951.

headed south toward Spain, then across the sea via the Azores, arriving in New York Harbor just in time for the season's first blizzard. It was eerie, sailing into the city at two in the morning under the cover of darkness and swirling snow. But of course nobody cared. The mad dash to get off the ship began the second our engines were secured and I gave the go-ahead. What all hands did with their month's leave, I have no idea, but I reunited with Allie and Tony Junior. Then we went out to spend some time with Mother and Tom in Westbury.

Summoned back to the Navy Yard a few weeks later, my crew realized we were off to the war again—but not all together. About one-third of my men were reassigned to newer LSTs so they could help train less experienced men. It cannot be said that they went willingly. In fact, there was nearly a mutiny—curses, tears, and pleas that I call the Navy Department and somehow persuade them to rescind the orders. After all we'd been through together—from the ship's commissioning to Normandy and all those trips across the English Channel—I felt so close to these men that I actually put in such a futile and ridiculous call, and of course whomever I reached questioned my sanity.

After the sad farewells, the crewmen were replaced by new men with little battle experience, so I knew there would be a new round of training ahead. Our top-secret orders were to head up the coast to Providence, Rhode Island, where we would take on two locomotives retrofitted to move on Japanese-gauge tracks. The Allies were bombing the hell out of Japan's rail system, and evidently these locomotives would eventually be used to transport our men and supplies once we won the war and were occupying Japan. I was fascinated by such forward-thinking (not to mention optimistic) war planning.

The locomotives weren't the only secret cargo. Shortly before we set sail, a machinist mate named Novack came to my quarters with a confession. Earlier that day, my mother—whom I'd kissed goodbye the night before—had made an unannounced appearance at the Navy Yard. Accompanied as always by Pat, she had somehow talked her way into the shipyard by saying she was "a friend of the admiral." I knew she had been there because I'd found chintz curtains on the port hole in the wardroom. What I didn't know was that it wasn't just curtains she'd brought onto the 530. According to Novack, Mother had strode up to a group of men and asked if anyone knew how to unscrew the bolts on a deck. Novack said he could, and the next thing he knew "the chauffeur" was unloading cases filled with gin, vodka, and whiskey. "This is for when we win the war," Mother said. "You'll have a nice celebration. Now, quickly. We've got to do it before Mr. Bones comes back," she said, using her old nickname for me. "He'd never permit it." Novack and a few other men snuck the contraband onto the ship, went into my quarters, unbolted the deck plates, and stashed the liquor underneath. Then they replaced the deck. When Novack told me about it, I could hardly believe Mother's audacity. "Jesus Christ," I said, "This better be the biggest secret of the war or we'll all wind up in the brig."

Secret cargo safely stowed, we shipped out one night in January, but not before a final, fleeting farewell. Based on our departure time, I realized I'd have the 530 passing right in front of the River Club on Fifty-second Street as we made our way up the East River on course for Long Island Sound and Providence. I called Mother and said, "I didn't tell you this but if you go to the River Club for dinner, step outside at around six-fifteen." We sailed past right on schedule, and as I sounded our horn, they all came out—Mother and Tom, Angier, Uncle Tony, and my cousin Nick. Great timing!

Thus began a most circuitous route to the Pacific war: stops in New Jersey for ammunition, Rhode Island for the locomotives and pontoon barges we were to haul to Japan, then Norfolk for our final orders, and a stop in Guantanamo Bay, Cuba, the highlight of which was a night of partying at a very excellent officers' club. The last stop before Japan was Hawaii. "Pearl Harbor managed to poke its nose out of the sea dead ahead one morning," I wrote a few years later in the 530's official history, "and on arrival all hands clambered ashore and did the usual taking over of the best liberty spots on Oahu. Coxswains Hopson and Hensley became hopelessly spellbound by some languorous penny arcade hula girls and spent two months' pay being photographed with them." Then I added, "Again the gloomy curtains of war began to draw around the ship as she sailed for Guam and Saipan with a load of 4,926 fifty-gallon barrels of high octane aviation gas destined for Okinawa."

Reaching the South Pacific, I was promoted to division com-

U.S.S. L.S.T. 530
Fleet Post Office
San Francisco, Calif.

27 January 1945

MEMORANDUM

From: The Commanding Officer.
To :   The Men Whom This Notice Concerns.

Subject: The tearing-down of posted notices.

1.   From time to time it is necessary that
notices be posted in order to inform the crew of something that
otherwise would have to be passed along at quarters.

2.   There seem to be either one or perhaps
several snivelling characters obviously of weak intellect, who
derive a certain fatuous self-gratification at slinking up to
the bulletin boards, and with a haunted glance over the shoulder,
snatching these notices down, and making off to some lonely spot
on the ship where no one else can read them. What takes place
after that is a challenge to the imagination. Perhaps they do
some sort of wild-eyed native dance before flinging the notices
to the wind, or it is even conceivable that they eat them.

3.   The picture of one of these crackpots
engaged in what he considers a glorious mockery is a first
amusing, but on second thought we see that the crew misses out
on getting the word on some subjects. If these notice-grabbing
monomaniacs continue their practice, they will force all their
shipmates to go to daily muster to receive such information even
though the ship is at sea.

A. D. DUKE
Lt. Comdr., USNR
Commanding

cc:
    All bulletin boards
    Wardroom

On the bridge of the 530 off Okinawa.

Dealing with an annoyance while on the way to the South Pacific.

NAVSHIPS (360)
NOS 597

U. S. NAVAL COMMUNICATION SERVICE

U.S.S. L.S.T. 530   SRS

HEADING: NR J3459-P-A- L6B 150204 D8N NPG NSS SNOW WAR -W- HUNG KATY
           KHYF S4G WTJ W4K ZL1C GR75 BT

DATE: 15 AUGUST 1945

RDO WASHN PASS TO BRITISH ADMIRALTY LONDON FOR ACTION X RDO
SAN FRANCISCO PASS TO PRESS ASSNS PLUS REUTERS X CINCPOA
COMMUNIQUE NUMBER 467 RELEASED AS OF 0200 15 AUGUST 1945 AS
FOLLOWS X

ORDERS HAVE BEEN ISSUED TO THE U. S. PACIFIC FLEET AND TO

OTHER FORCES UNDER THE COMMAND OF THE COMMANDER IN CHIEF

U. S. PACIFIC FLEET AND PACIFIC OCEAN AREAS TO CEASE OFFEN-

SIVE OPERATIONS AGAINST THE JAPANESE X BT 150204 AR

TOR: NPM/12375KCS/EWB/0605

*The communication that told us the war was finally over—
let the celebration begin.*

mander, with a dozen LSTs under my command. We were originally ordered to Iwo Jima, but that battle was finished by the time we arrived, and so we moved on to join the invasion of Okinawa, ultimately considered the fiercest sea-air battle in history. Hanson W. Baldwin, the military editor of The New York Times who won a Pulitzer Prize for his coverage of World War II, wrote that Okinawa was "an epic of human endurance and courage" that dwarfed the Battle of Britain. The Japanese lost 110,000 men and sixteen combat ships at Okinawa. On our side, there were 12,000 dead, more than a third of them Navy men. "Never before had there been, probably never again will there be, such a vicious, sprawling struggle of planes against planes, of ships against planes," Baldwin wrote. "Never before, in so short a space, had the Navy lost so many ships; never before in land fighting had so much American blood been shed in so short a time in so small an area. . ."

And the 530 was in the thick of it. It was at Okinawa that we experienced firsthand the terror of the kamikazes. We were at anchor in Buckner Bay early one morning when I went up to the bridge, still in my shorts, to chat with the men on watch. We were one of about forty ships in the bay. Most were amphibious but there were a couple of larger troop carriers and one destroyer anchored nearby. I was taking in this oddly peaceful moment when suddenly a low-flying Japanese Zero appeared just over the horizon. It was coming straight at us, flying at an altitude of less than a hundred feet. "General quarters!" I shouted to my gunnery officer, who pushed the button that screamed out the signal for the crew to get to battle stations. I yanked a cord attached to a bell on the flying bridge. Within seconds, men were pouring through the companionway onto the deck to man the anti-aircraft weapons. I had some great marksmen on my crew, and they fired on the plane until they hit her. Just as it was right on top of us, the plane took a sudden turn away from us—and toward another LST, the 534, that was anchored half a mile away. The kamikaze crashed into the middle of the 534's hull and blew up. Then came the aftermath: the smell of gunpowder and fire, the devastating realization that men had been burned and torn apart on that other ship. Bits of shrapnel struck my deck, but none of my men were hit.

Watching the 534 burn, I felt more depressed and weary than at any other point in the war. I felt older than twenty-six. Later that day, the kamikaze pilot was pulled from his plane, intact amid the wreckage, and laid on the beach with the other dead. I took a look at him as he lay there, trying to imagine what sort of culture required such sacrifice. As I later learned, the kamikazes damaged more than three hundred American ships and killed or injured some fifteen-hundred men, and it was at Okinawa that they exacted their greatest damage. Ultimately, the man who had conceived of the idea of a flying suicide squadron, Vice Admiral Takijiro Ohnishi, committed hara-kiri, leaving behind an apology "to the souls of those dead fliers and to their bereaved families."

After Okinawa, we prepared for what was to be the ultimate and bloodiest battle of the entire war: the invasion of mainland Japan. My fellow commanders and I were told by our admiral that we would be in the first wave of the invasion—we had been in the third and fourth at Normandy—and that we should expect a casualty rate of 90 percent. We would win through volume, we were told. How do young men cope with such a devastating prospect? How do you confront such a destiny? In my case, I simply convinced myself that I wasn't without some control of the situation. And what I told my men was: *Whatever time you've got, you're going to be better than you've ever been. God willing, some of us will get through this, but we've got to do our share better than we've ever done anything in our lives. Let's help each other, let our friendships show, and just be as well-prepared as we can.* I could tell that the newer men, those we'd picked up in Brooklyn, didn't know what I was talking about; not really. They hadn't been in battle yet. They didn't really understand what lay ahead.

With that, we waited for our orders, just as we had before Normandy. Only this time, something else happened, something extraordinary. The United States had dropped the bomb. Within days, Japan had surrendered. The war was over. It was really over. With the news, sailors on several ships began firing their weapons in the air to celebrate—without thinking that what goes up must come down. I remembered that the same thing had happened at Normandy, and the shrapnel that came raining down injured many men. So I told my crew to get below deck, but quick. There was so much firing in the air that an unknown number of men were killed in this most tragic and ironic fashion. The incident was covered up and didn't come out for many years.

To celebrate the end of the war I turned the ship in the direction of the nearest beach—I didn't give a damn where we were. It was finally time to break out the contraband Mother had arranged to be hidden under the deck of my office. We got two big barrels and poured in the vodka, the gin, the bourbon, the scotch, and gallon cans of juice. The crew got good and smashed on that beach, and I managed to stay sober enough to announce that no one could get back on board until they could walk straight. That took two-and-a-half days, by which time we'd received orders to go to the Philippines to pick up Japanese prisoners. We made two of these runs, and during the second one we ran into a typhoon that nearly killed us all. The ferocious storm was unlike anything I had experienced at sea. A mountain of waves pounded us. The ship became unsteerable, and we lost contact with other ships. Never before had I felt that the 530 was completely out of my control. We flooded our ballast tanks for stability, and somehow, by shifting engine speeds, course-changing—and hoping—we came out of it. We were able to refuel at sea, and aboard the tanker beside us I saw an almost hallucinatory sight. A young man was waving at me, shouting, "Hey, Mr. Duke! It's me—Frankie! I'll see you after the war!" It was one of the boys from my summer camp on Duck Island.

The dropping of the bombs on Hiroshima and Nagasaki saved my crew members and me from the invasion of Japan that seemed destined to decimate our ranks. For us, there was no debate such as the one that developed over the next few decades about the morality of the decision—a question that even some of my children raised twenty-five years later. My daughter Josie was particularly harsh, accusing me of all but personally dropping bombs on innocent people. "What did you think you were doing?" she asked. I replied, "I think I was trying to survive, and you wouldn't be here if I didn't."

That our ship not only survived but lost not one man to combat was fairly amazing. Dozens of LSTs were sunk during the war, among more than five hundred naval vessels of all kinds that were lost. A total of 56,683 American sailors and Marines were killed at sea and another 104,985 wounded. By the end of the war, the 530 had sailed nearly 45,000

After I'd been awarded the Bronze Star at the end of the war. It was the last time I was photographed in uniform.

Celebrating the end of the war—and our survival—off the coast of Japan, August 1945

miles. But Bob Reed, our supremely skilled chief motor machinist mate, kept our engines in such great condition that we didn't spend a day in dry dock for repairs the entire war. Nearly every other LST was out of action a few weeks a year, and you would always see one or two limping into port. Some never made it—sunk by submarines before they could get their engines repaired. Who knows how many lives Bob saved by doing his job so phenomenally well? But it's also true that we were just very lucky. The kids on my crew called the 530 a "miracle ship." While things were often going very badly all around us, we seemed to have a charmed life.

In August, just weeks after the Japanese surrender, I got a wire telling me I was now eligible to be discharged. Oddly, though I'd had more than enough of war, I found myself in no hurry to go home. The bond I had with my crew was stronger than I could have imagined. My five years in the Navy was such a deep experience that I strongly considered making a career of it, at least for a while. But when I wrote to headquarters in Washington asking what kind of duty I might have in the post-war Navy, the answer I got back didn't sound promising. The Navy was slated for a massive downgrading, with many ships going out of service. The future for someone like me seemed very unclear. Still, I wasn't ready to go home. I had a wife and a son waiting for me, and yet

I couldn't bring myself to leave my ship, my men—especially after several of my closest officers all but begged me to stay on a little while longer. We spent the next few months in Japan, ferrying Russian engineering groups who were beginning to restore the northern ports.

By December, half my crew had already been shipped home. Rather than stay on and train a bunch of green kids as replacements, I decided it was finally time for me to leave the Navy behind and return to my life— whatever that might turn out to be. When I was about to leave the ship we had a huge and incredibly sentimental good-bye gathering on board while anchored in Tokyo Harbor. My replacement, a fine young man who was an Annapolis graduate, arrived the next day, and I officially turned the ship's command over to him in a ceremony that only he seemed to enjoy. After serving with about half the men for more than two years— from the day we left New York, through D-Day and the battles in the South Pacific—it was finally over. What was left of my crew lined up on the 530's main deck to say farewell. I stepped aboard the LCVP that would take me to the battle cruiser Lexington, and simply could not look back as we got underway. It was a cold, gray day, the end of the biggest chapter in my life thus far. And I felt completely lost.

The Lexington brought me home to American soil. We landed in San Francisco, where the Navy put three hundred of us officers up in hotels. We put numbers in a hat to determine which of us got to get on the next train across the country to New York. Fifty at a time got aboard, and by the time my number came up, I had been in San Francisco for eleven days, most of which was spent carousing and swapping war stories. For all those two weeks I felt one thing was lifted from me but another was crowding me—a fear of going back to normal life. After all I'd seen and experienced, the idea of going home and resuming civilian life was somehow jolting and disorienting. The train stopped at a dozen towns or so. Everywhere we stopped, and returning servicemen stepped off the train to stretch, there were cheering crowds with "Welcome Home" signs and high school bands serenading us with patriotic tunes. And at each stop we'd be greeted by veterans who'd preceded us home, some of them still recovering from serious wounds. It was a sweet victory ride across the country, lubricated by drink and a joyous relief that was mixed, for me at least, with a certain unsettled feeling about the future.

SIX

From the Great War
to a Great Experiment

THREE DAYS AFTER DEPARTING San Francisco, I stepped off
the train at Penn Station, got a cab and told the driver to take me
to the Racquet and Tennis Club at 370 Park Avenue. I hadn't shaved
or even changed my clothes since leaving California, and I wanted to
get cleaned up before going home to Allie and Tony Jr. I'd been
accepted into this fine club when I was twenty-one—my stepfather
made sure to put me up for membership "before you do something so
terrible they won't let you in," he'd said. I checked in, took a Turkish
bath and a shower, and shaved my three-day stubble. Then, rather
than going straight home, I went straight to the bar to join my old St.
Paul's pal Walter McVeigh and a couple of other friends I hadn't seen
since the war started. After catching up for a few hours, I finally called
my wife and my mother and said I was home.

An older man got on the elevator with me, and as we rode down we
looked at one another with a note of vague recognition. I knew him
from somewhere but couldn't quite place him. Then he asked, "Are you
Angier Duke?"

"No," I said, "Angier's my brother. I'm Tony."

"Tony!" he said, breaking into a big smile. "I was looking at you up
at the bar and I was thinking you look like my late friend, Angier
Duke."

"You were a friend of my father's?" I asked. "What's your name?"

174

"Warner Jones," he said, extending his hand. "I saw you last when you were very young. In fact, it was the day you came on the boat with your Dad just a few hours before he drowned. You had a little friend with you and we had a great time. Later, we left you on the dock in Manhasset. You and your brother had an appointment with a portrait artist early the next day."

"I would really like to talk to you," I said. When the elevator reached the lobby, we stayed on and rode back up to the bar.

Over drinks, Warner Jones filled in so many missing pieces for me. "I knew your father most of his life," he said. "We did business together, hunted together; we were friends forever. I can tell you that he was one of the most wonderful men I've ever known. I sorely miss him."

Hearing this made me very happy. My mother's incessant warnings—"Don't be like your father"—had left me with a vaguely dark picture of my father. I thought of how odd it was to run into Warner Jones at this crossroads in my life. I asked him what else he could tell me about my father.

"Number one, he was a fine athlete, a great sport," he said. "He pitched for the Trinity College baseball team. That's now Duke University, of course. He was a tough businessman, he had a very good idea of what he was doing. At that time, he did not want to take the vice presidency of the two tobacco companies because he didn't feel qualified. He was working for the Sonora Radio Company."

What was his personality like, I asked. He was very well-liked, Warner said, though he could be "a little wild—sometimes he drank a little too much."

I asked him if he knew why my parents had split up.

"Your father was desperately in love with your mother and wanted to get back with her," he said. "Unfortunately, he was overcome by jealousy. Your mother was so beautiful and such fun, and she was very flirtatious without meaning anything. They would go to a party, and she was just very warm, talking to a lot of people, and he'd give her hell about that. I always tried to tell your father, 'Angie, try to get over this stuff.' I adored your mother, and at the time I was trying to get her to reopen the door to your father."

Warner's recounting of that day on the dock, the last time Angier and I saw our dad, made me realize why he looked familiar when he got on the elevator: everything surrounding that day twenty-two years earlier was frozen in my memory.

"I always wanted to tell you boys about your Dad because his death must have been terrible for you," Warner said.

"Yes, it was," I said. I told him how I'd always feared my own temper, because of my mother's warnings.

"Yeah, he used to get pretty upset," Warner said. "He had a bit of a temper, but so do a lot of other people. I think it would have all worked out with your mother. You must remember, she was so young in those days."

I didn't leave the club until after midnight, unable to avoid going home any longer. How thoroughly odd, I thought as I walked along Park Avenue in the cold night, that barely a few hours after my return to civilian life I should run into a man who would fill in so many blanks about my father, telling me things I'd wanted to know about since I was a kid. All I'd ever heard from my mother was that he was a jealous husband with a bad temper. Because I loved and admired her so deeply, her memories had a great impact on me. Now I had a little context, and I realized how badly hurt she must have been to think that my dad didn't trust her.

At ONE IN THE MORNING, I arrived at the apartment at 834 Fifth Avenue that Allie had moved into with Tony Jr. about a year earlier. Allie saw me standing in the doorway and threw her arms around me. After a long embrace, we went inside and woke up Tony, who was now four. We hadn't seen each other in nearly a year, and I was so proud and happy when I looked at him. It was a beautiful reunion, but I couldn't shake the uneasiness I'd felt since deciding to leave the service.

The next morning, Allie asked me what color curtains I thought we should get for the living room. This most innocuous question hit me like a mortar attack. It crystallized how hard a time I would have making the transition from the intense atmosphere of war to the mundane reality of domestic, civilian life. I had just come from Japan, where I'd had more responsibility than I could possibly have imagined. As a division commander of LSTs, I'd led six ships carrying thousands of infantrymen to what would have been a brutal ending to the war, had the atom bombs not brought Japan's surrender first. What color curtains? The question actually made me angry. And my reaction set the tone for what was to be an unhappy reunion.

A couple of months before coming home, I had sold the cattle ranch in Dutchess County by mail. I didn't know what I wanted to do, but I knew that cattle ranching wasn't it. Concerned about our future, Allie's father offered to get me started back in civilian life— in a big way. Nick Rutgers had a seat on the stock exchange. He was ready to retire, he said, and wanted to give me his seat. It was an extremely generous offer, and the only sensible thing for me to do would have been to say yes before he changed his mind. But I had neither a background nor interest in the Wall Street life. Even if I had, I wouldn't have felt right about starting at the top that way. I declined my father-in-law's offer, to his disbelief and frustration—and to my wife's. He pressed further and I declined again, this time somewhat aggressively. "Forget it, Nick," I said firmly.

My refusal was yet another sour note as Allie and I tried to resume our good life together. It was becoming evident that Allie and I were out of sync, and we never did find our way back to each other. Unfortunately, our marriage ended shortly after our second son, Nicholas, was born in December 1946. Allie was a lovely and wonderful woman, and when we split it was my loss. But our divorce did not diminish the powerful bond of love between my two sons and me.

Having turned down a free pass to Wall Street, I had to figure out what to do with the rest of my life. I had left Princeton after my sophomore year with an open invitation from the university to finish my degree after the war. But at twenty-eight, and after six years in the Navy, I wasn't inclined to go back to school. Instead, I pursued a business idea I'd come up with.

After the war, there remained in Europe huge amounts of mobile equipment that the United States military no longer needed. With a partner, and with financial backing from an investment company Angier had started, I went over to some of the big depots in France and Germany. For modest down payments I purchased surplus, second-hand equipment—trucks, Jeeps, and some maritime landing crafts. Then I arranged to sell the equipment to a Brazilian importing company that used it to carry freight up the Amazon. I made good money in a short time, and in retrospect I probably should have stayed with it a little longer. But at the time I saw it as a way to make some quick money while trying to figure out what to do with my life.

During my buying trip to Europe I met a girl named Betty Ordway. Betty was beautiful, exciting, and very well-off. Her father was Lucius Pond Ordway, a former Air Force colonel who was an early and crucial investor in Minnesota Mining and Manufacturing Company, commonly known as 3M. I met her in London through her brother, John, my partner in the import-export business back in the States. We became quickly involved—perhaps a little too quickly. We were married in Paris late in 1946. The rashness of my decision became evident when Betty insisted that I have nothing to do with my two sons. In fact, on our wedding night she asked me to sign a document promising never to see them again. She wanted the perfect little family, no complications. Incredulous, I told her I would never agree to such an intolerable condition. Whereupon she pulled her wedding ring off and hurled it out the hotel window. Betty eventually dropped her demand, but it laid the groundwork for a troubled marriage. I knew I had made a big mistake, but I was determined not to be twice divorced. And despite our problems, Betty and I had four wonderful children over the next five years. Cordelia was born in January of 1948, followed by Josephine, December, and John.

BEFORE LONG, THERE WERE other children in my life as well. Since leaving the service, I had been eager to resume my work helping underprivileged kids. My vision, first imagined while I was at Princeton before the war, was to start with a summer camp and to eventually build it into a year-round educational program, maybe even a school. It was idealistic for the time, and probably a little unrealistic, but I saw a clear need that wasn't being filled either by the city or by the leading social service organizations. The Boys Club did great work, but it was focused on keeping kids out of trouble and building character by engaging them in sports. There were the Boy Scouts and Cub Scouts, but they seemed geared to the exploding postwar suburbs. The boys I had in mind couldn't afford the uniforms.

Betty and I scouted out properties within a couple of hours' drive of New York, and found a small farm in Weston, Connecticut, seven miles north of Westport on a road called Lord's Highway. It had lately been owned by a farmer who had combined crop sales with the dairy output of thirty Holstein cows. We bought the place with some investments that had done well. It had a decent-sized house for my family and two cottages where tenant farmers had been living, and which could house summer campers. The property came with a swimming pool and a bunch of pigs, surrounded by eighty or ninety acres of virgin land. We were on a stream that ran down to Westport, on Long Island Sound.

ONE DAY IN THE SPRING OF 1947, Mother and I took the train down to Philadelphia to visit Granddaddy Biddle. Granny had died the year before, and his decline since then had been rapid. He was becoming frail—a sad change for anyone but a startling one in Granddaddy's case—and he was beginning to exhibit signs of dementia. My mother and her brothers, Tony and Livingston, discussed possible living arrangements. They decided the best place for Granddaddy was an apartment in a converted estate on the Main Line. It was a kind of rest home, to use the vernacular of that time. Today we might call it an assisted living facility.

Mother and I got off the train at the Thirtieth Street Station and rented a car. We arrived at the place around eleven o'clock and found a distinguished-looking gentleman seated at a table in the hallway. "We're hear to see my grandfather," I said. "Colonel Biddle."

Just then, we heard Granddaddy's voice echoing from somewhere in the back of the house. He was shouting out military orders. Straighten up! Come to attention! About face! "The colonel is exercising his companion," the man at the desk said matter-of-factly. "Follow that hallway to the end. His apartment is the last one."

We walked down the hall and Mother knocked on the last door, opening it cautiously. It was a sun-filled room, and Granddaddy was lying on a large bed. "Daughter!" he said. "Grandson Tony!" He looked weaker than the last time I'd seen him, but his voice still had plenty of spirit. "Say hello to Sergeant Willis. He's practicing his drills with me, and he's good. Just watch this!" The man was a retired Marine of about sixty who was employed by the home as a companion. He snapped to attention, saluted us, and with a smart about-face retired from the room.

"Now, we should speak softly," Granddaddy said in a low voice. "Granny will be napping in the next room and we mustn't awaken her. She's very tired, you know."

Mother and I exchanged a glance, but we didn't have the heart to remind him that Granny had been dead for more than a year. We chatted for a while, filling him in on various members of the family. Told that Uncle Tony was still in Europe as a top member of General Eisenhower's postwar staff, Granddaddy smiled faintly. Then he dozed off.

A few weeks later, Uncle Livingston decided that Granddaddy should live with him and his family in his house in Syosset, Long Island. Granddaddy spent his last year there, mostly in bed. One day I visited him with my oldest child, Tony Jr., who was seven at the time. Granddaddy was very vague in his conversation, but then suddenly he looked at us and said loudly, "There are three Tony's in this room. Isn't that something."

It was a moment both Tony Jr. and I remember vividly, and God knows I've thought of Granddaddy countless times in the years since. He died soon after that day.

GRANDDADDY LOVED THE NAME I'd chosen for my new camp: Lord's Highway. I didn't tell him it was simply the camp's address. Still, if anyone said we were on a mission of salvation, I wouldn't have tried to argue him out of it. I bought a beat-up old bus to bring the kids from the city and to take them on outings and to church. It's safe to say that church was the least favorite activity among the kids, but I thought it couldn't hurt. "I don't care who or what you pray to," I'd tell them. "Just say your prayers, keep quiet and sing a hymn. Then you can go swimming."

One Sunday morning I went out to get the bus for a trip to church. As I started up the bus, it sputtered and then stopped. One of my close friends, Tom Hollyman, lived in a little cottage next to camp. Tom, who had been a well-known war correspondent and photographer, told me that just before I arrived on the scene, he had spied a boy named Herby Shannon peeing directly into the bus's gas tank. Herby was a troublesome little boy whose favorite activities did not include going to church. Rather than accuse Herby, I wanted to see if I could get him to confess on his own. I gathered the boys around and told them somebody had messed up the truck. "Whoever did it is really detracting from our ability to move around and go on some good trips," I said. At first, Herby seemed as eager as anyone to solve the mystery of the stalled truck, but after a little while he admitted—not without a certain amount of pride—that he had peed in the truck. "I thought it would make it go faster," he said. I was glad he confessed, and gave him a relatively light sentence: no dessert that night. Chocolate pudding was on the menu. "I hate that stuff anyway," Herby said.

One day, a visitor appeared at camp. He was a tall, lean man in his early thirties. "Tony Duke?" he asked, extending his hand with a smile. "My name is John Hersey."

I recognized his name right away. Hersey was a famous writer who'd become well-known as a war correspondent for *Time* magazine, then won a Pulitzer Prize for his first novel, *A Bell for Adano*, in 1945. But he was most famous for the book he'd written the next year, *Hiroshima*, a first-hand account of nuclear devastation that took a strong stand against the bombing. So what was John Hersey doing at my door?

Hersey explained that he lived nearby and thought he'd drop by after hearing about the camp. I invited him in, and we wound up trading war stories and talking about Hiroshima and *A Bell for Adano*, which I'd read. "So tell me about your camp," he said finally.

I gave him the background, how I'd started before the war taking needy kids from the city and bringing them out to the country for a few weeks.

"And what do you do with them?" Hersey asked.

"Well, we have a good athletic program," I said. "We have a base-ball team. They do a little work on the farm. But I really see the camp as an educational experience. With all the kids, I get their school records and see where they need help so they can improve their prospects when they go back in September."

"Wonderful," Hersey said. "Absolutely wonderful."

He took a newspaper clipping from his pocket. "Did you see this?" he asked, handing it to me.

"No, I haven't," I said.

It was a letter to the editor in the Westport *Times*, from a man complaining that the stream that ran through his property was being polluted by "ghetto" children from a camp upstream whom he claimed were defecating and urinating in it. The man demanded that the town authorities prohibit such disgraceful behavior by closing down the camp.

"These children are doing nothing of the sort!" I told Hersey. I was furious.

Hersey asked if he could spend the day with us. I told him that nothing would please me more. He watched the kids tilling the soil and planting seeds. He watched them go on a treasure hunt and play baseball, and he looked in at a math tutoring session, and he stayed for dinner. He talked to the kids and the counselors, asked lots of questions. He wasn't here as a journalist, but it was easy to see why he was such a great one. He had a natural curiosity about people. "You've got a great spirit here," he said. "I think we've got to do something about that article."

"I'd like to go over and see who this fellow is," I said. "But we'd probably wind up hitting each other."

"I don't think that's the approach," Hersey said with a laugh. "Let me handle this."

The next day Hersey conducted an investigation of the situation. He looked at where we were, took a ride to the complainant's house, and checked out all the properties in between. He found that downstream from the camp but upstream from the letter-writer's house was a hog farm. For three generations the farm family there had raised these four-hundred-pounders that wallowed in the stream, using it as their personal latrine. The man hadn't cared about the hog farm all these years, but when he heard there was a camp with inner-city kids he demanded action. Hersey wrote his own letter to the editor. He said that a very fascinating and wonderful thing was going in the community, and went on to describe everything he'd seen at our camp. The result was a lot of positive attention from the community. After that, I went over to the letter-writer's house and tried to convert him. I invited him over to see the camp, but he had no interest. He sold his house and moved soon after. Hersey, meanwhile, became a friend and big supporter of the camp. He would often come over and have lunch with us in the mess hall, telling us about his experiences and career.

THE COUNSELORS AT LORD'S HIGHWAY included some from before the war and others I'd met along the way. All of them were great people with big hearts and much to offer. But none was more crucial to the creation and development of what was to become Boys Harbor than Paul Moore, a man of extraordinary wisdom and decency.

Paul and I were classmates and close friends at St. Paul's, but I had come to look up to him almost as an elder, a wise man. Some people born into great privilege never venture beyond that cocoon of wealth, stature, and cradle-to-grave comfort—not to mention an innate if unearned sense of superiority. But Paul was assuredly not one of those. Many at St. Paul's were to the manor born, but even there, few could match Paul's inheritance of wealth and prestige. His grandfather had helped found no fewer than four great American companies—Nabisco, American Can, Bankers Trust, and the Lackawanna Railroad—while one of his uncles headed the national Republican Party during the administration of President William McKinley. He grew up on a "gentleman's farm" in New Jersey with a Scottish nurse, a French governess, and a British butler. He was driven to scout meetings by a chauffeur. And he was imbued with the sensibility that blacks, Jews, and Roman Catholics—whom Paul only heard about—were assuredly not a part of his family's world. "Now, Paul," he recalled his mother saying before a rail trip, "on the train there will be men with black faces. I want you to be polite to them because they will be taking care of us." He later wrote in his autobiography, "A real class system was part of our daily lives."

Paul developed a keen sense of the social order at St. Paul's, in a way that would influence his life—and mine—profoundly. In his own autobiography, *Presences,* published in 1997, Paul observed that schools like St. Paul's instilled faith in a God that demanded courage, loyalty, and patriotism. "A rather simple, childlike faith remained with many St. Paul's boys throughout their lives," he wrote. "Understandably, the alumni of these schools were at their best in times of war. Most of them volunteered before being drafted, and many distinguished themselves through bravery and leadership. They fought for democracy against foreign foes but did not fight for justice and full democracy within their own land. They gave to the community chest, the hospital, the neighborhood house, and they volunteered in programs to help the poor. Social change to eliminate poverty, however, was thought to be dangerously liberal. Franklin Roosevelt was called 'a traitor to his class.'"

Paul went on: "The privileged prefer charitable giving to social action to empower the poor because charity makes the giver feel good and the receiver feel humbled; empowerment gives the poor a sense of dignity but threatens the advantages of the rich. For instance, if you give money to a settlement house for black people, where they can humbly beg for help when they are down and out, this assists them, to be sure, and it gives you a nice feeling inside. If, however, you help break the color barrier in your neighborhood, a black family buying a house will feel proud, but you will be criticized or even ostracized by your white neighbors. If you encourage a labor union to seek higher pay or better working conditions, you endanger the profit margin of your family's company and threaten investments."

It was in our fifth-form year, when he was sixteen, that Paul underwent what he described as a religious conversion. That year, an English monk named Father Wigram spent time at St. Paul's, and Paul went to see him in his guest quarters, a suite called Prophet's Chamber overlooking the waterfall. Paul was full of questions, and the answers he received put him on a new path. He was sure that God had pointed him in a new direction.

The summer after our graduation from boarding school, Paul joined me in working at the school's summer camp in New Hampshire. For him it was a revelatory experience of a different kind. It was his first encounter with people of a less privileged background—a lot less. Paul and I had similar reactions to the urban sons of struggling immigrants. We found them tough, sometimes nasty, but also funny, loveable, and full of potential. He observed that when you met these kids your impulse was to get to know them and enjoy them—not to feel sorry for them. That was because they didn't feel sorry for themselves. The seeds of my life's work were sown at the St. Paul's camp, and so they were for Paul as well. The following year, after our freshman year at college (me at Princeton, Paul at Yale), Paul joined me at the ersatz camp I opened at Duck Island in Southampton.

With the coming of the war Paul joined the Marines, and late in 1942 came the second turning point of his life. He was a young captain, leading four platoons—160 men—at Guadalcanal. Amphibious ships delivered them to the island, and early in the battle it looked as if they had the Japanese on the run across a narrow river. But when Paul and his men got to the edge of the river, the Japanese opened fire, killing half of them. As the battle became more and more intense, Paul and his men were completely pinned down. He looked to his left and saw that two of his men had been killed. A sergeant yelled that four more had been taken down by machine gun fire to their right. Paul located the source of the fire, grabbed a grenade, pulled the pin out, then got to his knees and threw it. "At that moment," Paul later wrote in his autobiography, *Presences*, "I felt a piercing, burning stab of pain going into my chest on the left side. I fell to the ground and realized I had been hit. The air was blubbering in and out of a hole in my lung. . . . I thought I was dying. I remember reading that your whole life passes before your eyes at such a time. Mine didn't. I thought, What a weird place for a person like me to die."

Somehow, Paul didn't die. The bullet went right through him, missing his heart but leaving him with the use of just one lung. A corpsman crawled to him, gave him some morphine and dragged him to a stretcher. They got him to an aid station, the first of many stops in his recovery: a naval hospital of Quonset huts in New Hebrides, a hospital ship called the *Solace* that brought him to New Zealand, a troopship that got him to San Francisco, and finally a cross-country train trip home to New York. At the Brooklyn Navy Yard hospital, a doctor examined the entry and exit wounds left by the Japanese sniper's bullet and told him: "Your heart must have been on the in beat when the bullet went by. On the way out, it missed your spine by two inches. You shouldn't be here!"

Paul eventually returned to duty, already having been awarded a Silver Star and the Navy Cross, and was sent to the Pacific as a company commander with the Third Marine Division. In the middle of 1945, I was on Guam as the invasion of Japan approached. One day, I was pulling my ship up to a dock to take on ammunition and cargo, and I couldn't believe my eyes. There, standing on the dock with some other Marines, was Paul. I yelled to him, and he looked up—a great smile came to his face. I had heard about his close call at Guadalcanal but hadn't seen him since. We had a wonderful two-day reunion in which we both got quite intoxicated. We were both to participate in the invasion of Japan, and who knows what might have become of us had two atom bombs not led to Japan's surrender first?

Paul came home and concluded that his narrow escape from death was more than dumb luck. The thought that he might become a priest had slowly been growing since St. Paul's, and he took his close call as further evidence that he was meant to spend his life serving God. Coming from his background, it wasn't an easy decision. The ministry was not a common career choice for people of his background. Paul's father referred to their local minister as "that little fellow at the church," as if he were a shoemaker. Not surprisingly, Paul's father did not take Paul's idea well. Make a living, he said, and then if you're still interested in the ministry you can take it up as a hobby. (Paul was such an influence on me that for a time at St. Paul's I, too, thought about becoming a minister. But ultimately I decided I was too fond of having a good time.)

During his seminary training in New York, Paul had done fieldwork with teenagers and their families as part of an outreach program at a church in Poughkeepsie. Calling on people he didn't know yielded little at the start, but Paul found that just showing up, letting people know that the church was there and that it cared about them, was worthwhile. He realized this was the only way to really get to know people; that you could tell so much by simply seeing the houses they lived in—the furniture, the knickknacks, the pictures on the wall. He concluded that these visits had a way of establishing a connection between a family and a clergyman, as well as between individuals and the church as an institution. It was a lesson that would come to profoundly inform my own vision.

Back in New York, Paul continued to pursue his natural interest in reaching families. With the blessing of the head priest of St. Peter's Church in Chelsea, which was half a block from the seminary, Paul, his wife Jenny, and some fellow seminarians roamed the streets of the parish, inviting kids for baseball games and trips to the beach. They started a vacation bible school and even held services on the sidewalk. Paul read about the "worker priests" of postwar France, and how they reached the lower classes by working with them in the factories and living among them in the slums—often without letting them know they were priests until they had gained their trust. Along the way, Paul became interested in the Catholic Worker Movement, which promoted social justice, and with the work of the NAACP, which was still years away from the height of the civil rights movement. As he approached the end of seminary school in 1949, Paul and his friends, full of idealism and enthusiasm, set out to get themselves assigned to churches in poor, urban areas where they could put their principles into practice. They wrote to several bishops, and the one in Newark responded with an offer to bring their work to Grace Church in Jersey City.

My camp was a natural fit with Paul's personal mission, and we became a virtual extension of his parish. Where most of the boys before the war came from the Lower East Side, now about half came from Jersey City. This was a fundamental change for me and my camp because it injected race into the equation. In the late 1940s, race was not something most white Americans thought much about. But for me, it seemed only natural. In college I had begun to develop an awareness of race and class, wealth and poverty, and to wonder how such extreme disparities could exist in a true democracy. Having come from the privileged class, I was more than a little curious about what it was like to be part of a downtrodden minority.

At Princeton I became an admirer of Paul Robeson, who had grown up there and gone on to become the country's most distinguished African-American performer. I read about how Robeson, brilliant and extraordinarily principled, had confronted racial discrimination at every turn—earning a law degree from Columbia in 1923, but quitting his first job after a white secretary refused to take dictation from him. He returned to his childhood love of drama and singing, and in 1928 he starred in *Showboat* on Broadway, famously altering the racist lyrics of "Old Man River" to turn it into perhaps the first civil rights protest song. One day I decided to write to Robeson and tell him how much I appreciated his music and admired him as a man. He wrote me back and invited me to meet him in New York. I went to his hotel and we had what remains for me the most poignant and inspiring conversation I've ever had about race in America.

The boys Paul Moore brought from Jersey City may have been culturally different from the European immigrants from the Lower East Side I'd worked with at camp before the war. But in the most important aspects they were probably more alike than different. There were boys who had reputations for being trouble, and some certainly lived up to their billing. In some of those cases, all it took was a little care and attention to change a kid's direction. Others seemed destined to be their own worst enemies. I heard years later that one of our boys snatched a woman's purse. The woman fell down, hit her head, and died, and he went to prison for manslaughter. But most were kids just trying to make their way in a tough environment. There was Frankie Golden, for instance, a small boy who had been beaten up by a gang and whose own home was no haven of love. As I got to know him, I sensed there was a boy of good character in there, and if we could just pump him up a bit we could improve his chances at life.

What I found most of all was a hell of a lot of kids, essentially no different from those who grew up in middle class homes, who simply needed guidance and encouragement. There is probably no better example of this than Albert Williams—"Albie" to everyone who knows him. Albie's brother Marvin had been one of Paul's first recruits when we started up the camp in Westport, and when I learned that Marvin had two younger brothers at home, I made a note to bring them to camp the following summer. In the spring, I went to Jersey City and

Teaching the sweet science at Westport, 1949: On the right is Niathan Allen, who went on to earn his Ph.D. and become a prominent educator, and has remained a lifelong friend to me.

Paul Moore outside church with some of his Jersey City kids.

found the Williams' tenement building. It was a walk-up where each hallway had a light that stayed on only a few seconds after you pushed the button, so that you had to get to the next light before the one before it went out. This was new to me, and I soon found myself in the dark. Then I heard a bunch of kids running past me down the stairs. I reached out and grabbed one, and it was Albie. He was happy to go with me to Duck Island, our new camp on Long Island.

Arriving at camp that summer, he couldn't believe his good fortune. From making a game out of running downstairs in the dark and hanging out on the Hackensack River, he had now moved on to swimming in a pool, boating, hiking in the woods, and sleeping in a cabin. Albie couldn't swim when he arrived but by the end of his first summer he was swimming two lengths of the pool. I kept a boat called the *Bulldog* in the marina in Westport, Connecticut. I picked Albie to be one of my crew members—a high honor among the campers—when I was making a trip.

Of course, the camp was not just fun and games, and Albie was one who appreciated the help he got from counselors who were also tutors. "I wasn't the best reader," he said during a conversation for this book. "I read a book that summer called *The Arkansas Bear*. It sticks in my mind to this day because that was the first book that I conquered." Albie went home to Jersey City excited about school, and at our annual awards night at the end of the following summer we gave him the prizes for reading and drawing. The award was a correspondence course with a well-known art school in Connecticut. His art teacher at camp would visit him during the year to see how he was doing. "Many of us who were having difficulty in school got the help we needed," Albie said. "There were counselors from some of the best colleges in the country— Yale, Harvard, Princeton, Columbia, Fordham."

Albie remembers himself as a rebellious and headstrong twelve-year-old. "To this very day I remember blowing up," he said. "I had a problem with a counselor. I wanted to beat up another kid and he restrained me. I got upset and found myself punching the counselor. He was white and I assumed it was because I was black. It had nothing to do with it, of course. But I went into a tantrum. By rights I should have been expelled." He was surprised that rather than sending him home, I sat him down and calmly explained that he needed to learn to control himself. "I was surprised I got another chance," Albie said. "That's not how it would be in Jersey City. And it worked because I valued camp so much and didn't want to get kicked out. It was such a rich experience that I saw it as something I didn't want to lose. I didn't want to lose the chance to be in the water, in the sun, to have clean clothes. The chance to be at such a caring place."

AT LUNCH ONE DAY in Westport, my mother, who often came up to camp, sat down in the mess hall between me and a boy named Richie Bates. Richie was miserable; he was usually miserable. I hadn't yet figured him out but kept him close, hoping to crack the code. Mother took note of this sad sack of a boy and tried to cheer him up. "Forget it," I whispered to her. "There's no way." Whereupon Mother took a bottle of ketchup and poured some of it over Richie's head. Everyone at the table froze, wondering how this doleful twelve-year-old would respond. He just looked at her. Then Mother poured some of the ketchup over *my* head. Now the kids started to laugh. And then she reached up and poured the remaining ketchup over her own head, sending everyone—including Richie Bates—into a frenzy of laughter.

Mother was always such a free spirit, and while I am not nearly the character she was, I do believe she passed on a smidgeon of her maverick ways to me. This was most clear in my choice to take a different path than my peers, an inclination that was, I suppose, a mild form of rebellion against expectations. Some of my boarding school friends worked with me at camp before the war, and they enjoyed the experience. But most of them went into law, politics, finance, and other careers you might expect of a St. Paul's boy. That was fine, of course, and I was proud of their accomplishments. But it wasn't for me. (As it turned out, I wasn't the only one who chose a life of service. Besides Paul Moore, there was Quigg McVeigh, my oldest friend, who ultimately became a Trappist monk and the abbot of a monastery in Oregon.)

If anyone understood me completely and supported me unconditionally, it was Mother. She was the world's best listener, and just about the only person I could talk to for hours about my ambitions to one day build on the camp experience by starting a school or center in New York City. There was nothing indulgent or disingenuous about this. Mother loved the boys. And they adored her, as much as anything for the way she exploded their myths of what a lady such as this—elegant and well-bred—should be like. "Oh, you monsters, you fiends!" she would say with delightful exaggeration. "What *awful* things have you been up to today?" And sometimes they would tell her.

It wasn't surprising that both Mother and Granddaddy were proud that I was doing something for society's betterment, or that I was pursuing an unconventional path. I drew my most embedded influences from them, in ways both deliberate and unconscious. In this book I've refrained from anything so self-serving and graceless as quoting other people about me. But I ask your indulgence for one exception, a lovely observation from an outsider that affirms the connections I've always felt deeply. It's by Patricia Linden, who wrote a profile of the Harbor and me for *Town & Country* in 1986:

> From his grandfather, the dauntless and utterly irresistible if eccentric Anthony J. Drexel Biddle, he learned to respect physical courage, God, America, the armed forces, boxing, the outdoors, and personal independence. His mother, Cordelia, who was no less powerful a personality, softened the edges. She gave him mirth, charm, zest and scampishness; a passion for helping people in trouble; and the gift of sensitive, understanding friendship.

And one day in the late Forties, my mother gave me rescue. It was during camp in Westport, and I had gone out riding on one of our trio of horses, a fine steed named Rex. While galloping across the meadow near our house, the horse either hit a hidden rock or somehow got his legs crossed. His body twisted as he went down, with me underneath. The horse apparently rolled over my body as he tried to get up, crushing my legs. I can't know this for sure because I hit the ground so hard that I lost consciousness. I was eventually found by a man who worked in the stable and who brought me to the hospital.

One of my legs was so badly damaged that the doctors wanted to amputate. Here I had survived Normandy and the rest of the war without a serious scratch, only to face losing a leg to a riding mishap on a Connecticut meadow. Mother arrived at the hospital and pleaded with the doctors, begging them to find a way to save my leg. They agreed to try something that was hardly conventional at the time. They operated on the leg, removing my twisted and shattered shinbone, and replaced it with a bar of steel. I was in a body cast for nearly a year, but thanks to my mother, I had my two legs.

IN MY EXTENDED FAMILY THERE WAS a precedent for a life of service to the disadvantaged, and it was a spectacular one. What makes it most significant—and what made it possible—is that it was on the Drexel side, the branch that produced a line of Wall Street titans.

Katharine Drexel was my great-grandmother Emily's first cousin—their fathers were the two Drexel brothers whose banking firm teamed with J.P. Morgan to start what became the first great house of Wall Street. Born in 1858, she inherited $15 million—roughly the equivalent of $250 million today—when both her parents died while she was in her early twenties. Katharine could have spent the rest of her life luxuriating in a family fortune rivaled by few in the country. But she chose instead to use it to help others. Her sympathy for the needy was both intrinsic and modeled. She grew up with a stepmother who opened the doors of their house on Rittenhouse Square three days a week to give food, clothing, and money to the poor.

After her father and stepmother died and she and her sisters inherited their millions, Katharine became in instant philanthropist. One day she received a visit from two missionary priests who had traveled from South Dakota to plead for help for Indian schools whose support from the federal government had been withdrawn. Katharine wrote them a check. A year later, during a private audience with the pope in Rome, she described the plight of the Indians in the American West and asked him to send more missionaries to their reservations. "Why, my child, don't *you* become a missionary?" the pope asked her.

The pope's suggestion resonated with Katharine, who had long felt drawn to a life of service over one of unearned privilege, and to faith over marriage. And so, in 1889, she became a nun. The front page of the *Philadelphia Public Ledger* screamed the news: MISS DREXEL ENTERS A CATHOLIC CONVENT—GIVES UP SEVEN MILLION. To her vows of poverty, chastity, and obedience, Katharine added one more: "To be the mother and servant of the Indian and Negro races."

After leaving the convent she started her own religious order, the Sisters of the Blessed Sacrament for Indians and Colored People. The order at first used the Drexel summer house in Torresdale, Pennsylvania, then moved to a new convent, Cornwells Heights. From there, Mother Katharine, as she became known, started a dozen schools for Indians in New Mexico, later touring them by burro and stagecoach. Her commitment to blacks was even greater. She used the income from her father's trust to build nearly a hundred schools for blacks in the South, including a university, Xavier in New Orleans, which she founded in 1915. It remains the only historically black Catholic college in the country. When she picked out the land on which she wanted to build Xavier, Mother Katharine had a lawyer make the purchase because she was afraid the owner wouldn't sell it if he knew she was the actual buyer. As the leader of an order committed to helping poor blacks, Katharine was a vilified figure in the South, but she took the disdain, and worse, in stride. When nuns in her order told her that whites taunted them with shouts of "Nigger sisters" as they walked the streets of New Orleans, she simply asked, "Did you pray for them?"

Mother Katharine lived to age ninety-seven, long enough to see the beginnings of the great civil rights movement. Of course, she had been conducting her own civil rights movement since the last century, trying to improve the lives of the oppressed since the time when the Civil War was as recent as Ronald Reagan's presidency now is to us. Six decades later, her inheritance was being used to pay for advancements like the NAACP's investigations of the exploitation of black workers. By the time of her death in 1955, the former Katharine Drexel had spent her entire fortune, $20 million with interest, on helping others.

In 1964, the Vatican began to consider Mother Katharine for sainthood. For her to be raised to this exalted status, there had to be proof of two posthumous miracles to demonstrate her saintly powers in heaven. One occurred in 1974, after a fourteen-year-old boy named Robert Gutherman lost his hearing to a virulent infection. Two operations didn't help, and with her son in terrible pain Robert's mother called the Sisters of the Blessed Sacrament, who encouraged Robert and his family to pray to Mother Katharine. Scared and alone one night, Robert did. The next morning, his hearing was perfect and the pain was gone. In 1988, after a thorough evaluation by the Vatican medical board, which took testimony from Robert's doctors and analyzed X-rays and other records, the church officially declared his recovery a miracle. A second miracle was recorded in 1996, after the family of a little girl who was born nearly deaf prayed to Mother Katharine and her hearing, too, returned to normal, with no medical explanation. In 2000, forty-five years after her death, Pope John II canonized Saint Katharine Drexel. I was among many family members who went to Rome to attend the canonization.

SEVEN

Three Mile Harbor

AFTER TWO SUMMERS in Connecticut, with the Westport area becoming more suburbanized, I decided to look for a more rural and spacious property. In the American Camping Association's bulletin I found a camp in Kingston, New York, that had run out of money and would rent its grounds for $500 for the summer. So we brought the kids up there for the summer of 1949. But it felt temporary.

One day the following winter, I went down to an airstrip in Flushing Meadows where there was a company that rented planes by the day to licensed pilots. For sixty dollars I got an Air Coupe, a wonderful little single-engine, two-passenger plane, and took off with maps showing everything within a 150-mile radius of New York City. I flew all day, looking for the right spot of land to build what I hoped would finally be a permanent camp. I had two main requirements: It had to be a wide open space with not much else around it. And it had to be on a body of water expansive enough that I could make teaching coastal navigation a mainstay of the camp. The Navy was still very much a part of me, and I envisioned imparting what I knew about the sea to kids who spent their lives in a sea of concrete and brick. I saw it as a way of opening up the world to them, showing them that there was more out there for them than what they knew. I wanted the camp to be a completely hands-on experience, where these boys from the inner city would learn about nature, about the seasons, about the sea.

From the air that day and later, I saw land on the shores of Rhode Island that looked good, and some in Connecticut. I would put down at local airports, where I'd get a cab ride to the properties. It turned out that most of the places I was interested in had already caught the eyes of developers, and that put the price out of reach. I was looking for a steal, and I was willing to look until I found one.

Finally, after all that flying around, I set my sights on a piece of property that was not very far from where I'd started out before the war. I flew out to eastern Long Island, and from the air I saw a beautiful harbor sheltered from Gardiners Bay and Long Island Sound by a spit of land. There were hardly any houses for miles around the bay. I landed at the little airport in East Hampton and called a friend of mine who lived in Sag Harbor. He picked me up and we drove over to look around. I learned that the body of water I'd seen from the air was called Three Mile Harbor, and the land around it was exactly what I wanted, only better. I could see it all in my head—boys out on the harbor, others building cabins, working in the vegetable garden. Over here, a cabin where counselors could tutor kids in math and science. Over there, a baseball game. A dinner bell ringing. Everyone gathering in the mess hall at the end of another great day of camp.

I went to see Jim Amaden, whose father had long been one of the big names in real estate in the Hamptons, and asked him about the land around Three Mile Harbor. "Oh, I don't think that's what you want," he said. "It's boondocks. Four hundred acres with no electricity and just a dirt road for access. It's not even for sale. What would you want that land for?"

I knew by now I had to be somewhat circumspect about what I was interested in. When I'd told a real estate broker in Rhode Island I was looking for land for a summer camp, that had led to all sorts of questions: What kind of camp? What kind of kids? Sorry, no land available here. There was also something else I had to worry about. People often assumed that because my name was Duke I was fabulously wealthy. That wouldn't help my negotiating position. So when Mr. Amaden asked what I wanted the land for, I told him I had a friend who was interested in acquiring some investment property. It wasn't exactly the truth, but I had a plan for making it so. I hadn't seen Paul Bianco since the war, but I thought he would make an excellent partner and front man.

The son of Italian immigrants, Paul had grown up in Sag Harbor and worked in construction before the war. We met on the island of Saipan when my ship put in for repairs as we prepared for the assault on Okinawa. Paul was then a noncommissioned officer serving in the Seabees, the Navy's construction force. He was in charge of a construction unit that was building barracks and mess halls for the troops that were pouring in from the States for the coming invasion of Japan. When we discovered our eastern Long Island tie, we became fast friends. Paul had just finished building a wooden structure designed to be a beer-and-Coke bar for officers. We christened it enthusiastically and one afternoon promised to get together after the war if we survived.

Now Paul was back in Sag Harbor and building houses. He'd built several around town and another on Sammy's Beach, which was on the piece of land at the north end of Three Mile Harbor. I called him with a proposition. I told him I was looking at a piece of property that we might want to go in on. He could build some houses to sell and I could have land for my camp and perhaps invest in a few houses myself. Since the property was completely undeveloped, I said, the selling price might be low enough for us to consider. I flew out to East Hampton a week later and Paul met me at the airport. We drove to Jim Amaden's office, and he took us out to the property, or rather to the edge of it. To get into the prime acreage we had to leave our car on Springy Banks Road and walk about three-quarters of a mile through tangled woods to the edge of Three Mile Harbor. There was a group of houses a mile or so to the east of the property, but other than that everything was pristine and inviting.

We found our way to the spot where I could envision building cabins, a mess hall, a house and dock right on the waterfront. "So who owns this land?" I asked casually.

"The Gerard Family," said Amaden. "They own about twelve hundred acres out here. Some in trust, some just open space. Mr. Gerard is also one of the main landowners on Shelter Island." He looked around. "I told you it was the boondocks." Later on, Amaden introduced me to an old friend of his who told me that the land came with a legend dating to Revolutionary War times. "They say there's an old man who lives out here and frightens people away," Jim's friend said.

"The legend is that he was a British soldier who was captured by the Americans. At the end of the war British prisoners were being shipped back to England, but he jumped off the skiff that was taking them out to the ship, And he's been living here the last couple of hundred years. He's reported to be seen skulking around from time to time. So that's the legend of Three Mile Harbor."

I smiled. It was a legend made to order for a boys' camp.

After looking the place over, Paul and I went to the village for a cup of coffee. "The property's perfect," I said, and asked if he would go in on it with me. "I would if we could get it for a fair price," he said. "But I don't think we're going to get very far."

"Well, let's try," I said. "Let's go back to Jim Amaden. But maybe you should go alone at first. My Duke name implies wealth, only a smidgeon of which I actually possess. So it's probably best if you do the bidding."

"I guess you're supposed to be some sort of tycoon," he said.

"I'm doing okay," I said. "But people seem to think that all the Dukes are like Doris. We're not."

Paul contacted Mr. Amaden, who reported back that we could probably get the land for between $150,000 and $200,000. It was obviously way too much. "Go back and offer him fifteen thousand cash," I said. Mr. Amaden laughed when he heard this. He said we should raise our bid if we were seriously interested, implying that we could probably acquire the land for a lot less than he initially thought. After a couple of weeks of haggling, we were able to make a deal for a very decent price, with a small down payment and a short-term mortgage.

Now all Paul and I had to do was figure out how to divide the land— who got what. I wanted the section that bordered both the harbor and a little inlet called Hands Creek. Paul said, "I won't tell you what I want and you don't tell me what you want—we'll just flip a coin." I won the toss, but it turned out well for both of us. Paul wanted to be a little closer to the main road to be near the eventual utilities.

Paul was not only my partner in the land but was to become a good friend and my right-hand man in building the camp—the first cabins as well as my small house. (Paul built his own house on his section of the property.) Over the next fourteen months we had some of the kids come out from the city and help out, clearing land, carrying lumber, and driving nails. The biggest task, though, was making a road to con-nect the campgrounds and the house to Springy Banks Road, which was half a mile away. The only way in was a dirt trail used by local shell fishermen and by bootleggers a couple of decades earlier. Apparently, at least some of New York City's illegal booze during Prohibition came in at the spot where I was planning to build my house and camp. There were stories in the area about gun battles breaking out during hijack-ings, including one in which several men were said to have been killed.

I came to enjoy the small and large tasks of building the camp, and became quite adept running a bulldozer. I cleared the trails, the base-ball field, and the road. It was a real hands-on operation. One day, I was sitting in Paul's house with my brother Angie, who remarked that the camp didn't have a real name. Up to now, wherever we'd been, I'd simply called it "camp" or applied the name of whatever location we happened to be in at the time—in Connecticut the camp was known as Lord's Highway while the Kingston camp was known as Kingston. It occurred to us that with the camp finally hav-ing a permanent home, it should have a real name. Sitting in Paul's house overlooking Three Mile Harbor, Angier suggested we call it Safe Harbor. "That's a beautiful thought," I said. "I like the implica-tion. The boys do consider it their safe harbor."

"Then why not call it Boys Harbor?" Angier replied.

I loved the name, even if I envisioned a little problem down the road. Eventually I wanted to expand the camp to include girls. But for now, "Boys Harbor" was perfect.

One weekend before our first summer I took Tony out to the prop-erty to get the feel of it and spend a couple of nights camping out. There were some fine trails on the property, and we used a compass to traverse the entire property. At the waterfront, we pitched a pup tent and cooked up some hot dogs and hamburgers. He was nine, and it was an exciting little adventure for him and a lot of fun for me to be with him. Tony was a wonderful boy, and always good company to boot. After we ate, I suggested we take a walk around. We hiked a trail that cut in from about a quarter-mile down the beach, then up a big hill. We saw a couple of deer, big bucks with huge antlers that seemed to Tony

just about the most amazing sight he'd ever seen. And then we encountered a two-legged creature—an old, bearded man. I waved to him, but
when our dog, Gendarme, ran up to him, the man stopped, raised his
arm, and pointed at us. Then he slowly turned and walked behind a big
rock. We circled the rock twice, but no sign of him.

I told Jim Amaden about the encounter, and he said, "Oh, that was
probably the mayor of Springy Banks."

"Who?" I asked.

"That's what they call this old man. He's a squatter who suppos-
edly settled on the land decades ago. He lives in a little hut on
Hands Creek, hunts and fishes. But you own the land now, so you
can evict him."

I wasn't inclined to do that. If he didn't bother anyone, what was the
harm? But it did give me an idea. Remembering how much fun and
excitement we'd had with the gorilla caper on Jessup's Neck before the
war, I hatched a new legend, which I made a highlight of the introduction to the new camp for the boys who arrived the first week of July.
The story conveniently combined an actual man—the "mayor of
Springy Banks" Tony and I had encountered—and a mythical one: the
British soldier of local legend. It went like this:

> One day, my son Tony and I came out to spend a night in the
> woods. We decided to hike all the way around the property, and as
> the sun was going down we encountered a man. He was old and
> looked as though he had spent his whole life here. He didn't speak;
> he let out a moaning sound, and we realized he had what looked like
> a hole or indentation in his chest. It was blood-red. When our dog
> went after him, he ran behind a rock and disappeared, leaving a trail
> of bloodstains. I began asking questions around town and learned
> that the man was said to be the ghost of a British prisoner of war
> from the Revolutionary War. He was very bitter that his fellow sol-
> diers had surrendered and that they'd all been captured by the
> American colonists. So while they were moving out in a rowing dory
> to meet a British-bound ship on the other side of Sammy's Beach, he
> flipped over the stern when the guard wasn't looking and slowly
> swam all the way back and into the Hands Creek Lagoon.

*When the settlers built a few cottages around the lagoon, he
would appear at night and frighten the children, and often the
adults, by making eerie, groaning sounds, hoping to scare these settlers away. They took to calling him the Lagoon Man. Well, one day
a farmer and his son got in their wagon to go up to harvest corn
growing in the big field bordering what is now Springy Banks Road.
They found the field smoldering from fire. They saw the man who
did it—the Lagoon Man. He was a British soldier, still wearing
pieces of his tattered uniform. They sped after him at full gallop, and
when they caught up to him he became impaled on the "gee pole" (a
rod attached by harness between a pair of horses drawing a wagon).
They went back to their village and announced that they had killed
the notorious and mysterious Lagoon Man. The people gave him a
proper burial, behind that big rock—right where Tony and I encountered him. So it seems that two centuries later he still doesn't want
anybody on his land. And he's not at all happy about Boys Harbor.
And he's going to do everything possible to scare us off. So if any of
you see him, come and tell us. Don't try to do anything yourself.*

I emphasized this last part, recalling vividly the rocks that came my
way when I used to don the gorilla suit. "We'll try to catch him," I said.

One day a group of boys was walking near Hands Creek and saw a
man they figured to be the legendary Lagoon Man (known as "Goon
Man" to later generations of campers.) They followed him to his hut
and threw stones at it. A few days later, I got a telephone call. "Mr.
Duke," he said, "I hear you're a nice fellow, and I must tell you I met
them kids over there in the woods and they followed me to my cabin.
So here I am back in the village calling you." It turned out that the
man we'd run into—"the mayor of Springy Banks"—was a fine local
man from East Hampton who was an ardent duck hunter and lived
the whole summer in the little cabin, complete with porch, that he'd
built out of driftwood on the edge of Hands Creek. He was a nice
man, and I had to tell the kids he wasn't the feared Lagoon Man, just
an elderly man who enjoyed spending summers by the creek. I had no
intention of making him leave. He wasn't bothering anybody—and I
thought he added an interesting touch to camp.

The legend of the Goon Man was to change and grow over the years, far outliving the man who inspired it. I passed the tale down through generations of counselors, who invariably added their own details to form countless versions of the same fiction. Its reputation preceded it. Each summer, new groups of boys would get off the bus wanting to hear the story, and I had to caution the counselors about overdoing it. Don't tell the really young children, I said, and don't make the story too horrible or bloody. And don't say we've seen him lately because the kids would spend the rest of the summer looking for him.

The "mayor" wasn't the only one I found on the grounds. One day that first year I discovered an entire family camping out—a husband and wife and two teenaged sons. It turned out they had been coming every summer for years. The man had a thick German accent and said he and his family were from New Jersey and had camped there every summer for years. I told him I'd bought the land and he began pleading to let them stay. "This is part of us," he said. "We've been coming here for fourteen years. My little boys grew up here. Are you going to make us leave?"

"Stop," I said. "Say no more. If we can live in peace and you realize it's now private property, I don't see anything wrong. You might not like the camp, though. I've got a bunch of kids here."

"Dot ist goot!" he said.

I decided not to tell Betty, my wife, about the family because she'd probably want them to leave. And sure enough, one day she detected a strong odor of sauerkraut and followed it into the woods, where she found the family from New Jersey sitting around their campfire. She insisted they be banished, but I wanted to let them stay. "He told me that any time he catches too many fish, he'll bring them over to the house," I said. That settled it. We ate lots of fish for the next several years.

IT'S FUNNY TO REMEMBER how relatively remote and undeveloped East Hampton was in those days, and how easy it was to do just about whatever you wanted with your land. When we started the camp, I went to see the zoning board and told them what I was doing. Nobody said anything against it. I put up a sign that said "Boys Harbor," bought an old school bus to bring kids out, and that was that—for a while, anyway. Eventually people caught wind of us, word started going around that this "Boys Harbor" wasn't like most camps. We weren't a camp for white kids from well-to-do families, and we weren't Boy Scouts. One morning, I found that someone had painted the words "nigger lover" on our sign. I quickly painted over it before any of the kids saw it. But I realized I might have a problem, especially when I started getting anonymous hate mail. There were threats: *Close up and get out of town, if you know what's good for you!* There were overwrought racist fears: *You're putting Negro boys in a community with white girls—they're going to get raped.* And worse. People seemed to know who I was. In town, some would deliberately step out of my way, as if being with ten feet of me would give them a virus.

One day I went into the little delicatessen store on Springy Banks Road that was known as Mary's. I introduced myself to Mary, and she said, "Oh, you're the man with those bad kids out there."

"Yes, I am, Mary, but don't misjudge us. They're American citizens and they're good kids. Why don't you come and visit us and see for yourself?"

Mary accepted my invitation and came loaded for bear. But as I introduced her around and served her lunch in the mess hall, I could actually see her presumptions melting away. "I had a very nice time," she said when she left. I told her she could come back any time. And she did—came to lunch every Sunday the rest of the month. "I want you to know that any time you want, you can come down to my place with these boys and I'll give them all Cokes and ice cream."

"Mary, that's great," I said. "So in other words, you don't see this as a 'nigger place.'" I was being purposely provocative. "You see it as just a nice place."

"Yes, I do," she said, "and I apologize for talking that way. Your boys are good."

I was relieved at how easy it was to win Mary over, but I knew there were others out there. I came right out and asked her who else might be upset about the camp. Without hesitation, she reeled off a few names—a bay fisherman, a couple of farmers, a plumber. Nor did she hesitate to make herself at home. A day or two later, she showed up with the fisherman, the farmers, and the plumber. We showed them around and invited them to stay for lunch. I'm not going to pretend that was all it took to turn around deeply ingrained racial attitudes, but it did seem to calm them down. At least they no longer saw our camp as an invasion of menacing young delinquents.

Each Sunday since camp opened that first summer, I had been driving forty or fifty boys to the Episcopal church in East Hampton. I sat with them in the back and admonished them to be quiet and respectful. But of course we got some looks that made them feel that "they're looking down on us," as one of the boys expressed it to me. However, in all fairness, we were all accepted. Because his daughter and her family lived in East Hampton, the nationally respected head of Pittsburgh's Episcopal church, Bishop Austin Pardue, was spending a few weeks as a visiting minister. After church on the second Sunday I introduced myself to him and told him a little about the camp. "I've noticed your kids in the back," the bishop said. "They're very respectful and well-behaved."

The bishop seemed very much interested in the camp, and so I asked if he'd like to drop by one day. He came calling on two evenings that week and sat with the counselors and me and listened to our ideas. I told him, as I told others, that I worried what would happen to our country if too many people slipped out of the system. "Too many people feel they're left out of the dream," I said. "We've found that children on the street have their dream. And they reach out for whatever they can find of value."

We talked about some of the kids, about their backgrounds, their problems, their personalities and talents and hopes. Then I told him about Mary and the other local folks, how they had visited camp and had meals in the the mess hall with our boys and counselors. I suspected, and the bishop agreed, that there were probably more townspeople out there who were wary because they didn't know us. "You know what you should do?" Bishop Pardue said. "You should have an open house out there and invite the whole town. And I'll help you. Why not do it next Sunday?"

How could I say no?

The next Sunday I loaded the boys onto the bus and drove to church, where they took their usual spot in the last two pews. "Before we begin this morning's service," Bishop Pardue said, "I'd like all of you folks in the first two rows to move back and I'd like to have the people in the last two rows move to the front." The last two rows, of course, were occupied by the boys of Boys Harbor. All at once, the church filled with the sounds of dozens of people rearranging themselves, while everyone else looked on with utter bafflement. When everyone was finally seated, the bishop reached under the pulpit and came up with a basketball. I looked around and saw that the congregants' puzzlement was turning to discomfort, even annoyance. For that matter, I was a little concerned myself. I didn't know what was coming next.

The bishop held up the basketball, then tossed it in the direction of the first pew. One of the kids caught it and threw it back to him. "Well," said the bishop, "it seems we have some young athletes here. They've been here the last two Sundays, and it's certainly wonderful that these children want to be with us, and we welcome them. By the way, they are all part of a wonderful camp run by Tony Duke and his friends out on Springy Banks Road. And this afternoon there's going to be an open house out there at five o'clock. I'll be there, and I'd really like to see all of you there. There's going to be food and cold drinks in the afternoon till seven in the evening, and believe me, you'll learn something. Now, how many of you will be going to the Boys Harbor camp this afternoon?"

There were very few hands. Now the bishop had the vestrymen appear to lock the doors. I couldn't believe what I was seeing: a congregation of East Hampton Episcopalians was being held hostage by the bishop of Pittsburgh until they agreed to show up at a camp for inner-city kids. "Anybody for tennis?" the bishop said. "How about golf? Well, if you want to get out of church and play, come to the Boys Harbor open house. Now, how many of you will be going to Boys Harbor this afternoon?"

Hands shot up throughout the congregation, including that of the mayor of East Hampton. The doors were flung open, and sure enough the open house was well-attended. It was the beginning of East Hampton and the surrounding community offering its approval and vastly important support for Boys Harbor and what it stood for. It seemed that any resistance to the camp was eliminated by my dear new friend the bishop's invitation to "come and see." By the end of the second summer, I felt a real difference in the attitude of the community. Not only was the Harbor accepted—we were embraced. Many in East Hampton and the nearby communities became significant supporters. One of the strongest was Bill Pickens, a fine young man from Sag Harbor who was a long-time counselor and later a distinguished member of the Harbor's board.

A DAY AT BOYS HARBOR always started with a gathering of everyone around the flag pole for the Pledge of Allegiance and a few minutes of sharing thoughts. Anyone who had something to say—about pretty much anything—was encouraged to step up and speak his piece. This was the beginning of what became standard practice and a virtual requirement at camp, and the seed for more formal instruction in public speaking that the staff and I gave for many years. The morning ritual not only helped many boys develop confidence and self-expression; it also encouraged the respect for one another that was always at the heart of my mission. The boys listened attentively to their campmates because they knew *their* time would come to speak and be in the spotlight. Over time, you could see the boys getting more comfortable. "Eventually, everybody would be jumping up, waving their hands to tell their story," my daughter December remembers. "They would talk about anything—if someone was mean to them or they had achieved something. Kids from the inner city learned to swim at Boys Harbor and they would get up and announce, 'I didn't sink to the bottom yesterday!'"

Occasionally, though, a kid would take a shortcut to self-esteem. Once, literally. We had a long-distance race once a summer—twice around the outer perimeter of camp, almost a three-mile course—and one boy seemed to win every year. This struck me as odd because he didn't look to be that fast. So I decided to run the race with him. This time, he finished far behind. With some questioning, he admitted to me that in the other races at a certain turn he'd cut through the woods, emerging just as the leaders were passing in the final leg. He'd fall in behind them, then use all the energy he'd saved to kick into high gear in time to pass the others.

I enjoyed being in the middle of everything, leading calisthenics each morning, playing in ball games, teaching sailing and boating, fishing, and swimming. I greeted every boy with a handshake as he came into the mess hall for breakfast, and made the rounds of the cabins to say sixty-five individual goodnights each evening. I found that my involvement and enthusiasm was rewarded in kind. If I was off clearing some brush or digging a drainage ditch, I was apt to be surrounded by boys wanting to help. Our house, meanwhile, was always open to the boys. They knew they could stroll up to the house whenever they weren't engaged in scheduled activities, to talk about a problem or simply to hang out. If a boy was with us on his birthday, he could pick six friends and bring them up for supper and a party. Betty was as open to all this as I was. She was the official camp barber, setting up shop on the porch. And my own children—Tony Jr., Nick, Delia, Josie, December, and John in those days—were part of the mix. They ate most of their meals in the mess hall, and camp kids would often invite them to stay overnight in their cabins. We were all a family. Looking back, I might have been taking a chance that my children would feel jealous or resentful that I was spending so much time with the camp boys. But those kinds of feelings never surfaced. In fact, most of my kids became very involved as counselors. As my daughter December says, "I grew up at Boys Harbor." And that's true for all of them.

Of paramount importance to me was to get to know the boys as well as possible—really know how they lived, what they thought and felt. I would talk to Paul Moore or to the head of the Boys Club, who also sent kids to Boys Harbor. I would make every effort to develop a rapport with the boys any way I could, and I would visit them in their homes after they left camp. I found that many of them lived positively Dickensian lives. There was a boy, one of nine children, whose mother was rarely home, whose apartment had no furniture, and whose dinner was typically a slice of bread dipped in grease. There was a boy whose alcoholic father beat him and his siblings routinely. Another boy would pretend to be asleep while his mother, a drug addict, entertained men

A Harbor ritual: Greeting the boys as they go into the mess hall in 1957.

Taking a spin across Three Mile Harbor aboard our legendary powerboat, Rum Runner.

in the same room. We had many boys—abused, neglected, or simply crowded out of their homes—who had lived on the streets.

I had no degree in social work or psychology, but transformed myself into a practical expert. While reading a book by a social work professor at Ohio State University named Leontine R. Young, I came upon a quote that struck a chord with me: "The attempt to make people be good has always failed. The only possibility for change is to help them want to be good . . . If the child is to learn that there is such a thing as adult interest in him for his own sake the worker must take the initiative and prove that interest, in action which can be bold, imaginative, and as flexible as the situation demands."

Considering the backgrounds of many of our boys, I believed that making clear that we considered education paramount in their lives— and putting that belief into practice—constituted bold and imaginative action. Besides counselors tutoring the boys, we began a long tradition of volunteers. One day I received a letter from a teacher who said she'd heard about our camp and offered her services as a reading teacher. I gladly took her up on the offer, and we became what I believe was the first summer camp with an accredited remedial reading program.

In the spring of 1954, at the suggestion of a public relations man I knew named Alfred Katz, I took a trip overseas to see how some other countries dealt with the kinds of children we served at Boys Harbor. I chose two countries whose cultures fascinated me: Japan, where I'd spent time at the end of the war, and India, whose magnificent leader, Mahatma Gandhi, had been assassinated six years earlier, just as the country had achieved its independence from Britain. When I arrived at my hotel in New Delhi, I was taken aback to find a note waiting for me from Gandhi's successor, Prime Minister Jawaharlal Nehru. Nehru had heard a bit about Boys Harbor from a reporter for *The New York Times* and was interested in talking with me about our work with disadvantaged boys in America. He invited me to meet with him, and out of it came a completely unexpected collaboration. I worked with an Indian teacher in creating a settlement house in the back streets of New Delhi, which began a long-running relationship with India. We supported the settlement house annually, and eventually began bringing counselors to Boys Harbor from India and other countries. (I also made visits to youth centers in Mexico, Puerto Rico, England, and West Germany.)

My approach at Boys Harbor became a blend of my own experience and what I learned along the way from others—Boys Club leaders, teachers, academics, and other professionals in the field, both in the United States and abroad. But perhaps most important were my own instincts, which came from my head as well as my heart. First, I steered clear of any outward displays of pity. I noted early on that it was wrong to assume that the boys were embarrassed or ashamed of where or what circumstances they came from. Some, in fact, seemed truly bewildered if someone implied that they would learn a better way to live at Boys Harbor, as if there were something wrong with the way they were being brought up. So instead of being judgmental, I found it best to be respectful. It was simple, really. By giving the boys consistent affection and setting a good example of behavior, we were able to give them a chance to see a world outside of the one they came from, and to find a way out on their own terms. It was as if we were showing them a path without pushing them down that path. They had their own legs.

From the beginning I applied many lessons from my Navy experience, while developing my own ideas of structure and authority. What I wanted to establish was an environment of openness, cheer, and real affection, while also recognizing the need for thoughtful discipline. In her first year of Boys Harbor, Betty came up with the idea of having a series of welcome parties in our home on the first three nights of camp. New boys were guests the first night, second-year boys (who had been with us at Kingston) the second night, and the veterans, who were coming to their third campsite in three years, on the third night. Now that we had finally found a real home, we wanted them to know that Boys Harbor was their camp as well as ours.

In the earlier weeks of summer I wanted to give the boys the chance to find their own places. If a boy showed little interest or aptitude for the conventional camp agenda of sports or boating, I would look for ways to adapt the camp to him. One seemed very interested in photography, so I arranged for him to spend afternoons helping a professional photographer in East Hampton. I had boys who loved to tend to the vegetable garden and others who were drawn more to the arts and crafts shop than to the ball field. I also eschewed the clockwork approach of most summer camps. I would often interrupt activities by taking a few boys sailing or for a spin into the village. This afforded a chance to hear what a boy was thinking about. I found that you could learn more about a kid by sometimes letting him do as he pleased— within reason—than by trying to squeeze him into a mold. Of course, there had to be a schedule. But I felt—and still feel—that it's sometimes a good idea to allow individuals, especially young ones, to diverge from it. The challenge was to find out what a boy would rather be doing, and if it was logical and useful to try to make time for it.

In choosing the boys whom I would invite to camp, I tended to avoid extremes. Boys with major behavior problems or serious criminal records, I felt, were better handled by places with trained, professional staffs. At the other end of the spectrum, I knew there were camps and schools that catered to exceptionally bright or talented children who were poor. I was more interested in the vast middle— the forgotten boys who could go either way and might be diamonds in the rough. Ignored, these boys would probably spend the rest of their lives in the neighborhoods in which they were born, with no feeling that they could move upward or forward. Worse, at any time the odds might tilt in favor of drugs and crime. The other kind of boy I was looking for was someone with the potential to be a leader among his peers. It was one thing for boys to look up to me, but as much of a role model as I tried to be, I felt they also needed to follow boys of their own generation who came from where they did. They knew the lives these boys were living in a way that I never could.

Albie Williams, who had first come to camp at Westport, was the essence of the kind of boy I had in mind—first as one of those middle kids who might be left behind and later as a leader among the boys—a harbinger of how his life would unfold. That first summer in East Hampton, we really built the camp together, all of us, and Albie and some others took on the task of creating a swimming hole. We had no pool as we did in Westport; instead we had a beach on Three Mile Harbor. Under Albie's watchful eye, the boys cleaned it up and we anchored a little floating dock that the boys could swim to and dive from. And Albie became an academic leader as well, from that very first summer. Without him knowing it, we built a remedial reading class around him, hoping the other kids would take note of his interest in reading and emulate him. Many did. As time passed, there was no doubt in my mind but that Albie was possessed of great intelligence and a powerful wish to do the right thing and lead others in the same direction.

Eventually Albie became a junior counselor and then a senior counselor. He took the central themes I tried to instill—respect for oneself and one another and pulling together—and made them his own operating principles. "We had cabin inspections and there was a competition for the cleanest," Albie remembers. "You had to line up outside your cabin as if you were in a boot camp. I wanted my cabin to be the best—I wanted it to be spotless—and I always stressed, 'Let's work as a team.' And when we went outside the camp—to compete in sports with another camp or to go into town or the beach—I wanted my boys to be the most sportsmanlike and the best behaved."

I remember a boy in Albie's cabin—I'll call him Richie—who clearly didn't want to be at camp. He invariably resisted pretty much every activity. On the way to swimming, or art class, or baseball, or boxing, Richie would fall back and grumpily, sometimes angrily, follow along. One day, he simply cut loose from the group and disappeared. Albie arranged for a substitute counselor to take over the group and went off to look for Richie. He finally saw him heading for the camp entrance and followed him out onto the road into town. Albie simply trailed him, staying a few paces behind. He didn't tell him to stop; in fact, he didn't say anything. When Richie turned left at a crossroad, Albie did too. In a little while, Richie finally stopped. He turned to Albie, and with tears streaming down his face, shouted, "I hate it here! No one likes me and I don't like them either. I want to go home." Richie, like Albie, came from Jersey City, and Albie knew that his parents were split up and that his home was not a happy place. Albie was determined to get Richie to stay, to learn new things and maybe even start to enjoy himself. I don't know how Albie did it, but he got Richie to come back, helped him learn to get along with his group, and to become a happy camper. Albie showed me then that he had a magic touch.

In 1952, Rev. Kim Myers, a long-time mentor and colleague of Paul Moore at Grace Church in Jersey City, was appointed vicar of Trinity

Church on the Lower East Side of Manhattan. Kim was one of the most socially progressive clergymen in New York, if not the country. Among other things, he persuaded Paul and other white clerics to join the NAACP as far back as 1950. As he was about to continue his inspiring work with underprivileged youth in Manhattan, Kim decided to take it a step further. He came to me and said he wanted to take in one of the children I had been working with. It would be a kind of extension of Boys Harbor. Kim asked if I could recommend any of my boys. I immediately thought of Albie, who was thirteen at the time. "He has great promise," I said. Kim met Albie and his mother and asked what they thought. With six other children to raise, Mrs. Williams agreed this would be a good thing for Albie. And it was.

Over the next few years, Albie had two homes—his family's in Jersey City and that of his adoptive family in the city, which came to include Kim, his wife, and two children they adopted from Korea, a boy and a girl. Kim sent Albie to a prep school in Connecticut and then to Wagner College on Staten Island, where Albie majored in history and ran track. He became so bonded to the Myers family that he added their name to his, and to this day he is Albert Williams-Myers. After college, Albie got married and he and his wife, Janice, went off to teach school on St. Thomas. Then they went into the Peace Corps, working at a children's health care project in the central African nation of Malawi. Inspired by his two years in Africa, Albie returned to the United States and earned a master's degree and then a doctorate in African history from UCLA. In 1973, by which time he and Janice had two children, Albie got a Ford Foundation grant to do research in Zambia. Since 1979, Albie has been a professor of African Studies at the State University of New York at New Paltz. He spent several years on our executive board and is still on the advisory board.

"I'll be up front with you," Albie said. "I still go to Jersey City because I still have family there. And people are trapped. I can honestly say that I would have ended up like most of my family if not for Boys Harbor. I might even have gotten caught up eventually in the drug scene."

Whenever I think of the kids who've made me especially proud— and there are hundreds—Albie is always among the first who come to mind. His experience at Boys Harbor became a springboard to a unique opportunity, and eventually to his own career as an educator. Many years later, Dr. Albert Williams-Myers would come to Boys Harbor and I would point to him as Exhibit A. "If you stick with us," I would say to the boys, "you're going to find you're like Albie up here. He started where you are, and now he's a professor. He's Dr. Williams-Myers."

For me, Albie is not just one of the Harbor's great success stories and one of the finest men I've ever met. On a personal level, he is one of my closest lifelong friends.

THOUGH I'VE BEEN CALLED a philanthropist, I never felt that word fit. It suggests someone who donates wads of money from afar. Not only was I involved in everything at the Harbor, but I only wish I'd had the kind of money usually associated with a philanthropist. Still, in the early years Boys Harbor had virtually no outside financial support. I had to budget very carefully because the camp ran almost entirely on my own funds. I did eventually begin to receive welcome contributions from friends and family members, but I realized that it wouldn't be until I could show results that I would be able to approach foundations and corporations. There was no question that if I wanted to expand the enterprise to include a year-round program I had to become an adept fundraiser. And doing that meant becoming an aggressive promoter and networker.

One of our first brochures had a cover featuring a photograph of a boy water skiing on Three Mile Harbor. But the text inside belied the notion of a camp that was all fun and games. We described the difficult circumstances from which many of the Harbor boys came—how they often arrived withdrawn and suspicious, viewing camp as just another stop in a world of cold and hateful adults. There was Jerry. Beaten brutally by the police and forced to confess to a crime he knew nothing about, he came to us with layers of mistrust and hostility that had to be peeled off. There was Bobby. His parents had turned him into a pimp at age eleven, only to be arrested and then expelled from school for doing what his parents told him to do.

As a fundraising tool, the brochure stressed the progressive nature of our program. It pointed out that our counselors had daily meetings

Original campers such as Tony Albarello and Fred Cicerelli went on to happy lives and successful careers, but always considered Boys Harbor their second family. They and others formed the Boys Harbor Alumni Society, which met monthly, raised money for an annual scholarship, and organized various volunteer activities for the Harbor.

The first group of campers and counselors is pictured above at Duck Island in 1937. Nearly twenty years later, by which point we had settled in East Hampton and become Boys Harbor, many attended the Alumni Society's 1955 annual dinner.

Front row: Howard Murther, Nick Carlaftes, Joe Janots, Eddie Indellicati.
Middle row: Roger Schafer, Rudy Kliemisch, Tommy Casale, Steve Andrews, John Meyer Jr., Tom Alongi.
Top row: Dick Wirth, Geroge Katsafouros, me, Tony Albarello, Lonsdale Stowell, Gardner Boothe

with a professional staff that included a social worker, a sociologist, and a psychologist, as well as visiting specialists who received postgraduate field training. "Is all this help advantageous?" we asked. "Is it necessary for seventy-five boys? Any estimate of the adjustment Boys Harbor youths have made and are making should be reckoned with consideration for the difficulties they must overcome. Without intensive help, many boys referred to Boys Harbor are destined for tragedy. With the right guidance they find the courage and strength of will within themselves to win out over circumstance and become good citizens."

We were able to point to some early results. We told of one boy, an original camper at Duck Island, who came to us with a stack of delinquency charges, including an arrest for playing a role in hijacking a truck. After three years at camp, plus year-round guidance, he served with distinction in the Navy during the war and went on to become a CPA and a father of four. Meanwhile, a Boys Harbor alumni association was started, led by Tony Albarello, another of the original twelve boys at Duck Island, who became an executive of a leather manufacturing company. With great enthusiasm and dedication, the alumni made sure to keep the current generation of boys on track with regular visits and events that kept the Harbor involved in their lives year-round.

Our philosophy resonated with many people in the emerging fields of social work and psychology. Through my cousin Nick Biddle, who had been a counselor at our first camp at Duck Island, I met Dr. Kenneth Clark, one of the most influential black voices in the country. He was the first African-American to earn a doctorate in psychology from Columbia University, the first to become a tenured instructor in the City College system, and later, in 1966, the first elected to the New York State Board of Regents. But his groundbreaking research on the effects of segregated schools was Kenneth's most important contribution to civil rights. In 1950, he went to South Carolina and studied a county school system in which three-fourths of the children were black, but they received only 40 percent of its education funds. It was Kenneth who famously showed sixteen black children between the ages of six and nine a black doll and a white doll and asked what they thought of each. Eleven of them said the black doll looked "bad" and nine thought the white doll looked "nice." Clark's testing demonstrated that many black children considered them-selves inferior. It was a centerpiece of the case Thurgood Marshall and the NAACP brought to challenge the constitutionality of racial segregation of schools. The case resulted in the Supreme Court's landmark 1954 ruling striking down the "separate but equal" doc-trine that school boards had long used to justify segregation.

Nick arranged for me to have lunch with Dr. Clarke and his wife, Mamie, who was also a doctor of psychology and often his professional partner. This was right around the time he was conducting his research in South Carolina but before he made his results public. The Clarks became very interested in Boys Harbor, pointing out it was one of the first educational agencies, public or private, that had adopted total integration as a matter of policy. They became big supporters of the Harbor, and over the next several decades Kenneth Clark regularly attended conferences I organized in an effort to build bridges with edu-cators and government agencies. At one of these, I remember a man—a black man, in fact—who stood up and asserted that we were moving too fast, that our principles smacked of communism. Kenneth Clark would have none of it, and responded with an eloquent rebuke. I learned much from both him and Mamie.

In these early years, Boys Harbor also received support and friend-ship from the great baseball player Jackie Robinson. The man who broke down one of the greatest racial barriers in the country's history felt that we were breaking down barriers too. He and I first met at Ebbets Field, when I introduced myself and a group of Harbor kids I had brought to a ballgame. Jackie later visited the Harbor and invited groups of boys to come to Dodger games and sit in a special box as his guests. He twice arranged for me to join him in television interviews, during which he praised the Harbor and further fueled my goal to keep on improving it.

Another celebrity who became a friend of the Harbor was Gary Cooper. After meeting in the locker room at the National Golf Club in Southampton, we played a round of golf and became friends. The actor who had portrayed Lou Gehrig in the movies would come to camp and play ball with the boys. He enjoyed hanging out and having long, relaxed conversations with the boys, who would ask him about his movie roles. "Jesus, Mr. Duke, he's a real person!" a thirteen-year-old named Matty Campagna marveled after one of Gary's visits.

With more attention starting to be focused on "juvenile delinquency," the city one year organized a conference at the Roosevelt Hotel. Mayor Robert Wagner attended. We got to talking, and of course I told him about Boys Harbor. He was very interested and introduced me to the director of the New York City Youth Board, a man named Ralph Whalen. I invited Ralph out to East Hampton to inspect camp, and he was impressed with what he saw. "You're giving these boys a sense that it's highly possible for them to have a decent future," he said.

Ralph, who later became one of my best friends, followed the visit by inviting me to become a member of the city's fourteen-member youth board. Mayor Wagner also became both a big supporter of Boys Harbor and a good friend of mine. He found it remarkable that we managed to run a camp for inner-city kids without turning it into a boot camp. "Tony, you've got some real hard core kids here, and the atmosphere is somewhat on the loose side," he said. "But it's a very happy place." The mayor often came out to East Hampton in his official city car with flags flying. It was wonderful local publicity for Boys Harbor. East Hampton's town fathers were honored to have the mayor of New York City in town, and would come out to greet him. He enjoyed talking with our campers, and they with him.

My service on the city's youth board led to many acquaintances and contacts through whom I was eventually able to start building a foundation of financial support. It also became a pipeline for the kind of boys for whom Boys Harbor could make a difference. For instance, I heard about a remarkable family court judge named Justine Wise Pollier. Her father was an important rabbi of the time, and she worked with Eleanor Roosevelt on many social welfare issues. I went to see her and told her about Boys Harbor, citing examples of boys who were doing better after joining the Harbor family. She came out to visit, and before long she started sending us two or three boys a summer. These were boys whom she thought had potential despite scrapes with the law, and who would be a good fit with us. In one case, she sent us a boy who had several robbery arrests. Instead of jail, she "sentenced" him to Boys

A visit to camp by New York City Mayor Robert Wagner in the mid-Fifties. Tony Junior is to my right, along with Roosevelt Harson and Richie Bates. On my left is Jim Karish, Mayor Wagner, Thurston Haines, and Albie Williams.

Original counselor Claiborne Pell returns to camp as a United States senator.

Harbor. And Judge Pollier became a key reference as I tried to promote
Boys Harbor with potential benefactors. Ask Judge Pollier what she
thinks of us, I would tell people.

LIKE MAYOR WAGNER, MANY VISITORS remarked on the unusual atmosphere at Boys Harbor. If it had been a camp filled with privileged white
kids, perhaps they wouldn't have found the happy, relaxed environment unusual at all. But this was too often perceived as a camp for
"juvenile delinquents," and people had their preconceived notions of
how you deal with such kids. To me, that whole premise was a misper-
ception. First, a good number of the boys came from absolutely wonderful families with solid moral values. And even those who had been
in trouble were hardly serious criminals.

   In working with the boys I relied on much of what I'd learned as a
military commander, when I'd had a bunch of kids who got drafted
and found themselves in a situation not of their choosing. I realized
you couldn't turn a civilian, still a teenager, into a disciplined Navy
sailor overnight. So I broke it down and conveyed a simple message:
Everyone had a job to do, and it was vital for each man to learn his
job well in order for us to survive as individuals and as a group. I also
made a conscious decision to allow a certain amount of latitude.
Other captains adopted a totally no-nonsense, militaristic approach.
It wasn't mine. For one thing, it wasn't in my being to be autocratic.
But I also thought it made perfect sense to put morale into the equation. One of my men exceeded his leave a couple of times. "You
know," I told him, "I can deny you leave for six months. I could even
throw you in the brig. But I'm not going to do that. And I'm hoping
that you will show your appreciation for this break I'm giving you by
not doing it again." I found that approach worked. I neither threw the
book at my men nor threw the book away.

   On my ship, I felt I could probably draw out more of the character
that was inside these young men, and their better instincts, if I gave
them a little slack rather than come down hard on them for every
minor infraction. Few of my men took advantage of this policy, and the
530 had a reputation for being a "happy ship." That meant there was a

mutual respect between the officers and the enlisted men, a closer personal relationship than existed on many ships. Often when we were on liberty I'd go out on the town with the officers or the enlisted men, or both, and we'd have a hell of a good time. And that's basically how I ran Boys Harbor. Of course, you couldn't compare summer camp to World War II, but my theory of leadership applied to both young sailors facing death and inner-city boys (and later, girls) facing life.

I adopted from my old school, St. Paul's, a system of students policing themselves. Routine infractions like disobedience, bullying, or smoking were dealt with by a camp court of half a dozen seniors who would mete out punishments such as denial of a movie or commissary privileges. More serious violations, such as stealing, were left to me. Usually, a stern talk and warning would suffice.

Just as I preached respect to the campers, the same went for counselors. Respect the kids, I insisted. Respect and understand their backgrounds. Appreciate that their behavior might have more to do with their lives at home or simply their lack of experience than who they really are inside. And just as important: get to know each boy as an individual. I would sit down with counselors and go over each boy— what kind of people he comes from, what sort of life he's been living, what kind of trouble he's been in, and—this was crucial—what his interests and talents might be. And in varying degrees, over time, the Harbor helped many boys and girls change for the better.

There was one boy, a Russian immigrant who was very, very tough, a real street kid who seemed to have a lot of experience with girls and with street violence. He was sent to camp and, not surprisingly, had quite an attitude about it. He belittled the whole thing, refusing to participate in anything and ever ready for a fight. But he did look after his two younger brothers, and from that I knew there was something truly good inside him. I made a point of keeping him close to me and by the end of the summer I could see a positive change. The following year, I made him an assistant cook, which I intended as a gesture of confidence. He took to it, and even began playing baseball. He was a hell of a good pitcher. By his third summer, Steve was not only a willing camper but an enthusiastic one.

Running the camp, I came to realize that certain things were out of my control. Boys Harbor, like any camp or school, was occupied by dozens of young people trying to figure their lives out—campers and counselors alike—each with his own personality and character, some with troubles, others with secrets. That meant that on any given day I would rise knowing that anything was possible—good, bad, unexpected. One day, an eighteen-year-old, brand-new counselor came running up to the house in a panic. He was being chased by a pack of boys and was trying to hide. What had happened, I quickly learned, was that the counselor was homosexual and had made a sexual advance on a thirteen-year-old boy. The younger boy had gathered his friends, and they were out for blood. I snuck the counselor out of the house and had him lie down in the back of my car, then covered him with a blanket as if I were carrying a load of booze during Prohibition. I took him to the train station and said farewell. I was unsettled by the incident, to say the least. The counselor had been highly recommended by his college dean, who had sent us several other candidates in the past who had been excellent counselors. This mistake could have had disastrous consequences for the camp. I realized then that, as in war, you had to expect the unexpected.

BY 1955, BOYS HARBOR HAD BECOME well enough known that the *Saturday Evening Post* sent out a reporter to write an article about us. The writer, George Wiswell, observed that an interracial camp was unusual enough, but one for disadvantaged boys run the way ours was, was unique in the nation. Wiswell was very complimentary and supportive, but he found that my unorthodox way of doing things didn't sit well with some people in the field of social services. "Some professional camp men and sociologists who have heard about Boys Harbor, and a few of those who have seen it, are critical about its seeming indifference to what the textbooks consider proper camping," Wiswell wrote. "The camp facilities, although growing, still haven't caught up to the population. The lax programming would give many orthodox directors the shudders. Executives of a couple of foundations whom Duke recently sounded out for possible support said they would be unable to help; they diagnosed his as a one-man

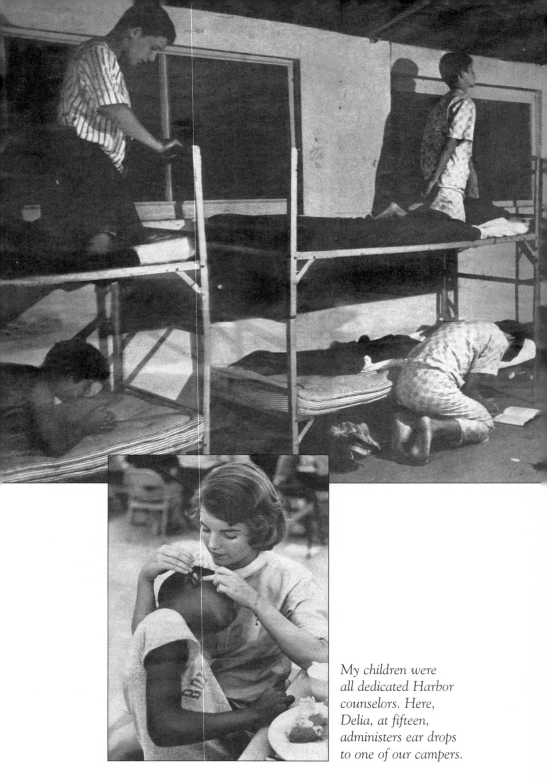

My children were all dedicated Harbor counselors. Here, Delia, at fifteen, administers ear drops to one of our campers.

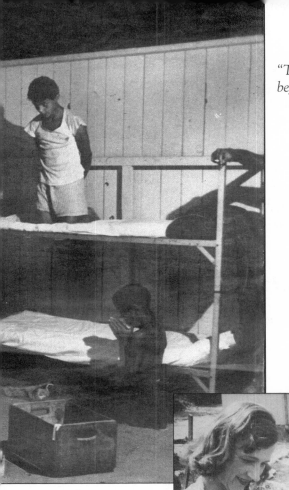

"The Lord's Prayer"
before lights out.

My mother loved Boys
Harbor, and the boys
loved her. Here she is in
the summer of 1959.

undertaking which might collapse without his leadership. Some authorities think the camp should have psychiatrically trained workers. And, since many of Duke's affluent friends drop in at camp, and others spend weekends and vacations serving as extra counselors, there have been questions about the wisdom of combining Southampton [sic] and Hell's Kitchen. According to its critics, Boys Harbor is short on efficiency and shaky in some of its theory."

It was true that Boys Harbor could have used more cabins, and the facilities weren't particularly distinguished. But without the help of those reluctant foundations it was all we could do to keep the camp running on the money I put into it, which was about $30,000 a year, plus the various contributions of time and equipment I managed to talk people into. Nonetheless, I was squarely opposed to over-institutionalizing Boys Harbor, which is basically what those critics were suggesting. Meanwhile, I had plenty of supporters. Among those was Dr. Justin Greene, who was the chief psychiatrist at Lincoln Hall, a school for probationary boys. "The outstanding feature of the camp is the complete acceptance of these boys as equal human beings," he told Wiswell. "This seems to result in a sense of relaxation and happiness."

We weren't always successful, of course. We had one boy from the earlier years who was later arrested for a postal robbery as an adult. When I heard about it, my first reaction was that we had let him down. Intellectually, I realized the fallacy of that way of thinking. But in my heart I believed that no boy was beyond redemption. And there certainly were many success stories, some large, some small. There was a boy named Hank, one of Paul Moore's boys from Jersey City. His was a typical story: poor family, little support at home, unlikely to finish high school. He had a good summer with us, and I thought we might have made a difference. But when he went home, he reverted to form. He wouldn't go to school and became increasingly hostile to authority. I heard from Paul that Hank had run away and was seen around Jersey City sleeping in doorways, snatching food from fruit stands, and running in the other direction whenever an adult he knew came near. As soon as I hung up the phone, I got in my car and drove to Jersey City. I walked around all night, street by street, checking alleyways and doorways. Finally, around dawn, I saw Hank crouched behind a parked car. He saw me but didn't run. I think he was so shocked to see me he just froze.

"Come on, Hank," I said. "Let's go have some breakfast."

He came and we talked. The trouble started, he said, when he had problems with his teacher. That caused trouble at home, leading him to run away and hide. Of course, it was more complicated than that, but I suggested we start by talking to the teacher. I drove him to school and we sorted things out with the teacher. Hank went back to school, returned home, and stayed on course the rest of the school year. In the long run, Hank did well. He simply needed concern.

Keeping tabs on these boys became a year-round activity. I'd drop in on them, take them out for meals, and nearly every weekend from October through June, Betty and I would have a few of the boys stay with us at our home in Locust Valley. Our Christmas party was always well-attended by Harbor boys. I felt that we'd lose some of the boys to the street if we didn't keep the connections we'd made over the summer. The boys needed to feel responsible to somebody, and they needed to remember that someone did care. I think of kids like Mickey Battles, who had a reputation as a fighter, a trouble-maker, but in whom I saw leadership qualities that could be developed. I think of Frankie Golden, a small boy who'd been beaten up by neighborhood gangs and had a very low opinion of himself. For many of the boys, summer camp was fine but it wasn't enough to really affect their lives in a fundamental, ongoing way. We needed to raise the Harbor to a higher level of involvement, and for that I give a lot of credit to Richard L. Williams, known to all as Lonnie.

ANY TEACHER WILL TELL YOU that some classes, some years, are just tougher than others. By luck of the draw sometimes you wind up with a group with more than its share of troublemakers. It could be that way at Boys Harbor. On the first day of camp one year, a bunch of new boys tumbled off the bus and immediately established their credentials as unruly street kids. Usually I would meet the new campers at the bus and have them all line up so I could give them a quick introduction to camp. But this group got off the bus and immediately ran off and disappeared. I grabbed a couple of counselors and as we approached the workshop, we heard a power saw going. Uh-oh, I thought. By the time we got there, these boys had sawed a row boat in half. With three dozen other kids to get settled, I needed a hand. I saw a new junior counselor and had an idea. He was sixteen, and big. "Lonnie, go up there and try to get some control of those kids," I said.

A few minutes later, Lonnie appeared, boys in tow. I don't know what he did or what he said, but they fell into line and listened to my welcome talk. "I think I have some kind of genius on my hands," I said to one of the senior counselors..

I took Lonnie aside. "Lonnie, you're sixteen, is that right?"

"Yes, sir," he said, "sixteen."

"Well, as of now you're twenty-one. And you're going to be twenty-one until you're really twenty-one." He nodded tentatively, trying to be agreeable but obviously baffled.

Lonnie Williams was one of the Jersey City boys brought to camp by my good friend Paul Moore. Paul had told me that he thought the Williams family was one of the best in his parish. The parents were solid, religious people. Mrs. Williams was very kind, while her husband was a patriarchal type who had a kind of unseen power that he transmitted to his sons. One of Lonnie's older brothers was on his way to becoming a teacher, and another had his mind on politics. I had taken an immediate liking to Lonnie when I first met him two years earlier, when he was fourteen. I had invited him to spend the summer with us at Boys Harbor, but he said he'd rather stay in Jersey City and play on a baseball team. He didn't want to come the following year either, but when he was sixteen he decided to check us out. By that time, of course, he was a bit too old to be a camper. My gut told me he was the kind of kid his peers looked up to, so I decided to take a chance and make him a junior counselor.

As the summer progressed, I saw on a daily basis that Lonnie had true leadership in his bones. He had a powerful personality and a sense of responsibility that I'd never seen before in someone so young. He had a certain magnetism as well, and nothing about it was phony or contrived. There was something about him that conveyed genuineness and strength of character. And because he had something to offer that

I could not—he was a young black man—I made a calculated decision to get him ready for a position of authority.

We had a boy named Reuben who didn't like white people very much, and we had a cook who was white and prone to racial insensitivity. One day the inevitable happened. The cook said something to which Reuben took offense, and Reuben picked up a bread knife and went after the cook. Lonnie stepped in, telling Reuben, "You're gonna have to kill me first." Reuben put the knife down. That was typical Lonnie: doing the right thing at the right moment. Practicing respect as a way of life. He was the embodiment of what Boys Harbor was all about.

In his second year, I made Lonnie the camp's assistant director. He took the responsibility and ran with it, becoming my right hand man year-round. Back in Jersey City, he became a big brother to the boys, even a surrogate parent. If a boy was having trouble at school, Lonnie would speak to the teacher. If a boy needed to see a doctor, Lonnie would get him there. He also cultivated a team of peers to act as "caseworkers," to use the term used in the then-burgeoning field of social work.

Lonnie's leadership and dedication was a powerful catalyst for moving the Harbor in the direction of my long-held conviction that education was the key. Staying in the boys' lives year-round was a start, but only a start. In fact, it only made more clear that we were falling short. We needed to work toward establishing a formal education program. The key to that, of course, was money. But it would be a few years before we would get there.

EIGHT

Bright Days and Dark

ASIDE FROM THE CAMP MONTHS, Betty and I were living in Locust Valley. But not very happily. The first problem in our marriage—her untenable demand that I forsake my two sons from my first marriage—continued. I'd lost my own father at an early age, and my stepfather had never really replaced him. So I was acutely aware of how important it was for me to see Tony and Nick as much as possible—and of how much I wanted to see them.

Betty and I eventually divorced, but not before a contentious battle for custody of our children that became, very unfortunately, something of a public spectacle. We think of today as the tabloid age, but even then the travails of public families were fodder for the newspapers. Betty ended up with custody of Cordelia, Josie, December, and John, and then moved with them to Florida. The children spent their holiday vacations with me, along with their summers at the Harbor, which turned out to be a wonderful bonding experience. I made the most of our time together, determined to build the strongest relationships with them, just as I had with Tony Jr. and Nick.

My work life, meanwhile, was also in transition. By the early 1950s, I had closed down my military-surplus business and moved into real estate investment and development. I rented office space in a building at the corner of Fifth Avenue and Forty-fifth Street and hired a secretary, a grandmotherly woman named Ray Goodman who was married to a CPA. Mrs. G, as she was known to everyone, including me, was very dedicated and efficient. The only problem at first was that she expressed some troubling racial prejudices. She said black people made her "uncomfortable."

"You know, if you're going to stay with me you've got to get over that," I told her directly.

"I'll try," she said. She not only got over it, she became a totally dedicated advocate of integration and a favorite of countless Harbor kids.

Getting to know the boys at camp made a big difference, but it was mostly the humanistic Lonnie Williams who wiped out Mrs. G's culturally-bred racism—to the point that I would kid her. "I think you're in love with Lonnie," I said. Said she: "Maybe a little."

Mrs. G was a strong-willed, mother-hen type who got involved in every aspect of my life, including my difficult marital situation with Betty. And she wasn't shy about offering her opinions. If she felt I was making a poor decision, she'd say so. Mrs. G was to stay with me for thirty-five years, becoming a legend at the Harbor in the process.

One day, Fay Neville, my uncle Livingston Biddle's stepson, came up to the office. "Fuzzy," as he was known to all, had been an outstanding counselor at camp while in college at Princeton, and had eventually worked his way up to head counselor. He showed up at my office with a classmate named Bill Carey who had gone on to the Wharton School of Business. They had in mind for the two of them to start up some kind of real estate holding company. They needed office space, and they knew I'd gotten a good deal as a tenant at 545 Fifth Avenue because the building was not fully rented. I had more space than I needed and offered to split it with them. They jumped at it. We signed an informal sublease agreement and bought a screen to divide the room. Out of that humble beginning grew W.P. Carey & Company, a hugely successful, publicly traded real estate investment firm. Bill Carey, a brilliant, kind, and sympathetic friend over the years, became so successful that his foundation endowed the business school at Arizona State University with a $50 million gift. In 2003, it became the W.P. Carey School of Business. (Fuzzy Neville went on to become a highly successful attorney in North Carolina.)

I saw Bill one day in recent years and he joked, "You know, you own half the company."

"I know," I said. "I've still got the papers in my desk."

"Uh-oh," he said. "Did I say something wrong?

Jokes aside, Bill's wonderful success, together with his friendship, would be good for Boys Harbor. Both he and his brother Frank became among our most reliable benefactors. (Bill's enormous generosity would allow the Harbor to open a high school within our building in East Harlem in 2005.)

I had high hopes for success in real estate, not only for myself and my family but for the Harbor, which in those days had virtually no constituency of support beyond me. As it turned out, my acquisition of the Three Mile Harbor property in East Hampton was a harbinger of success. I found I had a knack for knowing when and where to invest, and in the 1950s, it was Florida. I went down there and saw all this beautiful property and knew there would be a boom. I got myself a real estate license, bought a small building that looked like a gas station on Route 1 in Fort Lauderdale, and went into business as A.D. Duke Realty. Meanwhile, John Ordway, Betty's brother and my former business partner, again introduced me to a young woman in his family whom I found delightful: his stepdaughter, Diane Douglas. "Didi" and I were married in September of 1957. We would have two wonderful sons: Barclay, who was born in the spring of 1960, and Douglas four years later.

As I predicted, Florida was ripe for real estate speculation. For my first big deal, I found a piece of property north of Pompano Beach. I went up to New York and collected $10,000 each from twenty friends of mine, and bought it for $200,000. My firm laid out and created the infrastructure of roads, power, water, and sewers, then sold the land to a developer for more than $1 million. Then I had an idea. Along with a friend and partner of mine, John Morrison, I went to the telephone and utility companies and got maps showing where the utilities were five years before and where they were now. We could see that development was advancing up the coast from Miami. We'd drive around, look for signs of life—a gas station or grocery store—and then see if there was any land available within a half mile. We picked out seven parcels, each around fifty acres, then raised money in New York to buy them. We'd bring the bulldozers in to clear the land, and then John would lay out a subdivision that

Outside my real estate office in Fort Lauderdale with Delia, Josie, John, and December, in 1959.

This photograph of me with Josie and Delia appeared in Life, in 1949.

In 1967, I had eight children. In front are Barclay, Delia, Josie, December, and Douglas. Standing are John, Nick, and Tony.

could be hooked up for power and utilities. With the land ready for builders, we sold the properties one by one, usually for twice or three times as much as we'd paid. The biggest deal was a 150-acre parcel in Boca Raton that ultimately yielded a profit of more than two million dollars.

I wasn't quite as successful in a gambit to expand my business offshore, in the Bahamas. You couldn't buy land there, only lease it from the government. So Morrison and I, along with another partner, leased a large parcel split by a canal on the north coast of Nassau. We dredged the canal and cleared the land; I ran the bulldozer myself, We quickly sold a few of the larger lots, and on another section of the tract we built a dozen or so houses for low-income families. The prime minister came out and cut the ribbon when we were finished, and the houses went fast—we sold twenty the first day. But a week later, we found ourselves without power and water. It turned out that the prime minister and others with government connections saw our success and decided they wanted it for themselves. We were shut down and had to watch as another development—almost an exact replica of ours—was built by the insiders closer to town. We eventually sold our property to another developer, but we were left with a significant loss and the nasty taste of banana republic political corruption.

Not that I couldn't be enticed to another foreign land. In Florida, I sold a house on the Intracoastal Waterway in Fort Lauderdale to a wealthy Cuban-American woman who gave me a tip: take a look at Cuba. She cautioned that the political situation was unsettled, but if nothing radical happened I could find some wonderful opportunities. Out of curiosity, if nothing else, I flew to Havana and wound up talking business with the head of the Cuban National Bank. Together we scouted land around the bridge going east to the main road to Santiago del Estero. I took an option on a big piece of property with plans to build low- and moderate-income housing.

I was enthralled with Cuba, and in 1958 I took Tony, Nick, Delia and Josie on a hunting, fishing, and camping trip in the eastern provinces. We camped out and stayed in humble little places, and when we got back to Havana we checked into much more civilized accommodations at the Nacional Hotel. "Look for the swimming pool!" I bellowed happily to the kids as we arrived, and off the younger ones went while teenager Tony and I made our way to the bar to get some Cokes for the kids and a Cuba Libra for me. At the bar sat a man who was chatting with the bartender as he made our drinks. As we waited, a Cuban non-commissioned officer in battle fatigues walked up to the bar and ordered a rum and Coke. Then he turned to the man sitting at the bar, pulled out a revolver, and blew a hole in his head. For a moment, Tony froze in horror. Then he and I raced to the pool and threw the girls in, figuring they would be safer in the water than out should the man come looking for another target. He didn't, though; he just walked out of the hotel and roared away in his jeep.

We soon learned that the man in fatigues was a Castro agent, and the victim was a colonel in Batista's army—one of three high-ranking officers killed that year. About six months later, my banker told me he was pulling my loans. "There's going to be a revolution," he said, "and I'm getting out of here." That was my last try at doing business in Cuba.

WHILE I DABBLED IN FOREIGN AFFAIRS of a business kind, my brother Angier was starting to make a career of the political sort. In 1949, President Truman had appointed A. Stanton Griffis, an investment banker, ambassador to Argentina. Griffis owned a house in Southampton and had become friends with Angier; he thought my brother's facility with Spanish and experience as an American of social standing would make him an ideal assistant to help conduct the embassy's business and public functions. So Angier was off to Buenos Aires, to work in the very same building where I'd spent my early years in the Navy. Two years later, when Griffis was promoted to ambassador to Spain, he took Angier with him to Madrid. Angier worked so hard and did so well as an all-around diplomat that a year later, in 1951, Truman appointed him United Stated ambassador to El Salvador. At thirty-six, Angier became the youngest ambassador in American history.

Mother was proud that Angier was following in her brother Tony's footsteps as a foreign service officer. And just as she had sometimes helped Uncle Tony host receptions during his diplomatic days, so she did for Angier. She was a master at entertaining, and wasn't apt to alter her style to suit the occasion. At diplomatic functions she would break protocol by addressing people by their first names and generally by being her gloriously uninhibited self. "She just flabbergasted people," Angier said after one such occasion, admitting that it made him alternately nervous and amused and proud.

Angier worked hard in El Salvador, where his assignment was much different from a post in, say, Europe. As ambassador to a Third World country, his main job was overseeing the delivery of American aid to people who needed it. It was almost as if he and I were in the same general line of work. One newspaperman wrote that Angier "dedicated more sewers, slaughterhouses and clinics than half a dozen politicians." Politics being politics, though, Angier wasn't long for the job. A one-time Republican, he had converted and become an active Democrat. That was the right party when Truman was president, but not when General Eisenhower was elected in 1952.

I had visited Angier in El Salvador and was proud of the job he was doing—proud of his success in general. I hated to see him lose his job because of party politics. I had an idea: I'd met Ike—maybe I could put in a good word for my big brother. Of course, our Uncle Tony knew Eisenhower a lot better than I did, but I didn't want to pass the buck and put him in that position. He was still in the military, serving as special assistant to General Matthew Ridgeway. So I called the White House soon after Eisenhower's inauguration and began to explain: *My name is Tony Duke, and my brother Angier is ambassador to El Salvador. I met President Eisenhower at his headquarters in London three weeks before D-Day. I was there with my uncle, General Anthony Biddle . . .* Hold on, said the operator. A few seconds later someone else got on the phone, apparently a higher-level secretary. I repeated my introduction, adding that I wondered if I could leave a message for the president. Hold on, said this person. I waited several minutes, then finally someone else picked up the phone.

"It's Captain Duke, I assume?" said a friendly voice.

It was President Eisenhower himself.

"Why, uh, yes, sir," I said, once again trying to keep my wits after finding myself in an unexpected conversation with Ike.

"Nice to hear from you. What can I do for you?"

"Well, it's not for me, Mr. President," I said. "It's for my brother." I gave him a quick rundown of Angier's accomplishments as ambassador to El Salvador. "I understand tradition calls for him to be replaced, but is there any chance he could stay?"

"That's a very brotherly thing for you to do," Ike said. "Let me look into it."

"I appreciate that very much, Mr. President."

Angier got a call saying he would get six more months on the job. It made him very happy, and he was able to accomplish a lot in that extra period.

He came home to Southampton and spent the next eight years tending to business interests, working for the Democratic Party on a national level, and pursuing human rights issues around the world. In 1954, he became deeply involved in the International Rescue Committee, an organization dedicated to helping the victims of political upheavals around the world. The IRC had been founded in 1933 as the American branch of the European-based International Relief Association, which itself had been founded at the suggestion of Albert Einstein to assist Germans suffering under Hitler. Angier became president of the IRC in 1955. Over the next few years he helped make it the most significant nonsectarian refugee organization in the world. That year, he went to Vietnam to coordinate help for more than a million South Vietnamese refugees after the defeat of the French by the North Vietnamese. Angier arranged for food and medicine, brought tools to build housing, and spent time among the people at the refugee camps. Two years later I accompanied him to the Hungarian border, where he started a resettlement and relief program for refugees after their revolution was crushed by Soviet forces. Our close lifelong friend Claiborne Pell was also in Hungary at that time, working with my brother and the International Rescue Committee.

Angier's activism in the national Democratic Party during the 1950s led to a friendship with one of the party's bright young lights—Jack Kennedy. After JFK was elected president in 1960 he asked Angier to become his chief of protocol. It was a post for someone with outstanding organizational skills, impeccable social instincts, and an ability to keep straight the politics and cultures of all the world's nations. The duties included being in charge of state visits by foreign leaders, accompanying the President on trips abroad, accrediting foreign diplomats, and generally representing the United States at diplomatic functions. Though eager to work in the new administration, Angier noted that leading the protocol office, which was established in 1916, was a sub-ambassador job. He told the president-elect that he'd accept if the post was raised to the rank of ambassador.

"Hold on, you're getting a little ahead of me," Kennedy said. But Angier persisted. After all, he said bluntly, he'd been an ambassador. He was reluctant to take a lower-ranking position. As Angier later told me, Kennedy was a little taken aback to be negotiating terms of a secondary State Department position. Of course, that was the point: he didn't want to be a secondary State Department official. Kennedy conceded that Angier had a point. "You're pretty slick," the President-elect told Angier. "I need your kind of guts and experience." Angier became the first chief of protocol with the rank of ambassador (and, thus, the first to require Senate confirmation). The job still carries the ambassadorial rank.

Angier wasn't the only newly sworn ambassador in the family. Kennedy also sought out Uncle Tony, luring him back into the diplomatic corps with an appointment to the ambassadorial post in Spain. Uncle Tony had retired from active military service as a brigadier general in 1955 and returned home to Pennsylvania. He was serving there as adjutant general of the commonwealth—head of the state's National Guard—and chairman of its aeronautics commission.

Uncle Tony was flattered to be brought back to State Department service by President Kennedy. Sadly, though, his return was short-lived. Only a few months after reaching Madrid, he was diagnosed with lung cancer. He came home for surgery and treatment at Walter Reed Army Hospital, and he was optimistic all the way. But the cancer was much too advanced. He succumbed only a month later, a few weeks before his sixty-fifth birthday. His death was a huge blow to all of us, of course. But it touched so many beyond our family, in many countries. In *The New York Times* the next day, Arthur Krock, the winner of four Pulitzer

Prizes, devoted his column to my uncle. Tony Biddle had "three careers—diplomat, soldier and tolerant human being," Krock wrote, unintentionally evoking the Quaker roots of the first American Biddle. "This tolerance, which life-long possession of the advantages of birth, talent and personality such as his often subordinates to self-satisfaction, was a genuine product of his nature." Krock observed that Uncle Tony was a mirror of three centuries: "The elegance, grace and enlightenment of the eighteenth, the ruggedness and change of the nineteenth in which the composite American type was formed, and the fortitude that the twentieth has required of those who accept the high obligation of sharing its miseries with its blessings."

ANGIER MOVED TO WASHINGTON amid the optimism and excitement created by our young and charismatic new president and his dazzling wife, Jackie. One of Angier's first meetings in his new job was with the new first lady, with whom he knew he would have frequent contact as chief of protocol. Angier asked Jackie what she would like to do as First Lady. "As little as possible," she replied, in all seriousness. "I'm a mother. I'm a wife. I'm not a public official." She was determined, she said, to maintain a private life and keep her children out of the limelight.

Angier made the job far more than ceremonial. Early on, he realized that nonwhite foreign diplomats, important guests of our country, suffered the same discrimination that American blacks did. Seeking to break down these barriers, Angier took action. First, he publicly resigned his membership in the Metropolitan Club of Washington after it refused to admit black diplomats. Then, in advance of a visit by a large group of dignitaries from Africa, he took even bolder action.

Those were still the days when, shamefully, many hotels in Washington refused to accept black guests. Angry—and worried that there wouldn't be enough places to house the African diplomats—he called me for advice. He knew I'd had some experience with racial discrimination with neighbors of my camp, first in Connecticut and then in East Hampton. "I really need your help on this," he said. I flew down to Washington and found myself setting out to force a fundamental change in Washington culture. Angier virtually deputized me a representative of the United States government, and we went from hotel to hotel, asking the managers what their policies were regarding black guests. "We don't allow them," a troubling number of them replied. We would then inform the manager that the President of the United States would soon be receiving guests from Africa, that he expected them to be treated well, and that, unfortunately, we would have to go back and tell the President that their hotel was being uncooperative, very possibly putting the United States at risk of an international embarrassment. Suddenly flustered, the manager would try the timeworn excuse, "Well, it's not that we don't allow them. We've just never had any." To which I would say: "Well, you will now—rest assured of that!"

Amazingly, it was as easy as that. The policies changed overnight. At first, it was just the diplomats who were accepted, but it wasn't long before the racial restrictions were dropped entirely. Angier and I had lunch with the president soon after that, and he thanked us for our contribution to desegregation.

Angier's wife, Lulu, was killed in a plane crash that year, a tragedy for my brother and his and Lulu's children, Maria-Luisa and Dario. In 1962 Angier married Robin Chandler Lynn, a mother of two who had been divorced from Jeffrey Lynn, the movie actor. The reception was at the Georgetown home of Claiborne Pell, who was just beginning his remarkable thirty-six-year run as senator from Rhode Island. President Kennedy and Jackie stopped in, long enough for a photographer to take a picture of them in a merry moment with Angier and Robin, which ran in *the Herald Tribune*. Robin was an old friend of both Jackie and Tish Baldridge, the White House social secretary.

I had my own relationship with Jack Kennedy, dating back to the time I'd sailed with him and some buddies to Hyannis when we were all in our late teens. I'd seen him from time to time after the war, during his days as a congressman and then a senator, and we had always enjoyed each other. Indeed, I was no less under his spell than anyone else. When you were with Jack Kennedy, and he liked you, you couldn't help but feel swept up by his affection. I wasn't at all surprised that Jack had made it all the way to the White House, but it was somewhat odd to think of the power and responsibility the carefree teenager I'd first known now

The President and Jackie Kennedy offer their congratulations to Robin and Angier on their marriage in 1962, when Angier was the President's chief of protocol. Claiborne Pell hosted the wedding reception at his Georgetown home.

Catching up with the President, whom I'd first met when we were both teenagers.

held in his hands. In my mind's eye I could still see his father going around the dinner table, asking each of his children what they had learned that day—Jack talking about our sail from Southampton, Bobby reporting his strong performance in a basketball game, me stammering that I hadn't done anything worth mentioning.

Now that Angier was JFK's chief of protocol, he and I would occasionally have lunch with the president at the White House. During his second year in office, and after some long, hard thought, I made a decision. If I could come up with a graceful way of doing it, I would ask Kennedy for some government support for Boys Harbor. I'd managed to keep the Harbor on reasonably sound financial footing with my own funds, along with support from foundations, corporations, and generous friends and family. But we didn't have the kind of financial support we would need to grow in the way I envisioned. Knowing of President Kennedy's domestic social policies, I concluded that I should give it a shot. I seized an opportunity when, during one of our occasional lunches, Kennedy brought up the possibility of an ambassadorship, which seemed to him the family business. "Your brother's doing a great job, and your uncle was at the top," he said. "Why aren't you doing this sort of thing, Tony?" I thanked him for the honor of even thinking of me, but demurred. "I have enormous respect for my brother's work," I said, "but I'm doing what I feel I'm supposed to do and what I love to do. I'm going to stick with it."

I couldn't have asked for a better segue. I talked about the poverty I saw in New York, about the kids who fell through the cracks of the vast city school system. "There's so much wasted talent walking around that city," I told the President. "An awful lot of brains aren't getting fertilized because they're not getting a decent education. My little organization is making an effort to fill that void. But we could sure use some help." Kennedy knew about my work with the Harbor, but I'd never gotten into it so deeply, and I'd certainly never made such an overt pitch for money. To my delight, he seemed genuinely interested, asking good questions. Talk to the Agency for Child Development, he advised, giving me the name of its director.

One of the Harbor's administrators, Bob North, and I met with officials of that agency, and then wrote a proposal to use government funds to offer tutoring and other educational programs to supplement the public schools. Our proposal was approved, and we began to receive the first of what would eventually become major government funding. I never knew if Kennedy himself had helped grease the wheels, but being referred by the president surely didn't hurt.

ON THE FRIDAY BEFORE THANKSGIVING of 1963, I was in Washington for a meeting at the Department of Health, Education and Welfare. After the meeting I drove to Angier's office at the State Department, and we went to the Carlton Hotel for lunch. We had ordered drinks and started catching up when the headwaiter brought ours and every other conversation in the room to an abrupt halt. "May I have everyone's attention?" he asked, clearly upset. "President Kennedy has been shot." There was a collective gasp, and then shocked silence. We ran to the radio in the bar and heard the chaotic words from Dallas. And then the crushing, impossible words. Jack Kennedy, our friend, our president, was dead.

Angier was sheet-white—so was I—as we hurried to the car and drove back to the State Department. The building was in chaos, men and women in tears, and when we got to Angier's office he was besieged by staffers and colleagues, questions flying at him. Half an hour ago, it was just another day and we were chatting over lunch as always. Now my brother was about to be centrally involved in orchestrating a state funeral for the president of the United States. I knew I would just be in the way, so I told him, "Brother, unless I can be of some help I'll go back to the hotel." He grasped my shoulder and said he'd see me later.

For Angier it was the beginning of three nights without sleep, days of mediating competing demands and fixing problems, all the while trying to be of some comfort to Jackie, and delaying his own grief. Technically, Angier's chief responsibility was to supervise protocol for the world leaders who would attend the funeral. But inevitably he was to be in the middle of nearly every aspect of the hastily arranged farewell to the president. Even before Air Force One left Love Field in Dallas, as Lyndon Johnson was being sworn in with Jackie beside him, battles were raging in Washington over who should go to Andrews Air Force Base to meet the plane. Sargent Shriver, who was married to Kennedy's sister Eunice and was head of the Peace Corps, told Bobby Kennedy that "everyone" wanted to go. Bobby was appalled. "The last thing Jackie wants to see is a lot of people." Then Arthur Goldberg, one of JFK's two Supreme Court appointees, called Bobby and said the arrival from Dallas couldn't be private. This was the President of the United States. "I think we should all go," he said.

Bobby told Goldberg to go if he wanted to; he wasn't going to get into an argument about it. Angier told me about all this late that night when he came by my hotel to talk. Taking on his role as the official arbiter of protocol—if not a funeral director without portfolio—Angier ruled that nobody should go to Andrews, other than Bobby and whomever Bobby wanted with him. "And then Hubert Humphrey called me," Angier said. "He said, 'The hell with you. I'm going to the airport!'"

It had been a day unlike any other in the history of the presidency. After a lot of intensely emotional back and forth among members of Kennedy's staff and his family, Angier and his colleagues had begun making preparations for a private Mass for the family and close friends in the East Room of the White House on Sunday morning. It would be followed by the public Mass at St. Matthew's Cathedral on Monday. As difficult as anything would be the task of organizing the procession from the White House to St. Matthew's. Jackie had made one thing clear: she would not ride to her husband's funeral in a "fat black Cadillac." She insisted on walking behind the horse-drawn caisson. Much of the responsibility for the logistics of both the procession and the public Mass fell to Angier. We finished our drinks and said our goodbyes with a melancholy hug. I was going home in the morning to be with my family. Angier was headed right back to the White House. It was two A.M., and his work was just beginning.

The heartrending funeral procession that played out on the nation's television screens three days later would be instantly and indelibly stamped on our collective memory. But nobody watching knew what it had taken to pull it together. Jackie's insistence on walking behind the casket meant that everyone else would as well.

The idea of a phalanx of American and foreign dignitaries forming a pedestrian parade presented Angier with a protocol nightmare. He dispatched staff members to the Library of Congress to research precedents, and they came back with cartons of yellowed newspaper accounts of the processions that followed the coffins of Washington, Lincoln, Grant, and Theodore Roosevelt. Washington's body, he learned, had been followed by more than 32,000 veterans of the American Revolution. The accounts gave Angier models for who should follow whom. Still, the idea of the world's most important people walking those eight blocks made everyone from Dean Rusk to J. Edgar Hoover nervous—especially when warnings started coming in that French President Charles de Gaulle, already the object of four previous assassination attempts, might be a target.

At 10:30 on the morning of the funeral, the CIA director, John McCone, received a report that agents in Geneva had verified a plot to murder de Gaulle outside St. Matthew's. At the White House, McCone rushed up to Angier and said the general had to be told at once. Angier's French was good but McGeorge Bundy's was better. Angier found the President's special assistant, and the two of them approached de Gaulle. They explained the rumor and asked him to accept a limousine. As they put it, "It would be a courtesy to Mrs. Kennedy if you would not endanger your life." As Angier heard it, de Gaulle's response was that it would be a courtesy to Mrs. Kennedy to show disregard for his life.

De Gaulle joined his counterparts—there were nineteen heads of state in all—and Angier assembled them near the northwest gate of the White House. He managed to get them through in one rank, shoulder to shoulder. But at the cathedral, he found a snag over seating. Angier had personally gone to St. Matthew's the day before to calculate how many people could sit comfortably in each pew. Besides the heads of state, he was responsible for dozens of diplomats, government officials, and members of royal families from nearly a hundred countries. And now he found that some of them were being squeezed out. William Manchester vividly described the scene in *The Death of a President*, the minute-by-minute account of the assassination he wrote at Jackie Kennedy's suggestion:

This was Angie Duke's worry, and it was a stupendous one. The slight, sensitive chief of protocol had been working without rest for three days and three nights. Ahead of him, after the funeral, lay two crucial receptions—Mrs. Kennedy's in the executive mansion, and President Johnson's, at State. Nevertheless, it was his hour in church that was to be his hour of trial. First he found that the pews he had earmarked last night had been confiscated by Jack McNally for President Kennedy's staff. He was obliged to lead his chiefs of state off to the right, to St. Joseph Chapel—from which, he discovered in horror, the main altar was invisible. Angie improvised. He seized a church functionary and demanded a television set. There was one in the cathedral, he was told, but using it in church during Mass was unthinkable. It *had* to be thinkable, said Angier, arguing furiously; diplomatic relations with ninety-one countries were at stake. The set appeared and was plugged in. It would be the only one in the cathedral, he told his charges, and they looked immensely pleased.

Their pleasure diminished, however, when he started seating them. It was then he realized that in failing to allow for overcoats he had miscalculated badly. He had forgotten something else: the Emperor of Ethiopia, the King of the Belgians, and the husband of the Queen of England were all carrying bulky swords, more space-takers. Putting four bodies in a pew instead of five made a difference of twenty people—twenty world leaders who would have to stand. It wouldn't do. He would have to start cramming. Like a conductor on a crowded bus he kept urging them to move over. They complied, grunting.

Robin, meanwhile, was doing her part, trying to be helpful to her old friend, now the most famous widow in the world. Robin and Tish Baldridge sketched out an arbor of flowers for the grave and began a search for every rose in Washington—a plan Jackie later quashed. Robin's heart sank for the children, and one of her most enduring memories is offering six-year-old Caroline her hand as they were preparing to leave for the funeral.

Angier's last bit of finagling came after the Mass, when he found, once again, that Presidential assistant Jack McNally had appropriated space for White House staffers at the expense of his foreign dignitaries. That whole weekend he and others had tussled over pecking orders: chiefs of state versus the joint chiefs of staff; senators versus cabinet secretaries; Kennedy relatives versus Kennedy confidantes. To say nothing of Kennedy's two predecessors, Eisenhower and Truman. Now the problem was the motorcade from the church to Arlington National Cemetery. The scene outside St. Matthew's was chaotic. Manchester wrote:

> Limousines were like lifeboats after a badly managed "abandon ship." Once established form had been broken it became every man for himself. Mike Mansfield saw McNally and his wife entering the first White House car; despite Angier's anguished pleas Mike took off with the Congressional leadership. All semblance of order collapsed. Supreme Court justices and governors were running around like emerging theatergoers hailing cabs in a downpour. Most of them wound up hitchhiking rides from resourceful colleagues who had commandeered empty limousines.
>
> Charles de Gaulle declined to use his thumb. He looked down upon the melee and arched his brow at the American chief of protocol. Angier improvised brilliantly. Watching White House secretaries and servants occupying prime positions, he explained to de Gaulle and Haile Selassie that the President's family should, of course, go first. Naturally, they agreed. Doubtless they had heard, he went on, that the Kennedy family was very large. They nodded. Well, he said, extending his arm in a sweeping gesture, now they know how big it *really* was. This seemed to satisfy them. They may have wondered how on earth George Thomas—who was as black as Haile Selassie—could possibly be a Kennedy, but their sense of tact kept them mute.

After the funeral, Angier was struck by the change in mood at the White House. Lyndon Johnson was not wasting a moment establishing his presidency—Manchester went so far as to say that he was "enjoying himself hugely." Angier felt that the mood was suddenly electric. "We were moving into the future," he told Manchester, though his heart was still in the past. He was still very much on the job. He listened obligingly as Princess Beatrix of the Netherlands complained about having been squeezed between the Soviet deputy premier and his bodyguard at the church. Then the princess asked to meet Lady Bird Johnson, as did Queen Frederika of Greece. Angier brought the request to the first lady's husband. "Fine!" Johnson bellowed, and Robin volunteered to go pick her up.

For Angier, orchestrating the president's funeral was like packing a lifetime's worth of anguish, anxiety, and adrenaline into four days. He stayed on as chief of protocol, remaining until 1965, when President Johnson sent him back to Madrid to be our ambassador to Spain, the same post Uncle Tony had filled four years earlier. But after November of 1963, no job would ever compare with the one that put him in the middle of one of the most dramatic events in American history, arguably the most traumatic of the twentieth century.

The most memorable episode of Angier's two-year tenure in Madrid was a publicity stunt for Spanish tourism after an American B-52 accidentally dropped four unarmed hydrogen bombs in the Mediterranean Sea, near Palomares. The bombs, had they been armed, would have packed five hundred times the power of the bomb that destroyed Hiroshima. Unarmed, the only consequence was that the tourism season would be ruined by fears that the sea had been contaminated with radioactivity. So Angier and Spain's minister of information, along with their children and staffs, put on their swimsuits and took a dip in the chilly March sea to show that the water was fine. Angier came home from Spain at the end of 1967, served briefly again as President Johnson's chief of protocol, then was sent back to Europe to be ambassador to Denmark, a post he held until Johnson left office in January 1969.

ANGIER OWED SOME OF THE BEST YEARS of his career to Jack Kennedy, and in an indirect way Kennedy provided an opportunity to another member of my immediate family: my eldest child, Tony Jr. Tony had always been a hard-working and adventurous young man who insisted on making his own way. As a teenager he had mowed lawns and done road maintenance on Fishers Island, and spent a summer working as a tuna fisherman off the coast of northern Peru. During college he was a ranch hand out west and worked for the New York City Youth Board. Tony never had any thoughts of taking advantage of his name or trading on any family contacts. "You helped me get educated, and that's as far as I need you to go," he told me after he graduated from Penn in 1964.

Tony had thought about joining the Marines after college. No doubt it would have pleased his great-grandfather. But with troops starting to be sent to Vietnam, I was unenthusiastic. "Tony, I've had so much war," I said. "I would really love it if you did something different."

As it happened, President Kennedy had begun a new branch of service that could satisfy a young man's inclination for adventure without putting him in harm's way. It even had a name that a parent could find comforting: the Peace Corps. Given the commitment to Boys Harbor that extended to my mother, my brother, my wife, and all my children, the Peace Corps was arguably more in keeping with family tradition than the Marines. Tony liked the idea, and in an awful irony, he took the foreign service exam on the very day of President Kennedy's assassination.

After being sent to Indiana to be trained in the modern methods of raising chickens, Tony was dispatched to Uruguay to teach what he had learned. He traveled by horse between farming towns there, and became known far and wide as the young American chicken-farming expert.

I made plans to visit Tony during his first summer in the Peace Corps. Besides seeing where he was living and working, I wanted to take him to the country next door—Argentina—to show him where he was born and where he lived the first two years of his life. I was excited when we arrived in Buenos Aires, but the feeling evaporated as soon as we stepped up to the immigration counter. When we showed our passports, the officer looked at Tony and started flipping through sheets of paper. "You were born here?" he asked. Tony said he was. "Did you do your military service?"

I jumped in, explaining that Tony wasn't an Argentine citizen. He just happened to have been born here while I was stationed in the country at the beginning of World War II. The man said it didn't matter—under Argentine law, if Tony was born here he was an Argentine citizen, and all Argentine males had to fulfill military service. I tried to explain the situation again, but it only made the man agitated. He became wild-eyed, yelling, "He must serve!" He turned to Tony. "You must serve!"

Tony was remarkably but characteristically calm as the authorities put him in a little room. Meanwhile, I tried to figure out what to do. I thought I had an out. I had gone to Argentina in 1941 as a member of the Navy, but once the war started I was put under the aegis of the U.S. Embassy to cover various aspects of my job. That gave me—and my family—diplomatic immunity. I called the embassy and explained the situation to a sympathetic staff member. He managed to convince the determined immigration officer that Tony had diplomatic immunity for life as well. He released him, and we had a marvelous time, even sharing a few laughs at the irony of the episode—Tony following my advice to join the Peace Corps rather than the Marines, only to find himself conscripted into the Argentine army. I showed him where we'd lived and took him to our favorite places, but we didn't linger. I wanted to get back to Uruguay before the Argentines changed their minds.

MOTHER FOUND TONY'S NEAR-CONSCRIPTION a hoot. It was the kind of preposterous episode that could have come straight out of her father's life, which she had documented a few years earlier in a book that became a play that was soon to become a movie.

Mother had teamed with Kyle Crichton, an engaging man who was a member in good standing of the New York literary world. He was about Mother's age but could not have come from a more different background. Crichton had grown up in the Pennsylvania coal-mining country and had worked as a miner, lathe operator, and open-hearth puddler—whatever that was—before coming to New York to be a writer in 1929. After the Depression hit, Crichton joined the Communist Party. For a decade he led a kind of double literary life. As Kyle

Crichton, he worked as an editor under Maxwell Perkins at the Scribner's publishing house and later at *Collier's Weekly*. As "Robert Forsythe," he wrote two notable books and hundreds of articles for the *Daily Worker* condemning modern capitalism. But in 1940, outraged by the Stalin-Hitler pact, Crichton quit the party and began writing on less serious subjects under his own name. He was best known for a biography of the Marx Brothers published in 1945, and would later write a book with the wonderful title *Total Recoil*, a memoir about the people he'd met during his life as a New York writer.

Crichton was a deft writer known for his light and entertaining prose, which seemed like a good match for my mother, whose life had been nothing if not amusing and occasionally downright hilarious. But when Crichton came up to my office to interview me after he'd had a few meetings with Mother, he mentioned that she was not as forthcoming as he hoped or needed her to be. "Really?" I said. I almost wanted to ask him if he was sure it was my mother he was talking to. Perhaps she's a little intimidated, I said, and offered to join them at their next session. Maybe I could get her to relax and help him draw her out.

The next afternoon, we met at the apartment Mother and Tom owned on Park Avenue. They had a little bar on one side of the living room, and behind the bar was a montage of pictures of the buildings my stepfather had designed. "Mom, tell him about these buildings," I said as I mixed a pitcher of her favorite drink, Dubonnet and gin. Before long she was opening up, sometimes with my prompting. "Tell him about the time your father got dressed up as a lion and went to his cousin's house," I said, and she smiled and picked up the thread. "Oh, yes, he was going to scare all the kids. But his cousin didn't like him very much so he told him to go a mile down the road and hide and he'd bring the kids down. Of course, he never brought the kids and Father was absolutely livid. He came back up and broke right through the library—still in his lion costume—and started to strangle him. He almost killed him!"

After a couple of hours, Kyle turned to me and said, "You know, I wish you would come up every day." Over the next few weeks, with some prompting from me, Mother told her life story and Crichton turned it into a highly entertaining book titled *My Philadelphia*

On publication day of My Philadelphia Father *in 1955. Mother donated her share of the royalties to Boys Harbor.*

Mother with her other children and her long-time aide-de-camp Pat Hoban, in Old Westbury.

Father. One of my happiest moments came when I opened the book and saw the dedication:

> *To Tony's Boys Harbor*
> *Father Loved it*

The book was named by *The New York Times* as one of the most notable books of 1955 on the strength of a glowing review by Cleveland Amory, who wrote that his only criticism of the book was its title. "Tony Biddle was called, as his biographers tell us, the happiest millionaire alive," Amory wrote. "I wish that this phrase, or the idea of it, might have been in the title . . . This phrase tells, as simply as Mr. Biddle himself was simple, just what was so remarkable about the man. In contrast to the selfish, pontifical, persnickety skinflints who dominate our literature of millionaires (often they even show these qualities in books they have paid their biographers to write), Mr. Biddle was a rollicking rover boy."

Amory got his wish when Kyle Crichton turned the book into a play and retitled it, "The Happiest Millionaire." I wasn't thrilled by Amory's suggestion. I had always lived with people thinking I had much more money than I did, and putting "Millionaire" in the title of a play about my family wouldn't seem to diminish that assumption. But Mother didn't share my concerns. I didn't press the issue because it wasn't my decision.

Crichton set the play entirely in my grandparents' home at 2104 Walnut Street and used my parents' courtship in 1914 as the action around which Granddaddy's life swirled. When it was announced that Walter Pidgeon would play my grandfather, I was skeptical. Physically, they were nothing alike. Pidgeon, tall and dashing, reminded me more of Granddaddy's son, Uncle Tony. But he learned Granddaddy's language and managed to capture the extreme things he did to entertain people, especially himself. My teenaged mother, meanwhile, was played by a young actress named Diana van der Vlis, who was making her Broadway debut and went on to win the Tony Award for Best Featured Actress in a Play. "She plunges into the temperamental whirlpool of Cordelia's adolescent emotions and makes a stunning performance out of them," wrote Brooks Atkinson in *The Times*. It didn't surprise me that Mother was a character worthy of a Tony Award.

Taking some dramatic license, Crichton had written my father as an insecure suitor baffled and a little terrified by Cordelia's father and the circus over which he presided. The role was played hilariously by George Grizzard, with whom I became good friends. Preparing for the role, he wanted me to tell him everything I could remember about my father, my parents' relationship, and my grandfather.

"The Happiest Millionaire" played in a few cities out of town before opening to positive reviews at the Lyceum Theater in November of 1956. The fun of seeing my family portrayed in all its wonderful eccentricity by renowned actors on a Broadway stage was wonderful enough. But the play also made a great gift to Boys Harbor. My mother—who had donated her share of the royalties from the book to the Harbor—arranged for the proceeds of a preview performance of the play to be donated as well. She and Tom gave a late dinner party in their apartment after the show for the cast and producers, along with dozens of their friends.

The show ran for 271 performances, from November to the following July, which made it a true hit in those days. But that wasn't the end of it. A few years later, Mother learned that Walt Disney was interested in turning "The Happiest Millionaire" into a movie. When she said that Disney "has some ideas" about changing the script—for one thing, he wanted to turn the straight comedy into a musical—I became a little concerned. Kyle Crichton, who had since died, had stayed close to the truth he and Mother had put in the book. But by selling the rights—with the proceeds going to Boys Harbor—Mother gave Disney complete liberty to turn my grandfather into anything he felt would sell a movie. As with "Mary Poppins" three years earlier, Disney himself would be the producer of "The Happiest Millionaire." It would turn out to be his last production.

This time, Granddaddy was played by an actor even less like him than Walter Pidgeon: Fred MacMurray. Greer Garson was my grandmother, and playing my parents were two fine young actors making their feature-film debuts, Lesley Ann Warren and John Davidson. Both would go on to successful careers in Hollywood. The music was composed by Richard M. and Robert B. Sherman, who had also done the score for "Mary Poppins." Writing in *The Hollywood Reporter,* James Powers found that Granddaddy's story rather lent itself to a musical. "The Biddles were apparently a freewheeling family, so one more touch of eccentricity does not seem out of place," Powers wrote. "A man such as the pater familias of the Biddles who keeps pet alligators in the conservatory of the family mansion and a collection of punchy ex-pugs in the recreation room, is not stretching his character if he suddenly communicates in verse and song."

The world premiere was held in Philadelphia on October 22, 1967. According to Enid Nemy of the *Times,* Mother upstaged the movie stars: "Mrs. Robertson . . . swept out of the late afternoon sunshine into the dark, paneled Urban Club in a new, floor-length Norwegian blue fox coat by Max Kahn. 'I'm mad for it,' she announced in her Eastern finishing school voice (although Mrs. Robertson is the first to admit that she never finished school of any kind) and swinging her long fall of auburn-colored hair. 'I shall never take it off,' she added and promptly proceeded to remove it, sliding it casually over an arm encircled with an impressive diamond bracelet inherited from her mother."

A fleet of antique cars brought us from the Urban Club to the premiere at the Boyd Theater, with Didi, Mother, and I riding with Fred MacMurray in the back seat of a 1929 Lincoln and my son, Nicholas in front. Later, I danced with Lesley Ann Warren, the very charming twenty-one-year-old star who played my mother at sixteen. A week later, we all attended the New York premiere, the proceeds of which were once again donated to Boys Harbor.

AFTER TAKING A SWIM IN THE OCEAn one day in the summer of 1962, my stepfather Tom told me he wasn't feeling very well. We went to the club, where he had lunch and a bourbon on the rocks. Feeling dizzy, he felt something was wrong and asked me to take him to the hospital. He died there that night, of heart failure. I really loved Tom.

For Mother, Tom's sudden death was an especially difficult blow because it came only nine months after that of her beloved brother Tony (and a year after the plane crash that killed Angier's wife, Lulu).

Devastated, Mother found it too painful to go back to the house in Old Westbury that she and Tom had bought soon after their marriage nearly four decades earlier. She asked her brother Livingston, who was in real estate in Nassau County, to sell the house as quickly as possible. Having done well in real estate myself by anticipating rising values, I knew it was a bad move. With twenty acres of prime Nassau County land, she would have gotten millions for the property had she waited a few years. But Mother's emotions were too raw and overwhelming to give way to business sense, and I wouldn't even try to talk her out of it. The bar that was built for Tom toward the end of Prohibition wound up on my porch in East Hampton.

With Mother ensconced in Southampton, in the house called Wyndecote, I saw quite a lot of her during the summer, especially on the tennis court. We'd played since I was young, and she was still very good, a perennial tournament champion at the Meadow Club and a much sought-after doubles partner. Anyone who played with or against her realized very quickly that she was all business on the court. When she served, she didn't fool around. No bouncing the ball or asking her opponent, "Ready?" She'd walk briskly to the service line, toss the ball and serve, accurately and hard, to an opponent who might not even see the ball as it passed him. Then she'd quickly move to the other side, announcing the score as she went, then spin around and serve again. Bang—another ace. Eventually opponents would learn to be ready on time. If not, they simply lost, fair and square. She wasn't much easier on her doubles partners. She could accept a missed shot, but not the apology that followed. "Don't ever say 'sorry' to me," she would say to someone new. "Just get in position and play better." One very nice man was completely flummoxed by this rule—he kept saying "Sorry," then apologized for continually apologizing. We never saw him again, at least not on Mother's side of the net.

Though you might not know it by watching her on a tennis court, Mother was a remarkably forgiving and nonjudgmental person. She once told a reporter: "The only thing I dislike is a bore," then quickly changed her mind. "No, I cannot dislike. I forgive a bore. They're rather fun, actually." The worst you might get for less-than-exemplary behavior would be her trademark comment: "Well, dear, that's not very *attractive* of you, is it?"

IT WASN'T LONG AFTER MOTHER became a widow that my marriage to Didi was coming to an end. My third divorce would begin the longest unattached period of my adult life. Of course, by "unattached" I don't mean alone—not with eight children. By 1965, Tony Jr. was the only one on his own, working overseas in the Peace Corps. Nick was in college at Vanderbilt, while Delia, Josie, December, and John were all in high school. And then there were the little ones, Barclay and Doug, my two wonderful boys with Didi.

All my children spent their summers with me at camp, and all have been part of the Harbor in varying degrees and in different ways. But of all eleven of them, the one who was the most closely attached to the Harbor—the one I came to regard as my likely successor—was Barclay. When he was a little boy, Barclay insisted on sleeping in the cabins with the campers. Like any kid, he wanted to go to camp, and sleeping in his own bed in his own house would mean he wasn't at camp. He developed close friendships with many of the kids, and this continued when he became a counselor. He was as diligent as any counselor we've ever had. As he got older, he truly grasped the mission and believed in it. The work came naturally to him—especially when it came to the water. He spent hours out on the harbor, teaching kids how to sail and navigate.

What came less naturally to him was formal education, and that was another way in which he was like me. When I was young, it always took me longer than the other kids to do my schoolwork. But while I may have had a learning disability that went unrecognized in that era, Barclay was diagnosed as dyslexic. Still, he worked hard and persisted. Because of his learning difficulties, Barclay was the one of my children who reminded me, in a way, of some of the children who came through Boys Harbor. I felt a tremendous desire to help him through, not with pity but with love and encouragement, and with my time. He eventually went to Warren Wilson College, a small, nurturing school in North Carolina. I remember going down there at one point and spending two

Walking and talking on summer days at camp. That's Barclay and a pal around 1972.

days in a motel room with Barclay, helping him study for his finals. He responded with a determination that made me very proud. It took him five years to complete his degree, but he did it, and with flying colors.

After college, Barclay went to trade school to learn carpentry and other skills, and he came home to East Hampton and started a construction business with a partner. But his heart belonged to the Harbor. He taught carpentry and boating, and as soon as camp started every July, he would put his business aside—in the most lucrative time of the year for a contractor—and spend nearly all his time at the Harbor. I knew it would always be an important part of his life, and hoped that he might one day take over as director.

NINE

Miracle on 104th Street

TO THIS DAY, FUNDRAISING puts a knot in my stomach. I've gotten fairly good at it—I've had a lot of practice—but it's something I've always found to be kind of unpleasant and daunting. Unfortunately, it's absolutely necessary. It wasn't until the late 1950s—nearly a decade after Boys Harbor opened in East Hampton—that I had my first real success in attracting a sizeable sum from a major philanthropist.

The catalyst for my effort was the growing realization, shared by my protégé and then friend and partner Lonnie Williams, that we needed to expand from a summer camp to a full-fledged year-round educational institution. We needed kids coming to us five or even six days a week during the school year, rather than *us* dropping in on *them* when we could. To do that, of course, we needed a place for them to come. And that's how we get to the first time I really had to ask for money— serious money.

To tell this story I have to go back more than a hundred years and talk about the Gibson Girls. Around the turn of the last century, an artist named Charles Dana Gibson became famous for drawing illustrations of beautiful, refined women. Though the original "Gibson Girls" were composites from the artist's imagination, it was a portrait of his wife, Irene, that led her to become known as *the* Gibson Girl. Irene was one of the celebrated Langhorne sisters of Virginia. The others were Nancy, who married the son of a British Lord and, as Lady Astor, became the first woman member of Parliament in 1919; and Nora, a free spirit whose many admirers were said to include F. Scott Fitzgerald. She wound up marrying a British architect named Wilton Phipps and had two children, including a boy named Thomas. Tommy was my best friend for many years.

Tommy was in the Air Force and stationed in London shortly before D-Day when we met one night at White's, a famous and exclusive club that dated back to the mid-1700s. Tommy had been a screenwriter and amateur golf champion; among his movies was "A Yank at Eton," which he based on his own experience at the British school, and which starred Mickey Rooney. He was one of the most delightful and amusing people I'd ever met. After the war, Tommy was a prolific writer of television dramas, including a collaboration with Truman Capote on a TV version of "Laura." He also wrote dozens of one-hour plays, many for "Robert Montgomery Presents." He became my best friend after the war, and I was present when he married Mary Chesebro, a beautiful and well-known model from Florida.

One day Tommy and I were having lunch at the Racquet Club in New York and I started talking about how much the Harbor was growing, and how much more it *could* grow—if we only had the financial backing. "Somehow or other I've got to get the money to find space so we can be become a serious educational center," I said. "We need a place big enough for classrooms, athletics, and office space."

"Well, you know," Tommy said, "I've got a friendship with Brooke Astor."

Brooke Astor was perhaps the city's most famous philanthropist. In 1953, she had married for the third time, to Vincent Astor, the last powerful American member of the Astor family and the elder son of Colonel John Jacob Astor IV, a hugely successful real estate magnate best known to today's generation for having been the richest victim aboard the Titanic. Vincent was listed as the twelfth-richest person in America by *Forbes* in the 1950s. But he was, according to Astor family biographer Derek Wilson, "a hitherto unknown phenomenon in America: an Astor with a highly developed social conscience." Only twenty when his father went down with the Titanic, Vincent dropped out of Harvard and set about to completely transform his family's image from one of the country's most avaricious to one of its most altruistic. Vincent built a large housing complex in the Bronx and turned a valuable piece of land in Harlem into a big playground for children. When Vincent died in 1959, Brooke took charge of the philanthropies to which he left his fortune, and over the next three-and-a-half decades she would donate more than $193 million to charities.

Tommy's initial connection to Brooke Astor had been indirect, to say the least: His aunt Nancy, his mother's sister, became Britain's Lady Astor after marrying Lord Waldorf Astor, whose cousin was John Jacob Astor, whose son was Vincent Astor, whose widow was Brooke Astor. So Tommy was some kind of distant, twice-removed cousin by two marriages. But he had come to know her well enough to arrange a meeting and to give me some valuable coaching. "You have to be careful with how you approach this," he said over lunch before my meeting with Mrs. Astor, which he'd scheduled for four o'clock. "You have to be very well-versed in what you want and a little wily about how you ask for it. You must make her feel that whatever you want her to do is her idea entirely. Ask for her ideas. She's a very intelligent person."

"I think I understand," I said.

"If you don't, you're not going to get any money."

Tommy, the playwright, began to script the meeting and rehearse me. "Okay," he said. "I'll be Mrs. Astor. What do you want?"

"Well, I want a place at the south end of Harlem and near the subways," I said. "Our kids come mostly from Harlem and East Harlem, but we've got many from downtown too."

"And what are you going to do with the space?"

"I'll use it to help inner-city kids get ahead with their schoolwork," I said, "and to tutor those who fall behind. So I need rooms for them. And I'd like to have an athletic program that teaches self-discipline. And I would need an office for an executive director who would work with me. We probably need room for several staff people."

"In other words, you're going to add curriculum to what you're already doing," Tommy said. "Now what you've got to do is make her feel these are all her ideas, not yours."

"How do I do that?" I asked.

"Here's how," he said. "You do a lot of pondering. You talk about what you've been doing and you ask, 'What's the best way for me to hang on to these kids from year to year? How do I make sure they're doing their homework and staying away from drugs and crime and all that?' She's a bright woman. *She's* going to tell *you* what you need. And you just look surprised and pleased. Oh, and one other thing, Tony. Don't be upset by her silence. She won't say much when you're talking, but she's absorbing it. She's a brilliant person."

Arriving at the Astor Foundation's offices in a private residence, I found Mrs. Astor gracious and welcoming. Tommy had obviously told her enough to get her interested. She asked me how I'd started Boys Harbor and I gave her the background, all the way back to St. Paul's School. "I'm trying to somehow formalize all these things I've been doing," I said, trying to follow Tommy's script. "What I'm trying to figure out is what steps I can take to create some kind of year-round center for these children."

She was utterly silent as I talked—and it was a good thing Tommy had warned me about this. It would have been a little unsettling had I found myself giving a monologue without so much as an occasional murmur of interest from her. Finally, Mrs. Astor spoke. As Tommy had also predicted, she started throwing out ideas—all the things I wanted to do, plus a few new ones. "You've got to have a place where courses can be taught," she said, "where tutoring can go on and where perhaps the families can get medical advice. Any number of things you would want for your own children. That is the kind of center you want. A school has to be part of it!"

"You're right!" I said. "All these things I'm doing. My aim is to set up a comprehensive, ongoing program that will challenge these young citizens to continue their education and work hard at it. So many of them are much more intelligent than they even realize. What else do you think?"

"Obviously, you need a proper office for your staff."

"Oh, yes," I agreed. "The problem is I have been funding this myself for many years," I said. "So what I would need is some kind of a grant."

"Well, as you know the foundation is inundated with proposals," she said. "But you'll be hearing from me."

A few days later, a letter came. It was brief and to the point. "I will help you get located," Mrs. Astor wrote. I wasn't sure exactly what that meant, but when we found a good-sized house on East Ninety-fourth Street, just off Fifth Avenue, it turned out to mean exactly what I'd hoped. She bought the place for the Harbor.

The house had belonged to a doctor whose office was on the first of its four floors. He and his wife had raised four children in it so it had large, deep rooms and a little garden out back. There was a swimming pool in the cellar. With her connections, Mrs. Astor was able to negotiate a good price: $175,000. I hired a contractor to reconfigure the house, dividing some of the bigger rooms so we could create classrooms, counseling rooms, space for karate classes and other fitness activities, and office space.

The building quickly filled up with life. In the summer, kids went to camp in East Hampton for two-week sessions and could take part in activities on Ninety-fourth Street the rest of the summer. The building was a base for day trips to the park, museums, movies, baseball games. In keeping with our mission, we put major emphasis on education—all day long, kids would come for help in English, math, science, and history—as well as on behavior and the importance of mutual respect.

Though Mrs. Astor's gift was historic for us, and by far the largest and most important single donation we'd ever received, it wasn't the only instance of generosity by a major New York-based foundation. We received reliable help from the Haydn, Ford, Rockefeller, and Kresge foundations, among others, most of which had board members or executives whom I knew. That support begat more success stories, which in turn begat more support. Some of our financial supporters also joined our board. We had monthly meetings, and one I'll never forget was on a rainy November night in the mid-1960s. The board members arrived to find a young man checking hats and coats and directing them to the stairs leading to the meeting room on the second floor. When they descended the stairs after the meeting, their hats and coats were nowhere to be found—nor was the unknown young man who had "checked" them.

After buying a building for us, Brooke Astor became a good friend of the Harbor—until one disastrous event. When the wife of one of our board members organized a benefit at an art gallery, Mrs. Astor volunteered to chair it and host a party. But at the appointed time on the appointed night, the gallery was empty but for the organizer and a few board members. I asked the organizer what was going on (I will keep her anonymous out of politeness). She admitted that she "must have forgotten to send the invitations out." Mrs. Astor dropped us for a while after that. But the foundation continued to support Boys Harbor, and eventually, our friendship was restored.

In those years the Harbor received many gifts from well-known people, but none so dramatic as the one we got from John Hay Whitney. "Jock" Whitney was a financier, philanthropist, and diplomat who was ambassador to Britain during President Eisenhower's second term. He was also the last publisher of the New York *Herald Tribune*. We met at a social function, and naturally the subject of Boys Harbor came up. "I've heard about you," he said. "I understand you've got quite a sailing program." I talked a bit about Three Mile Harbor and how we took boys who couldn't even swim and turned them into sailors. Then Whitney shocked me with an offer: He said he wanted to donate his famous yacht, Aphrodite, to Boys Harbor.

Whitney had had the 74-foot Aphrodite built in 1937. He used it to commute from his estate in Manhasset to his Wall Street office, and to entertain many of the big celebrities and business and government leaders of the day. Fred Astaire, Katherine Hepburn, and Laurence Olivier were among the many members of Hollywood royalty who'd been on the yacht, and Shirley Temple once had a birthday party aboard. The day after the attack on Pearl Harbor, Whitney offered Aphrodite to the government for war service and she was commissioned in April 1942, though not exactly for combat operations. Aphrodite spent the war as a Coast Guard auxiliary vessel, ferrying dignitaries up and down the Atlantic coast and transporting President Roosevelt to and from his home at Hyde Park on the Hudson River.

Whitney got the yacht back after the war, and his offer to donate it to Boys Harbor was an incredibly exciting and generous gesture. But there was one problem. We couldn't possibly afford the fuel and maintenance for this huge vessel with its big Packard gasoline engines. Whitney said that was no problem at all: he'd pay for gas for ten years. He had somebody make some calculations, then presented us with the yacht and a check for $40,000. So after twenty-five years hosting the

Teaching coastal piloting and navigation aboard the Aphrodite, a gift from Jock Whitney. Leaning on the table is my nephew, John Biddle Brock. Sitting to my right is Julian McKee Jr. And that's Lonnie Williams standing over my shoulder.

Learning something new myself: karate.

rich and famous, Aphrodite spent the Sixties as a classroom at sea, a tool for teaching coastal navigation and seamanship to kids from the most humble backgrounds, who had never set foot on a boat.

One of these kids was a boy named Ron Jackson, who was eleven when he came to camp for the first time in 1965. Ron's brother, Charles, had a friend who was a Harbor boy and he wanted Charles to come with him to camp. Unfortunately we had no room in that age group—but we did have an opening in the eleven-year-olds' bunk. So we asked if Charles' little brother wanted to come out. "I didn't want to go," Ron said. "I thought the world was between Seventh Avenue and Lexington. That was my world. Finally they convinced me."

Ron was one of those kids you remember. He had a thousand-watt smile, an earnestness and eagerness that was contagious. One day, I had Ron out on the boat and decided to give him a thrill—or a fright, depending on how you looked at it. "Young man," I said with mock formality, putting my hand on his shoulder. "Take the helm. I've got to go down below and check the charts. I'll be back in three minutes."

Ron looked panic-stricken. "Mr. Duke, Mr. Duke," he said, "I don't know how to steer the boat."

"Just put your two hands on the wheel and get us through that channel," I said. "Then through the cut and out into Gardner's Bay."

"But Mr. Duke, I don't know where Gardner's Bay is."

"Just follow the channel markers"

"Channel markers—what are channel markers?"

"Those things out there. The ones that're red, leave 'em on the left. The green or black ones, leave 'em on the right. Think you can do that?"

"No!" Ron protested.

"Well, try," I told him.

With that, I went down and watched him. I knew it was the first responsibility of that kind he'd ever been given, and that it would be an experience he'd never forget.

About ten minutes later—not three—I came back up. "Congratulations," I said. "You're doing great. You're right on course."

After that, Ron couldn't stay away from the water. He asked me day and night to take him out on the boat and let him steer.

But steering a power boat was one thing—real sailing was another. Ron's cabin counselor, Charlie Dean, had taken an immediate liking to him. One day, Charlie told Ron that he wanted to teach him how to sail. "I know you know how to maneuver in the streets of the city," Ron recalls Charlie telling him, "but I want you to learn how to do that on the sea. I want you to be a sailor like me."

Charlie was Howard Dean's younger brother. As followers of Howard's 2004 presidential campaign learned, Charlie died tragically in Cambodia in 1974 after he and a traveling companion were captured and then executed by guerrillas. But a few years earlier, he was a wonderful counselor at Boys Harbor, a man Ron always admired and never forgot.

"Take Howard and multiply that three times—that's Charlie," Ron says. "He was extremely caring and didn't like unfairness, even something as simple as cutting in line at the mess hall. He had a sense of fairness and justice that I carry to this day. We had a lot of talks about how America was changing, about the civil rights movement. We talked about Malcolm X and Adam Clayton Powell, who was our congressman."

At the end of his first summer, Ron went home to Harlem and told his friends he'd learned to sail and water ski. "They're giving me these looks—'Yeah, right, water ski.' The closest we came to water skiing was a Bobby Darin movie." Ron came back to camp for several years, and he became good friends with my son Barclay. I remember the first time I invited him to have dinner with us in the house. "Oh, no, Mr. Duke," he said. "I can't come to your house for dinner."

"I'll see you at six o'clock," I said.

He came dressed up, and from then on, to this day, he's been one of the family. Both his children and grandchildren would later become Harborites, and Ron says the Harbor "gave me my life." I don't know if it did or not, but it certainly gave him a lot of confidence and expanded his world, which had consisted of ten square blocks before he came to camp.

AS THE BUILDING ON NINETY-FOURTH STREET put us on the road to expansion, and our fundraising efforts began to succeed, it was clear that I had the need and the means to bring on full time staff. Though I felt Lonnie could become a real guiding light for the Harbor if I could manage to keep him, I didn't think he was old enough to take on the administrative duties of an executive director. I brought in a man who had a fine background in public education. But after I noticed that he seemed to engage primarily with white children, I decided I needed to replace him. I came up with a man who was very popular with the kids, black and white. I found out one reason why when I discovered he was smoking pot with some of the older boys in his house at camp.

Finally, I decided, it was Lonnie's turn. And he didn't disappoint me. On paper, Lonnie didn't have the background of his predecessors, but he brought a true sense of purpose and what people today call "emotional intelligence" that compensated for any lack of formal education or administrative experience. Lonnie started out going to college at night, earning credits toward a degree. He wanted to work. He got a job with a state youth agency in New Jersey, while continuing his Boys Harbor casework at night and on weekends. His capacity for hard work was equaled by his ability to get positive results.

Given how we were stressing education with our boys, Lonnie's lack of a degree might seem odd, even hypocritical. But that's only if you believe that a diploma is the only mark of an educated person, or that Lonnie contributed less because he lacked one. We've never held that everyone who comes to the Harbor must strive for a college education. Our goal is to help kids discover what they enjoy and what they're good at, and to help them make the most of their lives. I also think that there are many ways to become educated. After all, with war coming, I myself had left Princeton to join the Navy and had never gone back. By the time I was discharged after the war, I was nearly twenty-eight and eager to start my civilian life. It seemed, at the time, too late to finish college. I figured I had a solid foundation of formal education, a hell of a lot of life experience, and, most important, an open and curious mind. Education to me is a lifelong process, and that's how Lonnie saw it as well. Working at Boys Harbor was very much a learning experience for him, a form of self-education that was no less valuable than taking classes and writing papers. I held this conviction so firmly that I eventually arranged for Lonnie to get an honorary doctorate degree from

Southampton College. It was a wonderful event, and our respective families joined forces to celebrate. Lonnie's beloved wife Hazel managed to rent a big bus for the day, and we all convened at my mother's house before going out to the college.

That he came from where the boys came from certainly helped make Lonnie a great role model. But this caused me a slight concern in the realm of fundraising. Lonnie spoke in the dialect and vernacular of the streets that produced him, and I felt the need to tell him that there were times, as an executive of Boys Harbor, that he needed to be a little more aware of his audience. "With the kind of people I'm trying to raise money from, I think you have to speak their language perhaps a little more," I said. Lonnie could have misinterpreted my awkwardly conveyed instruction as an effort to make him more "white," but he took no offense, and understood my point. His sincerity, decency, and intelligence drew people to him. And it was clearly to Boys Harbor's benefit. In one instance, Lonnie and I went to pay a visit to one of the real titans of Wall Street to ask him to make a donation to a capital campaign we were running. I thought maybe he'd give us $100,000. When we got to his office, our donor said, "Let me speak to Lonnie alone for a bit." I sat outside, and a while later the door opened and the financier said, "Tony, come on in, I've got a check here for you." It was for five million dollars.

The generosity of individuals and foundations was wonderful and vital, but it was the money that became available from the federal and city governments that really helped us take off. When domestic social policies begun by the Kennedy administration were expanded under the Great Society programs of Lyndon Johnson's presidency, the flow of dollars from Washington made us eligible in turn for grants from New York City. That allowed us to expand our after-school academic enrichment program. (Parents who could afford to pay were charged on a sliding scale according to their means.) As Lonnie once told a magazine writer, "This is not day care. We're education-oriented, with an emphasis on critical thinking. Because if you can think you can do anything."

Within a couple of years of establishing ourselves in the building on Ninety-fourth Street, we began a major growth spurt that challenged our ability to keep up with the demands of our success. In earlier times,

Lonnie Williams.

our boys had come almost exclusively through referrals from churches, the courts, and various child-welfare organizations. But as our reputation grew, through word of mouth, the media, and our own promotional activities, the Harbor became so popular in the Harlem community that we had to take applications and make decisions based on factors such as need. The board and I decided that once a boy was in the program, he could stay until he was fifteen, at which point we would give his spot to a younger boy. But, of course, that meant turning many away. By the mid-1960s, we had about five hundred kids a year in our various programs—and hundreds more on our waiting list. Meanwhile, our government funding increased, eventually to 75 percent of our budget, allowing us to expand our programs.

BY THE LATE 1960S, DRUGS HAD BEGUN to transform the communities we had been serving since the camp's beginnings. Needless to say, the changing culture forced us to confront new realities. We didn't change our message so much as update and intensify it. I found more and more boys and girls who had no power in their lives, who had nobody to steer them in positive directions, away from drugs and gangs. The message we tried to convey was that they did have power, they did have a choice. If you want to be dead by the time you're twenty-three, we were saying, then by all means go ahead and get into that life. Make some money on drugs, spend it on yourself, have a good time. But if that's your ambition I can guarantee you won't survive. You will have a very short life. The approach was to talk about those choices constantly, drumming it in—brainwashing, if you want to call it that—an admittedly heavy-handed method that paradoxically put the responsibility on the kids. It works, and we have never stopped doing it.

Meanwhile, for the first time we were being challenged by some in the primary community we served. Though we still had a very strong relationship with our East Harlem neighbors, a radicalized political culture was spreading at that time. It made some people who didn't know us suspicious of our motivations and goals. This came to a head one day when I was in my office and heard a banging at the front door. I went downstairs and opened the door to four black men wearing battle fatigues and berets. "We're Black Panthers," one of them said contentiously, as they barged their way in. "Who's in charge here?"

"I am," I said. "I'm Tony Duke, and I'm the president of Boys Harbor. I teach here, too."

They were young and angry, and it was obvious they were looking for a fight. But I had no interest in giving them one. "Come on up to my office," I said cordially. "You can tell me what's on your mind." I recognized one of the Panthers as a former Boys Harbor boy. He was the only one of the four who looked slightly uncomfortable, avoiding eye contact with me.

"Look," I said when we got upstairs, "why don't you tell me why you're here? You must have come for a reason."

One of the Panthers noticed that outside my window were two flags. One had the Boys Harbor insignia, the other was an American flag. He pushed the window open, grabbed the American flag, and pulled it in. He pulled out a little can filled with gasoline, poured it over the flag, and took a match to it. When the flag caught fire he threw it out onto the street.

"That's a shame," I said. "We bought that flag about three years ago, and it's a good one. Or was."

They looked at me with an attitude that said: *What are you going to do about it?*

I knew exactly what they wanted me to do. They hoped I would pick up the phone and call the police so we'd have a great riot right then and there. I'd seen it happen before. The Black Panthers had taken over the Grosvenor Neighborhood House, a long-standing and highly regarded settlement house on the Upper West Side, because they felt—correctly—that its board didn't have enough community members on it. I served on the mediation board that was appointed to resolve the issue. So I was careful not to allow myself to be goaded into a serious confrontation. I resolved to avoid saying or doing anything that might provoke my visitors.

"I know what you fellas want," I said, "but you're not going to get it here. That's not going to do any of us any good. Look, we live in a very complicated time and a lot of what you're saying in the Panther movement, I'm in total accord with."

"Yeah, I bet you are," one of the Panthers said sarcastically.

"Really, I have no fight with you. I just happen to feel, and maybe you feel the same way, that education is one of the things that's going to help people. And education is what we do here, along with other helpful things."

I can't quote the Panthers verbatim but their basic premise was that I was a limousine liberal—a rich white man who had no place in the lives of black children. I was like a plantation owner, they asserted, and the kids who came to the Harbor were like slave children. To them, I was putting a little ointment on their wounds to make myself feel good. The young man who had been a camper looked as if his heart wasn't in this, as if he had been bullied into it. But I stifled any impulse to ask him if, based on his personal experience, he agreed with his friends. I didn't want to put him in that position.

"Look," I said finally, "with all this rhetoric about what a bad man I am, maybe you can do better here. I'll tell you what. I'm going home. There's a bunch of kids coming in here this afternoon, and if you want to stay here and sell them on your ideology, that's up to you. These kids are doing pretty well. Some of them have problems in school and we're tutoring them in their math, and we're trying to work on their attitude—"

"What do you mean by *attitude*?" the leader interrupted.

I knew I had used a word they would seize on, but ignored it. "It'll be about an hour before the after-school kids start coming in, so you may want to prepare a program for them. What they expect here is some math tutoring, and one of them has a drug problem, so I hope you can help him with that. In fact, maybe it would be better if you took the whole place over and ran it. It's a little expensive. We owe some money. But we have some very good teachers and many volunteers who share their skills with the children. We're interracial here, and I have people who fully understand what the young people who come here need. I think I know it, but it might be better if it comes from somebody who's black. Anyway, I'm going home. I may go to the movies on the way." I straightened the papers on my desk, got up, and left. The Panthers looked stunned and baffled. I knew this encounter reflected the racial schism in the country, and that was serious. But a part of me kind of enjoyed the chance to square off with such adversaries.

From what I heard later from the kids and tutors who arrived that afternoon, the Panthers offered their party line on the white establishment, to little or no effect. The kids told them how much they enjoyed coming to the Harbor and to camp, how much it helped them. I also heard later from the Panther who was a graduate of our program. He apologized and confirmed my suspicion that he'd been somewhat intimidated into participating in what was supposed to be a newsworthy confrontation. But best of all, we wound up taking in many children of Black Panthers over the next few years. They did well.

One day, I was on my way to the Harbor when I saw a commotion around a church and began talking to a young Hispanic man. He said his name was Felipe, and that he was the founder of a community activist group called the Young Lords Party. I invited him up to the Harbor, and he was surprised by what he found. "I thought you were some rich guy who didn't know what the hell he was doing," Felipe said. I found him to be highly intelligent and interesting, and I told him I hoped we could stay in touch. This happened, and Felipe became a supporter of the Harbor as he softened his radicalism and assumed a well-rounded point of view as a broadcast journalist. Felipe Luciano became the first Puerto Rican news anchor of a major television station. In response to some of the concerns raised through the activism of the late Sixties and early Seventies, the Harbor formed an advisory board to get ideas and feedback from community members. Felipe spent many years on the board.

REVOLUTION, OR AT LEAST EVOLUTION, did come to the Harbor in 1972. That year, we invited our first girls to summer camp. This momentous development came about the way most important things have come about at the Harbor—with someone coming to me with an idea that made perfect sense.

The inclusion of girls had its roots in an incident that occurred a few years earlier, when Vincent Henry's younger sister came up to me one day at the Harbor building in Manhattan. Vincent was one of the best kids in camp in those years. He was an athlete, musician, and all-around wonderful character. (Years later, I went to see Vincent playing in a Broadway show. During intermission, he came down from the stage and climbed over rows and rows of seats to greet me. I felt honored.)

One day in the late Sixties, Vincent's sister, Ayanna, asked me why there wasn't some place that she and other girls could come to after school—just like their brothers came to Ninety-fourth Street. It was an excellent question. "Well," I said. "You're here now. Your wish is granted." That was it. No board meetings to discuss including girls in Boys Harbor. Eventually we turned the camp coed, and in the mid-1980s we officially changed our name to The Harbor for Boys and Girls. In 2001 it became Boys and Girls Harbor.

One of the girls in that first group was a nine-year-old named Tanya Robinson. She and her older sister lived with their parents in the Colonial Housing Project in Harlem, and she was enrolled in our day camp program in the city before we offered her a spot on the bus to East Hampton. "I remember my first day," she told me. "I was standing out on a patch of grass in front of the mess hall, and I saw all these kids running up all excited to greet an older white man. I was suspicious. Why did this man get such a big welcome? And what were these kids after? I didn't get it."

Tanya, an exceptionally bright and effervescent young girl, went on to spend three summers with us as a camper before getting her very first job—as a junior counselor. She moved on to college and then law school. "When I walked through the doors of St. John's University's School of Law in 1986, I had never even met a lawyer," she recalls. "But I had known since I was fourteen that this is what I wanted to do with my life. I did not let the fact that I had no knowledge of what it would be like prevent me from giving it everything I had. I'm pretty sure I had never set foot on a sailboat before Boys Harbor, either, so in my mind, what was the difference?"

After graduating law school, Tanya went to work as an assistant district attorney in Manhattan. Later she went into private practice. But she likes to say that she's taken the Harbor with her everywhere she goes. All her interests were cultivated there, in part with the help of members of my family, with whom she became close. Tanya polished her boating skills with John, Barclay, and Doug, and she's still an avid boater. Having taken lessons in no fewer than eight instruments through the performing arts program the Harbor initiated in the 1970s, she still counts music as an important part of her life. She learned photography, and now when she needs photos for her trials she takes all the pictures herself. "To this day, I apply the values I attained at the Harbor to my daily interaction with others," Tanya says. And she has given so much back: as a fundraiser, speaker, and then as a member of the Board of Directors.

THOUGH LONNIE WILLIAMS HAD a great deal to do with our initial transition from a summer camp to a year-round urban center, it was one simple but dramatic push from a young man named Eduardo Padro that put us on track to become a serious educational and social institution.

Eddie came to camp as an academically gifted young teenager in the late 1960s. After three years as a camper he graduated to junior counselor and then counselor. I watched him grow in every way over those years, and when he called to tell me he had been offered a scholarship to Yale I was as proud as I'd ever been of a Harbor boy.

In the summer of 1973, I gathered the counselors in the mess hall for a series of after-dinner meetings on the subject of the Harbor's future. I had talked often about my dream of making us a complete educational institution, and I wanted to hear their ideas. "I'm wide open," I said. "Just let it out." No one was more into the discussion than Eddie Padro. Up to that point, our year-round program at the building on Ninety-fourth Street was built around tutoring—certainly a helpful service but a relatively modest supplement to the education the boys and girls were receiving in public school. Eddie was outspoken in his conviction that we could and should be so much more.

After one of these mess-hall skull sessions, we all said our goodnights and I went up to the house to go to bed. At three in the morning, I woke up to the sound of broken glass. Someone was throwing pebbles at my window. I got up and looked outside to find Eddie saying he needed to talk to me. "All right," I said, "but first, I want two dollars for that window."

Eddie had some things to take care of at Yale for a couple of days and was heading into the city to take an early train to New Haven. "I've got some things I need to say," he told me, "and it can't wait till I come back. Because I may not *be* back. When are we going to start seeing the things you've been talking about?"

In the middle of the night, I couldn't offer much of an answer. But I probably wouldn't have had a good answer no matter what time it was. Eddie issued a challenge—actually, a threat. If I didn't start taking steps to make education the main thrust of the Harbor, then he wasn't coming back.

"Well," I said, "that's what I'm going to do."

With his bold challenge, Eddie lit the fire that got me to finally take the steps necessary to realize my goal. It was a goal, I now realized, that was shared by some of the boys who had already made the most of their Harbor experience and wanted the boys behind them to have even more.

Most obviously, it would mean undertaking a major expansion of space and staff. Lonnie Williams, Bob North, and I started looking around the city and found an intriguing site just ten blocks north, at the corner of Fifth Avenue and 104th Street, in the southwestern corner of East Harlem's Spanish-speaking El Barrio neighborhood. The building, a five-story neoclassical brick structure with arched windows on the street level and a U-shaped courtyard facing Fifth Avenue, had once housed an orphanage. It was erected in the 1920s to house the Heckscher Foundation for Children, an outgrowth of the Society for the Prevention of Cruelty to Children. It had been seized by the city for nonpayment of taxes in 1945 and been given the kind of attention—or inattention—such a transaction implies. When we went up to see it, the building was filthy and seemed to be occupied by squatters. While walking around, we were approached by someone who asked us for heroin. There was a swimming pool that was empty but for some garbage and the inevitable rats. But the building, as they say, had a lot of potential. We could expand all we wanted to and still have space left over. And the squalor could work to our advantage. We could probably get a good deal on a lease.

I went down to City Hall and talked to Abe Beame, the newly elected mayor. He was very warm and supportive and put me in touch with the commissioner of real estate. We were able to work out a long-term lease, under which we were designated a "local development corporation," or

LDC, making us the main tenant. We made a handsome profit on the sale of our building on Ninety-fourth Street to a private school and used the proceeds to start paying the rent ten blocks north. We arranged to have the city make some of the necessary repairs, enlisted a bunch of senior boys and volunteers to paint and fix up the building, and the Otis Company renovated the elevators as a contribution.

We took over about 75 percent of the new building, leaving space for a literacy program and a few other small, nonprofit social agencies. Eventually they were replaced by El Museo del Barrio, a Latino arts organization. El Museo was formed in 1969 by a group of Puerto Rican and other Latino parents, educators, artists, and community activists. They had started in a public school classroom and then occupied a series of storefronts before moving into the Heckscher building. El Museo has since become New York's leading Latino cultural institution and the last stop on Fifth Avenue's Museum Mile. It's also been a fine complement to the Harbor.

Moving into the Heckscher building was the catalyst for an unprecedented period of growth for the Harbor. One of our earliest and most important new services was an Upward Bound program, funded by the federal Department of Education. The program aims to help young people get to college and graduate. To qualify, we had to provide instruction in math, science, composition, literature, and a foreign language. The Upward Bound program changed the Harbor fundamentally. It made us much bigger in every way: we had more kids, more young adults, more staff, a bigger budget. But more than just numbers was the fact that it allowed us to keep our boys and girls much longer. Rather than disappearing as they got to be teenagers—the very time they most needed guidance—Harbor boys and girls now stayed with us through high school. There was so much temptation out on the street. The lure of a quick buck from selling drugs was formidable. Now we had more power than ever to influence these young citizens. We were able to help them choose courses that would lead them into professions or trades, and we taught life-survival skills, things as basic as how to handle a job interview.

But the heart of it all was a school program that fundamentally transformed our kids' educational experience. From humble beginnings we

Over the decades we've taken countless group photos at camp, our version of a "Where's Waldo?" game. Here's one of them, in 1976. Try to find my daughter Lulita. (Hint: she's head and shoulders above her father.)

now had a staff of eighty people, many of whom were teachers, counselors, and caseworkers rolled into one. Interestingly, quite a few of them were alumni, drawn to our newfound mission to educate. Our enrichment programs, offered before and after school at five different locations around Harlem, included classes in science, computers, math, writing, history, current events, world cultures, languages, art, music, and a host of special topics ranging from Greek mythology to legal procedure. Meanwhile, we addressed the future by running parallel programs for teenagers. Upward Bound helped those who had academic ability and desire get to college and graduate. For less academically-oriented kids, we had a career counseling service that guided them into fields that suited and interested them, including business and the arts.

In the early Seventies we began building from scratch a performing arts program that has since become widely recognized. Now called the Harbor Conservatory for Performing Arts, it was built and is still run by Ramon Rodriguez, an extraordinarily talented and dedicated musician and teacher who took the germ of an idea and ran with it. The Conservatory has grown so much over these thirty years that some 1,500 people participate each year—young children, teenagers, and even adults who play in the Conservatory's renowned Latin Big Band. Administering a program with classes in dance, theater, voice, instrumental music, and ethnic arts and culture, Ramon established himself as one of the leading lights in New York's multicultural life. Among his many honors is a distinguished service award from the Alliance of New York State Arts Organizations. The Conservatory is respected worldwide as a center of Latino music.

By the 1980s, the Harbor was touching the lives of more than 2,600 children a year. Its collection of programs was considered the most comprehensive of any organization of its kind in New York. One of the keys was consistency. Whatever part of our program kids participated in, the vast majority of them stayed with us year after year. We were able to work closely with their families, their schools, their churches. That our kids enthusiastically came to classes early in the morning or after a full day of school was a tribute to them—and to our committed, talented, and imaginative staff. Lonnie Williams told a magazine writer in 1986, "We make a lot of demands on our young people, and we never let up on them. We know they can meet higher standards than the public schools, and we insist that they fulfill their potential." The title of that article in *Town & Country* was, "Miracle on 104th Street."

Of course, miracles don't come cheap, and we were blessed with a solid fundraising apparatus that gave us support that was both deep and wide. We were also very fortunate to have Tony Jr. as our financial overseer. Tony had become a major success on Wall Street—a career path set, ironically, during his stint in the Peace Corps. On vacation in Brazil at one point, he had run out of money. He had an epiphany of sorts that he later said made him realize that financial security was important to him. After leaving the Peace Corps in 1967, Tony enrolled in an executive training program with Bankers Trust. Three years later, he went to work for Fiduciary Trust, where he was to remain and advance for eighteen years—eventually becoming the youngest senior vice president in the firm's 100-year history. But even while holding down a high-profile position on Wall Street, with all the pressures that entailed, Tony found time to serve countless hours as the Harbor board's vice president of finance, watching over our books with the sharp eye we needed.

Aside from the government and foundation funding that we had long relied on, money was coming in from all kinds of sources, including many individuals. Tito Puente, the legendary Latin jazz musician, donated an annual scholarship. Harbor alumni of every economic class remained loyal contributors. And we could count on tens of thousands of dollars each year from people and organizations in East Hampton, the community that had been wary of our arrival in the early 1950s.

One of our most prominent local supporters was my friend George Plimpton. He and I had first met in Paris in the Fifties, when a mutual friend suggested I give him a call while I was there on business. George was living on a barge on the Seine River and editing the *Paris Review*, and we became instant friends. He had a wonderfully gentle sense of humor and never used it at anyone's expense. I've known few people better at getting grouchy people to be ungrouchy. But from my point of view as a mentor, I always thought that one of George's great skills was picking out young writers with promising futures and helping them establish their careers.

George was one of East Hampton's most notable residents, and each summer he would put on a fireworks show at a public beach to benefit Guild Hall, an art museum and theater. One year, a man was burned on the shoulder by a spark and, in the American way, threatened to sue for several million dollars. "Any man with an arm that valuable should be pitching for the Chicago White Sox," George later joked. The following year, when East Hampton officials told George he couldn't have the fireworks show on town property anymore, I offered him an alternative. Why not turn it into a fundraiser for the Harbor? He could stage the show on our property.

The show had always been put on by the famous Grucci fireworks family, led by its patriarch, Felix Grucci Sr. Felix's great-great-grandfather started the business in Italy in 1850, and he joined it as a seventeen-year-old apprentice in 1923, by which time the family had emigrated to America and settled on Long Island. Felix became a master and an innovator, inventing a way of displaying fireworks without dangerous fallout. He also developed an atomic device simulator that the Defense Department used for troop training. The Grucci fireworks cost $35,000, but George assured me the benefit would raise far more than that. Mr. Grucci sent me a contract and I signed it. On the day of the event, after they finished setting up, he asked if it would be all right if he took a look around the camp. "I'd like to see what you do here," he said. Be my guest, I said.

A few hours later, Mr. Grucci came back to the house. "Let me see that contract," he said. I asked him if there was a problem. "No problem," he said, "just go get the contract."

I went upstairs to my office, came down with the contract, and gave it to him.

He ripped it in half.

"I've been talking to your kids up at the camp," he said. "I like what you do here. I'm gonna do the fireworks for free. For the rest of my life I'm not gonna charge you. And I'm gonna put the same commitment on my son."

Thanks to the Grucci family's generosity, the fireworks show became an annual fundraiser, one of the highlights of the year for the Harbor. It grew to attract crowds of more than eight hundred people who paid between $18 and $300. After Felix died in 1993, at age 87, his son, Felix Jr., kept his father's promise and continued providing the fire-works as the family's annual donation to the Harbor. He became a fast friend to the Harbor and to me. George, meanwhile, was the official host until his death in 2003. He loved the Harbor, and always made it seem as if I were doing him a favor, rather than the other way around. He joined our board and, besides the fireworks show, served as ring-master for an annual benefit by the Big Apple Circus. He even once donated his winnings from a harness race to repair our tennis courts.

George was happy to see that besides raising money for the Harbor, the fireworks show became something of an annual camp reunion. Alumni from every decade would come out, and it was wonderful to see our Harbor family ties stay strong. Among the many alumni who attended each year was Eddie Padro, the man whose middle-of-the-night challenge led to our miracle on 104th Street. I've watched with admiration and joy as Eddie moved up in the world. After Yale, Eddie went to NYU law school and began a career in the judiciary. In 1993, Mayor Rudy Giuliani appointed him to a judgeship on the New York City civil court. In 2002 the voters of Manhattan would make him the Hon-orable Eduardo Padro, justice of the New York State Supreme Court.

IN THESE YEARS, I HAD RESPONSIBILITIES with another venerable institu-tion close to my heart. In 1974, I had been asked to join the board of trustees of the university to which my family name has always been closely associated. The very first endowed scholarship established after Trinity College became Duke University in 1924 was named for my father, who had died a year earlier. More than eighty years later, the Angier Buchanan Duke Scholarship remains one of Duke's most pres-tigious. Angier B. Duke Scholars, or ABDs as they are known, receive a full four-year scholarship, study abroad (including a six-week summer program at Oxford), and are given research funding. Each spring, the university's admissions office nominates forty high school seniors who have been accepted into the following fall's freshman class. The stu-dents come to Durham for a weekend, after which the selection com-mittee picks the winner. Since Duke has become one of the most competitive universities in the country, *everyone* accepted is among the nation's top students to begin with. So the forty nominees are among the cream of the cream, and the eventual winner of the Angier Buchanan Duke scholarship is very special indeed.

Of all my Duke relatives, it has been my cousin Mary Semans who's been most closely associated with the university. Mary is actually my double first cousin: Her mother, also named Mary, was my father's sister, while her father was my mother's brother, Uncle Tony Biddle. Mary has always had a special place in my heart—ever since the day she very possibly saved my life when we were kids. I was eleven and Mary was nine, and we were taking a walk together on Flying Point Beach in East Hampton when I stepped on a broken bottle. I looked down and saw blood spurting all over the place from a deep gash in my foot. Mary sprang into action. She tore off a piece of her dress and used it to make a tourniquet. After stanching the bleeding, she ran to get help and came back with Pat Hoban, who got me to the hospital. The doctors said I cut a vein and could have bled to death.

When Mary was a teenager, after her parents' divorce, she and her mother moved from New York to Durham, where they lived with Ga-Ga, our grandmother. Mary was extremely bright, and a year later, when she was just fifteen, she enrolled at Duke. Not only was she probably the youngest student on campus, but she was the first of our generation—the first descendant of the university's founders—to attend Duke. She graduated with honors and stayed in Durham, where she married a doctor, Josiah Trent, and had four children. (After Josiah died in 1948, Mary married another physician, James Semans, and had three more children.) Meanwhile, she served on the Durham City Council and, in 1970, became vice president of the Duke Endowment. She would later become president and chairman of the Endowment. Since stepping down in 2001, she's remained active as chairman emeritus. Through these three-and-a-half decades, Mary has been a major force in the financial growth and well-being of Duke.

Mary was very supportive when the university's president, Terry Sanford, asked me to join Duke's board of trustees. I had known and admired Terry for thirty years, having first met him in London while we were both training for the Allied invasion. Terry had spent two years as an FBI agent before volunteering for service as a paratrooper. He was in the famous 82nd Airborne and managed to survive action in five separate campaigns, including the Battle of the Bulge. After the war, he became active in North Carolina's Democratic Party and in 1961 was elected governor. He was Hubert Humphrey's national campaign chairman in 1968. A year later he was named president of Duke.

Terry was a beloved figure at the university, a man of great effectiveness, style, and humor who became known affectionately to many as "Uncle Terry." Whenever I'm at a large meeting, my mind flashes to one of my first board meetings at Duke in 1974. A bishop who was leaving the board started the morning off with an invocation that was eloquent but very, very, very long. When he concluded, a weighty silence hung in the air. President Sanford drew himself up, looked around, and in perfect deadpan fashion said, "The meeting is adjourned."

Terry Sanford contributed greatly to Duke's progress in becoming the great institution it is today. He took over during a time when black students were clashing with Durham police. Terry managed to diffuse the students' anger then and later, by listening to them. While war protests closed down many colleges, Duke was open—because Terry was open. He didn't call for the National Guard. He sat in a chair in front of the chapel and invited students to bring their complaints to him. In his own quiet way, he was a great civil rights leader. In 1972, some Duke students pushed him to run for President, and he decided to throw his hat into the ring. I worked on his campaign committee, but we didn't get very far. It wasn't a full-fledged campaign, and he dropped out after he failed to win his home-state primary, losing to George McGovern. He tried again four years later, but dropped out for health reasons before the North Carolina primary. But Terry was just as happy to stay at Duke. In his fifteen years as president he brought the university to greater national prominence and presided over enormous growth in its endowment. (Terry was elected to the Senate in 1986 and served one term. He died in 1998.)

Aside from taking part in the normal business of overseeing a great university, I tried as a trustee to find ways to make my own contribution. I followed my natural inclinations and worked on ways for Duke students to get involved in improving Durham's inner city and creating better relationships between the university and its hometown. I won't defend smoking or monopolies but the fact is that Duke Tobacco and later American Tobacco were once huge employers that made Durham a mighty industrial city. When the government broke up the monopoly, the city began a long decline, just as the university was growing in size and stature. The relationship between the wealthy university and the poor city was complicated, to say the least.

As head of the board's student affairs committee for fifteen years, one of the things I tried to do was to get more students involved in doing good works for the community, such as tutoring inner-city kids. By way of example, I tutored high school students in Durham myself. I also encouraged the head of Duke's jazz studies department, Paul Jeffrey—a renowned saxophonist and composer who has performed and organized major jazz festivals all over the world—to start music-outreach programs in inner-city Durham.

Since I've never been able to give much money to the university, I found another way to contribute financially, by offering my experience in real estate. In the 1980s I fought against a plan to sell the university's golf course. Instead, my cousin Ben Holloway and I pushed an idea to add to it. We came up with a plan to build an upscale hotel next to the golf course and name it the Washington Duke Inn, after my great-grandfather. Others thought the university shouldn't get into the hotel business, so Ben proposed that an outside hotel company run it. After the inn opened in 1988, my brother Angier got involved, studying Durham and Duke family history to come up with names for the inn's suites and public areas. The inn wasn't a great success under the outside company, but when the university eventually took back management, it became a highly successful and extremely profitable hotel. I think of it as my financial contribution to Duke.

Not too long after I joined the board, I was elected vice chairman, which meant running meetings when the chairman wasn't there. At one point Terry and some others began talking to me about becoming chairman, but I demurred. I felt it was too big a job for me, especially without living down there. I also felt, though I could not prove it, that my popularity was due in some part to my relationship with the university's most sought-after but reluctant benefactor: my cousin Doris Duke.

For many years, Doris, who had inherited $80 million when she was only thirteen, had remained aloof from the university established by her father, my great-uncle Buck. The reason, I knew, was that she was sick of being asked for money. She was sick of that all her life, and few institutions felt more entitled to ask than Duke University. Finally, she had pretty much broken off her relationship with the university altogether. Terry Sanford told me he'd had no luck at all in getting her to bestow so much as a visit. He found it strange, considering that her parents had personally overseen everything from the campus's layout to the variety of trees planted on the Main Quad. That's Doris, I said. Over the years, she'd visited Boys Harbor on occasion and given moderate financial support.

Though I was six years younger than Doris, she and I had been close when we were young. We'd had a warm relationship through the years, and she was very fond of my mother. So I told Terry that I would make a tactful overture. The next time I spoke to Doris I told her I'd been named vice chairman of the board, that I'd love it if she would come down sometime. She was noncommittal.

Having some sympathy for anyone whose job entailed fundraising, I had another idea: I'd arrange a meeting between Terry and Doris. I'd make it as comfortable and low-pressure as possible by doing it at my mother's apartment in New York City. And just as Tommy Phipps, years earlier, had arranged for me to meet Brooke Astor and had prepped me so that I would maximize my chances of getting financial support for Boys Harbor, I coached Terry. I told him I had one instruction that absolutely had to be followed. Do Not Mention Money. "Just invite her down to Duke to see what's become of what her father started, to see how much it's grown. Just make sure you don't bring up money. That would kill it!"

Terry flew up from Durham and arrived early. While waiting for Doris, Mother offered him a drink. Terry accepted and Mother served him a huge vodka martini, which he seemed to enjoy. Doris was still absent when he finished it, and Mother asked him if he'd like another. "Be careful," I said warily as Terry, who was a very moderate drinker, downed his second martini.

By the time Doris arrived, Terry was, as they say in some circles, flying. The conversation barely started before he blurted, "We're building a new gym. I'd love to name it after you if you could see your way clear to paying for it."

Doris stiffened. "I don't think that's the kind of thing I'd be particularly interested in," she said. I chuckled nervously.

Then Terry started listing other buildings the university needed. "We need your approval, Doris," he said. "We need your knowledge, your taste . . ."

"And what else, President Sanford?" Doris asked.

"And, yes, your support," Terry said. "I think ten or twelve million would do it."

With that, Doris threw her napkin down, stood, and made for the door. "Cordelia," she said to Mother as she stepped onto the elevator, "I will speak to you later."

And she was gone.

"Oh, God," Terry said, twitching a bit. "I did it."

"I think the martinis did it," I said.

"Oh, Terry," Mother said, "that wasn't very brilliant of you."

Heartbroken and deeply embarrassed, Terry went back to Durham and, to his credit, admitted his failure to the board.

That night, Doris called me and said she'd never felt so set up and trapped. "Tony," she said, "our relationship is over."

And so it was. We spoke just once after that—when Doris heard that our mutual and much-loved cousin Nick Biddle was ill and she called me to ask what hospital he was in. We had a little chat, and I mentioned that I was putting in a grant request for Boys Harbor to her foundation. "Good luck," she said coolly.

Duke survived just fine without Doris's name on any of its buildings. Terry Sanford swore off vodka martinis and built the university's endowment into one of the nation's largest. The biggest victim of Mother's martinis was Boys Harbor. I had always hoped that Doris would someday give the Harbor a major gift, even if it was in her will. But when she died in 1993 and left $1.2 billion, not a penny of it was for Boys Harbor.

TEN

Passages

IN 1974, I WENT TO FLORIDA to be best man for my son John, who was marrying a lovely Cuban-American girl named Betty Alcebo. At the wedding I met Betty's sister, Luly. It wasn't long before I decided to give marriage another shot. In the grand tradition of the Biddle-Duke entwinements, with my marriage to Luly I was now my son's brother-in-law. And when John and Betty had children, two wonderful daughters named Camila and Natalia, it also meant that I was my granddaughters' uncle.

Luly (whose given name is Maria) was Cuban-American, twenty-eight years my junior. Like many Cuban-Americans of her generation who lost their homeland, she had a family history that was both dramatic and sad. Luly was born in Havana in 1946, the year I left the Navy. She grew up in an upper-middle-class family that was in the sugar business. In 1952, when Luly was six, Fulgencio Batista, a former Cuban president who had retired to Florida, returned to Havana and seized power, declaring himself president again. Batista presided over several years of unprecedented prosperity, during which Havana became a dynamic city with a lot of American investment and tourism. Public works projects rivaled our own post-war boom, and the economy boomed. Havana had more TV sets and Cadillacs per household than any city in the United States. Batista wanted gambling casinos, and the American mafia was eager to be his new partner.

Of course, I had seen firsthand evidence of Cuba's growing turmoil while on duck hunting trips in the late 1940s and while exploring real estate possibilities in the Fifties. By the end of that decade, university students and elements of the middle and upper classes were growing weary of the corruption and repression of the Batista regime—disenchantment that allowed long-time guerrilla leader Fidel Castro to foment a revolution that finally put him in power. On New Year's Day, 1959, Batista fled Havana and Castro proclaimed himself premier. I was fortunate in getting to Cuba too late to invest in real estate. After taking power, Castro seized more than a billion dollars in American assets.

Luly's family was politically neutral, and initially they held out hope that Castro's coup might be good for the country. One reason was that Luly's uncle, her mother's brother Jorge, had grown up with Castro. He and Fidel were classmates in El Colegio de Belén, an exclusive Jesuit school, and also at the University of Havana, where Castro was a law student and political provocateur. In fact, Jorge had once saved Castro from being arrested. His anti-government activities had gotten the attention of the authorities, and when they came to the university to seize Castro, Jorge hid him in the trunk of his car and drove off. Who knows how history might have been different if he hadn't done it. Jorge wasn't involved in Fidel's politics; he just did it because they were old school friends. So after Castro's coup Luly's family was ready to give him a chance. But that didn't last long.

Throughout his revolutionary years, Castro had promised to form an honest and open government, with freedom of the press and the respect for individual rights and private property that was guaranteed by the Cuban constitution. But after taking power he wasted no time demonstrating he was as totalitarian and iron-fisted as his predecessors. He executed more than a thousand of Batista's followers and began turning Cuba into a socialist society. He declared himself a Marxist, spouted virulent anti-American rhetoric, and began to accept aid from the Soviet Union and Communist China. Days before he left office, President Eisenhower broke off diplomatic relations with Castro's Cuba.

Jorge felt betrayed by his old friend and made plans for his family to join the many others who had fled Cuba for Miami. In November of 1960, Luly boarded a plane with Jorge, his daughter Leli, and their grandparents. Luly's and Leli's parents planned to join them with their younger children later on but wanted the older girls to go ahead so they could get started on an American education. As the plane took off and gained altitude, Jorge looked out the window and said to the two girls, "Look down, look at Cuba. You might not ever see it again."

The family found an apartment and Jorge got a job at the Miami Jai-Alai. But one night in March of 1961, Jorge didn't come home from work. It was a week before Luly's grandparents heard any information about their son's whereabouts. The word they got from the Cuban-American grapevine was that he had boarded a boat with some other men. That was all: nothing about who they were or where they had gone. Jorge's wife in Cuba had not heard from him, and she was frantic.

On April 17, news broke that 1,300 Cuban exiles armed with U.S. weapons had landed at the Bahia de Cochinos—the Bay of Pigs—on the south coast of Cuba. As the world later learned, the CIA had been training counter-revolutionary Cubans for a year, and only weeks after taking office President Kennedy approved the invasion. The plan was for the exiles to land at the Bay of Pigs, get support from the local population, then cross the island to Havana to remove Castro by whatever means necessary. But the operation, of course, was a colossal failure, partly because expected United States Air Force assistance failed to materialize. Castro himself took command of his army and defeated the exiles almost immediately, killing 114 of them and capturing nearly all the rest.

Though Jorge was not a particularly political person, it seemed obvious to Luly's grandparents that he had been involved somehow in the failed invasion. But it was several more weeks before they got the news of Jorge's arrest—from the Cuban-American newspaper *Diario Las Americas*. Jorge, it turned out, had been recruited in Miami to join a group of exiles who would sneak back to Cuba in advance of the invasion and try to drum up anti-Castro support for the American-trained commandos. Jorge wasn't captured immediately, and friends and relatives in Cuba pleaded with him to leave before he was. But he stayed too long, and was arrested. In Havana, Luly's mother and aunt, Jorge's wife, watched in horror as Jorge was paraded in public as an example of the consequences of opposing Fidel. They feared the worst, and for good reason.

Over the next six months, Luly's relatives worked furiously to save Jorge's life. They were a well-off family whose sugar business gave them contacts with influential people in many countries. The president of the Dominican Republic called Castro on their behalf, as did a high official in Brazil. Luly's mother and aunt tried to get messages to Castro himself, reminding him that Jorge had once saved him. But old ties meant nothing now. Castro judged Jorge a traitor, and in October, after a show trial, Jorge was stood before a firing squad and executed. Castro's government wouldn't even tell his widow where he was buried. A month later, Luly's mother and younger siblings, including Betty, left Cuba to join her in Miami. Her father came a few months later. Jorge's wife and younger children, meanwhile, were unable to leave.

Luly graduated from a Catholic high school and attended community college. She had a brief marriage that ended in divorce when her daughter, Lulita, was still a toddler. Meanwhile, though she had been in the United States for a decade, Luly still wasn't quite sure where her true home was. While some who fled Castro made their way north to New York and set their sights on American citizenship, Miami's Cuban exiles were an insular community of nationalists who lived on the hope and belief that one day they would go home. Cuba's twentieth century history featured one coup after another. Sooner or later, they believed, Fidel would go the way of others. Until then, they would stay close, do what they could to generate anti-Castro sentiment in the United States, and wait. "In Miami," Luly said, "it was always, 'Next year we will go back to Cuba.'"

Lulita was three years old when Luly and I were married. I immediately fell in love with her, and right off the bat Lulita became a full-fledged member of my family. Luly and I also had two boys, Washington and James. Washy was named for my great-grandfather, who planted the seeds for the Duke tobacco business in North Carolina. James was named after Washington's elder son, my Uncle

Buck. He was born in 1979, when I was sixty-one. It brought my brood to eleven—seven sons and four daughters, born over the course of thirty-seven years.

While Luly's life in New York distanced her from the Cuban exile population in Miami, our marriage had the opposite effect on me. I had been to Cuba several times and had good friends there, but Luly's family history added to the connection I felt. This became most affecting in April of 1980 when my son John and I left our wives, the Cuban-born sisters, to help in the Mariel boatlift.

It all started when word spread around Havana that the Peruvian embassy would give refuge to people who wanted to leave Cuba. After a bus rammed through a fence surrounding the embassy, throngs of Cubans began to flood the gates. Within a couple of days there were more than 10,000 people seeking asylum. A week later, President Jimmy Carter announced that the United States would accept up to 3,500 Cubans, with priority to be given to released political prisoners. Then, in an unexpected and historic move, Castro announced that members of the Cuban-American community in South Florida could come by boat to Mariel Harbor and take their friends and relatives back to the United States. From dinghies to shrimp boats, a mass flotilla quickly got underway toward Cuba. John had become a truly resourceful sailor and sea captain—I served under him on several sailing ships—and we made plans to join the Mariel boatlift.

My family and I had been part of political rescue missions before—Angier was in Hungary with the International Rescue Committee in 1956 and twenty years later I went to Vietnam and Cambodia—but this time it was more personal. We would not be bringing any of Luly and Betty's relatives back—their aunt, Jorge's wife, and their younger children did not want to leave at this point in their lives—but it still felt as if we were doing something meaningful for them. Aboard John's 38-foot schooner, Sea Breeze, we sailed for Mariel Harbor with a young man whose mother and sixteen other relatives were in Cuba. We arrived to a scene of corruption and chaos. Cuban officers were basically selling people. A man could buy members of his family if he had the money. Meanwhile, American shrimp boat captains used the situation to make money. They were charging $1,000 and more for transportation from Cuba. Castro had opened the prisons up, and there were stories in the press that boats were filled with dope addicts and prostitutes. But that was a vast exaggeration. Most had been in jail for minor offenses or for criticizing the government.

We spent nine unsettling days in Mariel, during which we saw a Cuban gunboat sink a vessel for reasons that weren't apparent. We also saw many people drown when a minor hurricane ripped through our anchorage. Using our ship's radio, I called the State Department in Washington to let authorities there know what was happening. I suggested they send a Navy battleship with a giant Red Cross flag draped around its bridge. But it had the same effect as the letter I wrote to the same department in 1941, warning about the Nazis in Germany after Gustave Glück stowed away to Argentina. We left with thirty-five refugees, mostly laborers, though two were computer experts. They had a hopefulness about coming to the United States that was poignant. We tried to tell them not to expect too much. Their lives in America would not be easy.

MY BROTHER ANGIER RETIRED FROM THE FOREIGN SERVICE in 1981 after a final tour as ambassador to Morocco under President Carter. That June, the National Committee on American Foreign Policy made Angier the first recipient of the Hans J. Morgenthau Award for his "exemplary foreign policy contributions to the United States." It was a special night for our entire extended family, harkening all the way back to our forebears. The presentation dinner—attended by more than four hundred people—was held in the stone mansion at Fifth Avenue and Seventy-eighth Street that our great-Uncle Buck and his wife Nanaline had built in 1912, the same year their only child, Doris, was born. (The building was donated to New York University in 1958 and now houses NYU's Institute of Fine Arts.)

The New York Times treated the occasion as a major social event, the kind to which newspapers used to devote much attention:

With Washy (left) and James in East Hampton.

Coaching James' hockey team, 1989

Seventy years or so after we sat for portrait artist Harrington Mann, Angier and I were still posing together.

"Neighbors gaped out their windows," the *Times* story opened, "possibly transported back to the times before income taxes . . . There was a traffic jam of limousines, the extra-long variety, and their elegant occupants well suited the Beaux Arts architecture of the James B. Duke House." (That is, they all did except for Ben Duke, Angier's eighteen-year-old grandson, who wore size 15 white Pro Ked basketball sneakers and sported four stalks of asparagus in the breast pocket of his dinner jacket.) Many of the women wore the kind of opulent jewelry "not normally seen in public," the *Times* said. My mother wore a black taffeta dress with rubies and diamonds in her hair, "and her wrists glittered with many bracelets of pave diamonds."

The dinner was a virtual family reunion, with about twenty-five Dukes and even more Biddle-Duke combinations, branches on a family tree made hopelessly confusing by the marriage of my father's sister Mary to my mother's brother Tony in 1915. As Angier's oldest son Angier Junior (Pony, as he's known) told the bewildered *Times* reporter, the only thing important to remember was that "Cordelia Biddle Robertson is the boss, make no mistake about that."

Among the non-Dukes and Biddles who came to honor Angier were many foreign diplomats and notables including Brooke Astor, John and Mary Lindsay, Henry Luce III, Cornelius Vanderbilt Whitney, Governor Hugh Carey, and Pat Kennedy Lawford. Henry Kissinger opened the ceremonies, saying that Angier "represents the idealism that has made our country the hope of the world." Not bad for a guy whom people had regarded, however incorrectly, as a rich playboy when President Truman appointed him ambassador to El Salvador. Angier himself was characteristically humble. "I thought they should have picked a more eminent figure than myself for the Morgenthau award," he told the *Times* afterward. "Not that I'm being modest, just realistic."

Actually, Angier was both realistic and modest. After his retirement from the diplomatic corps, among the pursuits he considered was writing a book. But he wasn't sure he had a perspective worth sharing. "I don't want to write a book that merely says, 'I was there,'" he said. He never did write one. Instead, he took one last job. After he and Robin converted a barn into a residence on Mother's four-acre property, he agreed to become—at a salary of a dollar a year—chancellor of Southampton College, a campus of 1,200 students that was part of Long Island University. He stayed for five years and made his mark, improving the college's financial condition and raising its profile. He started an annual Global Economic Forum that brought major political, intellectual, and financial figures to the campus. Angier enjoyed the campus life; he relished being close to the students. He could often be seen jogging around the campus in shorts and sneakers, and his door was always open. He and Robin personally led a drive to raise money so the college radio station, WPBX, could build a new tower. (Robin, by the way, had become a notable figure on the national stage herself. She was a director of several foundations, served as president of the National Abortion and Reproductive Rights Action League, and was appointed by President Carter to chair the American delegation to the U.N.'s education, scientific, and cultural organization meeting in 1980. And in 2000, she would be appointed ambassador to Norway by President Clinton.)

Though he was retired as a diplomat, Angier stayed tuned to international affairs. In 1992, after leaving the college, he was elected president of the Council of American Ambassadors, an organization of current and former diplomats. He was particularly interested in events in Latin and Central America, where he had begun his ambassadorial career as our envoy to El Salvador. Cuba was particularly on his radar.

Angier didn't expect the United States to restore full diplomatic relations with Castro's government, but he wished there could be a way for the two countries to at least open a dialogue. In his leadership role with the ambassadors' council, and with the approval of the State Department, Angier made an overture to Havana. He proposed to bring a group of former ambassadors to Cuba to discuss ways in which there could be some level of communication. He was overjoyed when Castro's government responded with an invitation.

Angier's forthcoming trip struck a nerve in Luly. She had met a young woman, a lawyer, who had been encouraging her to revive her feelings for her homeland. After some thought, Luly told Angier she wanted to go with him. And after some thought, Angier said no. He thought her abhorrence of Castro was undiminished and told her that he didn't think she was emotionally ready to go back. Angier's decision made Luly quite angry. But his trip was a turning point for her: it marked the beginning of a change of heart and led her to begin to make an intellectual separation between Castro and Cuba. "There had to be more to the country than one person," she said. But it would be another five years before she would finally set foot on Cuban soil.

On April 29, 1995, Angier died after being struck by a car while rollerblading in Southampton. It was a tragic accident, of course, but few of the thousand people who attended his funeral were surprised to hear that, at seventy-nine, my brother was still living life to the hilt.

For Luly, Angier's inspiration lived on. A few months later, she, Betty, Lulita, and I flew to Havana. It had been thirty-five years since Luly's uncle Jorge had told her on the plane to look down because it might be the last time she ever saw Cuba. For her, it was of course an emotionally jarring experience. Her first thought was that it was sad to see the country in such a state of disrepair. A friend of hers had a phrase to describe it: preservation by neglect. But the most emotional moment for Luly came when we visited her relatives left behind: her cousins, Patricia and Carlos, Jorge's younger children.

Luly returned from that trip doggedly determined to do what she could to encourage ties between her native and adoptive countries. The governments might not be the best of friends, she thought, but why should the people suffer? Luly thought it was time to move on. In 1998, she founded her own nonprofit organization, *Fundacion Amistad*, which translates to Friendship Foundation. It was devoted to bringing the two countries together in all ways but politically.

BETWEEN MY OWN FOUR WEDDINGS and serving as best man for my sons and friends, I've spent more than my share of time at the altar. My mother, on the other hand, never had much desire to marry again. After Tom Robertson died in 1962 she spent the next twenty years as a merry widow. Though marriage didn't interest her, the attentions of men certainly did. Young, handsome ones were preferred, but there were no age restrictions. One summer, she made the acquaintance of a wealthy older gentleman named Harry King, who fell madly in love with her. Harry was in a wheelchair, but Mother saw past that. One day they were together at the Beach Club in Southampton when my nephew Pony, Angier's son, passed by and said, "Hi, Grandma." She paid no attention and kept on batting her eyelashes at her geriatric Romeo. When Pony persisted, she smiled brightly at him, then turned to her suitor. "Poor boy," she said. "He thinks every woman here is his grandmother. Sad, isn't it?"

Harry arranged for a florist to make so many deliveries that he might have been better off buying the shop. One day he rolled up to my Boys Harbor office in the city in his wheelchair. He said he wanted to know whether it would be all right if he asked my mother's hand in marriage. "Well, I don't know, Harry," I said. "I suppose you'd have to ask *her*." He did, and she declined. But their wonderful friendship continued until his death.

Mother never lacked for company, especially from her beloved dogs. In Southampton at any given time, she had eight or ten of them, and twice that many in photographs, water colors, and sculptures. When one of the dogs died she would have him buried beside the house. The dogs could literally do no wrong. Once, my son Barclay noticed that one of Mother's terriers was relieving himself inside, on a very white rug. "Grandma, Salty's peeing on the rug!" he shouted. "I think that's wonderful!" she answered. "She'll feel much better now."

Though she had a passel of pooches, the one with whom she was most associated was Peaches, a miniature brown dachshund that she would hide in her handbag when she went to lunch. Once, while we lunched at the well-known Colony Restaurant in New York, the maitre d' approached our table, clearing his throat. "Mrs. Robertson," he said, "are you aware that we do not allow dogs here?"

"Of course," Mother replied.

"Mrs. Robertson, you have a dog in your purse."

"That's not a dog," Mother said matter-of-factly.

"If it's not a dog, Mrs. Robertson, then what is it?"

"I'm not about to tell you," Mother replied.

The maitre d' was so flabbergasted that all he could shoot back was a look of confusion and consternation. He gave up and returned to his post. Eventually, the staff at Mother's regular spots either accepted her position that Peaches was not a dog or just pretended not to see her.

There were other times at restaurants when the tables were turned and it was Mother on the offensive. Once, when the practice of announcing the day's special dishes was custom in France but not yet in the United States, Mother found herself captive of the head-waiter of a French restaurant whose litany of specials went on and on and on. Finally, she couldn't bear to hear the details of even one more entrée. She grabbed the poor waiter by the nose and used it to shake his head. "Don't ever talk to me like that again," she said. Somehow, they remained friends.

As she reached her eighties, Mother achieved a kind of exalted status in Southampton. People began referring to her as a *grande dame*, but she detested such talk. As my great friend Tommy Phipps liked to say, she was more of a Peter Pan—younger at heart than anyone of drinking age and doing everything possible to deny nature. She stayed out of the sun, maintained an adolescent's figure, and wore her hair in a style that was popular when she really was young.

Mother divided her time between New York and the Hamptons house at the corner of South Main Street and Gin Lane. She was just about the most well-known and revered resident of Southampton, famed for her parties, many of which she threw to support the Harbor and Southampton Hospital, and for her inclination to say and do whatever popped into her head. If she liked something or someone, she would rave. A person she was especially fond of was "a real peach." A peach was usually someone who was "bright, fun, and full of beans." On the other hand, if she *disliked* something, she'd leave no doubt. One thing she didn't like, oddly enough, was being mentioned a little too often in the society columns. Each spring, the *Southampton Press* would announce, "When Cordelia arrives from New York, you know the season has properly begun," or some variation of that entirely correct observation. "I don't want to be talked about," Mother would say, after being talked about her entire life. Naturally, she avoided giving interviews, but in 1979, a persistent young reporter from *Newsday* coaxed her into one. They sat in Mother's pastel-colored living room as the dogs wandered in and out, and she explained, between coos and kisses with the dogs, why publicity did nothing for her. "I don't give a hootin pootin what people think of me," she said.

Like everyone else, especially young people, the reporter, Susan Giller, got a big kick out of Mother. She saw her as a character from an age and a society that no longer existed, and as someone who refused to grow old. "Mrs. Robertson was dressed in size 6 red slacks, white silk blouse and white espadrilles," Miss Giller wrote. "Her mid-length brown fall was parted with a diamond and ruby barrette. It is difficult to believe she is an octogenarian with 11 great-grandchildren. . . . She moves and talks with such flair that one feels like applauding when she finishes."

Though Mother didn't like being written about in the papers, she didn't mind at all that she was a favorite subject for essays and writing assignments by her grandchildren and great-grandchildren. Barclay once wrote in a composition: "My grandmother lives on Bufferin, booze and BenGay. She's about no age at all and has one hell of a sense of humor. The one thing I can't figure out is how she can be so healthy after drinking so much Dubonnet and smoking for sixty-five years! If you're sitting with her at dinner and she starts to look for something, whatever you do don't ask her if she needs any help. She'll probably say, 'Finish your dinner!' or 'Worry about yourself, not me!' But she says it in a way that you can't stop laughing." Barclay, like all of Mother's grandchildren, loved her deeply.

My nephew Biddle, Angier's son, wrote, "When I was a boy she made me squirm; I was baffled by her outrageous behavior and girlish humor . . . She was scary-thin, with the waistline of an adolescent. Her dark brown hair always hung in a shoulder-length bob. In later years, as it thinned, she replaced it with an identical wig. When I approached, no conversation Grandma was having was too important to interrupt. She would utter a little coo and stretch out her hands. After the embrace she'd ask about my life, or more likely whether I'd brought my friends—girls in particular." Biddle recalled bringing a "ballerina girlfriend" to Thanksgiving dinner at Mother's apartment one year. "Grandma looked her over, sat her down and spoke to her for a few minutes," he wrote. "She then declared that I should marry the girl." Biddle was seventeen at the time.

Thanksgiving at Mother's apartment in the city was a family tradition, and it was a highlight of everyone's year. There were always fifty or sixty people. Besides family there would be the usual assortment of "socialites, New York royalty, struggling writers, failed actors," as Biddle described the crowd. "After most of the adults had been lubricated sufficiently, guests would rise and offer toasts. For the younger generation, this was a painful test, intimidating in a family of born orators and witty conversationalists. No words went unrewarded by my grandmother, who would shake her head and laugh quietly and jangle her braceleted wrists."

Now that I, too, was aging, Mother had a piece of advice for me. "As you get older, Tony," she said, "you'll find that people will come up to you and say, 'Hello, Tony! I'll bet you don't remember me.' You'll say, 'Of course I remember you.' They'll say, 'What's my name?' So you look at them and say, 'My dear, if you don't know it by now I'm certainly not going to tell you.'" I've taken her advice many times.

In 1984, Mother was eighty-seven. Her health was finally getting the better of her. She was ill all summer and became progressively weaker through the fall. "I never thought this could happen to me," she said. It seemed that the Thanksgiving tradition would finally have to end. She was in no condition to host the usual throng. But she would hear nothing of it. In fact, she insisted on a party that was bigger than ever. She wanted everyone, no matter how far they had to come, and from this we knew that she intended it to be her last party, her big farewell. And so they came in droves—from Philadelphia, Florida, North Carolina, Alaska, even Delia from Spain. Mother had to stay in bed, but she insisted that all the small grandchildren and great-grandchildren come to her so she could give each of them a little present. There were thirty of them, and they made a line into her bedroom as if she were Mrs. Claus. The little ones sat on the floor around her bed playing with their new presents. It was an unforgettable and bittersweet day.

Having fulfilled her last wish, Mother was ready to leave us. And so, two days later, on Saturday afternoon, she went.

MY MOTHER'S DEATH WAS CERTAINLY SAD and difficult, but it did come with the knowledge that she had lived long and joyfully. Hers was a life to be celebrated, with no regrets. But four years later, my family and I had to endure a much more anguishing and emotionally complex death.

After his graduation from Warren Wilson College, my son Barclay came home to East Hampton and started a construction business with a friend. But come July, he would put his business aside to spend his summer at his beloved Harbor, where he would teach the kids carpentry and boating, and just hang out with them.

One year, Barclay went on a hiking and bicycling vacation to the Dominican Republic and became captivated by the island and its people. He spent time in a remote poverty-stricken village where he met a girl from New Jersey who was there as a volunteer. They got engaged, and Barclay asked me to be his best man. After the wedding, they came back to East Hampton, where they bought a small piece of land and Barclay built a house. Meanwhile, they made trips to the Dominican Republic. During one, Barclay and his friends there built a medical clinic for the village.

If Barclay had an Achilles heel, it was his oversensitivity. He reacted emotionally to hurtful situations, a tendency born of his own reactions to his learning disabilities. As a child, he was very sensitive about always getting mixed up, and as he grew up he sometimes applied that emotional reaction to other kinds of difficult situations. When he was having a rough time in boarding school, he started seeing Dr. Harold Koplewicz, a wonderful child and adolescent psychiatrist who was on the board of the Harbor. Harold, a dear friend who later became the founder and director of the NYU Child Study Center, worked with Barclay and was so proud of his accomplishments.

Barclay as a counselor at the Harbor.

He told me once how much he admired the relationship I had with Barclay.

One night in 1988, when he was twenty-eight, Barclay came with me to a theater benefit for the Harbor. He looked badly, as if he were getting sick. I suggested he take a couple of days off, but he shrugged his shoulders and said he'd be all right. He asked if he could talk to me. I told him I couldn't right then. I was taking my two young boys, Washy and James, to New Jersey for a two-day hockey tournament. "We can talk when I get back," I said. I called him the next morning, but couldn't reach him.

While I was in New Jersey, I got two messages from Barclay but each time when I called back there was no answer. A dark shadow seemed to surround me. I sensed that something terrible had happened. Washy, James, and I headed back home following the boys' game that Sunday, and as we approached the George Washington Bridge the car phone rang. It was Tony Jr. "Dad, I have very bad news," he said. "Hold on to yourself. There's no other way I can tell you. Barclay committed suicide."

Tony's words pierced my soul. I nearly crashed the car when I heard them. Washy and James burst into tears when I told them the news. *"Why did he do this to us?"* eleven-year-old Washy shrieked. He loved Barclay dearly, as did James and his sister Lulita. In fact, all my children loved Barclay. They couldn't help it. He was that special kind of boy and man. It was the longest ride home of my life.

In the days and weeks after Barclay's death, I tried to piece together some clues about how it could have happened. I might not understand it—in fact, nearly twenty years later, I still don't—but at least I could find out what events led up to it. What I learned was that a few days before, Barclay had found out that his marriage had been destroyed by his wife's betrayal of him with his close friend.

When I saw him at the benefit before taking the boys to their hockey tournament, I thought Barclay looked pale and sad and ill. But I misread the symptoms as signs of physical illness, not mental anguish. But now I knew what he needed to talk to me about. In my mind's eye, I could see his face and register something in his eyes that should have told me he was in distress. I realized the second of his phone calls was just a few hours before he took his life. Apparently he spent three hours watching television in the camp's recreation room, then went up to my office in the house. He wrote a brief note, and shot himself with my shotgun. The note said: "I am deeply sorry. You have my love. Barclay."

It has been impossible for me, ever since, to stop thinking about how I might have prevented Barclay's suicide. His emotional sensitivity, his nemesis, made him react to the disintegration of his marriage in a way that a much younger person might. But I've always felt I would might have gotten him through it had I been there. Over the last two decades, I've had no choice but to live with Barclay's death, and with my unending regret. It is the hardest thing I have ever done.

ELEVEN

Onward

IN MY LIFE, I HAVE BEEN FORTUNATE to have had several families, distinct groups of loved ones from different parts of my life who have often intersected. There is my own family, of course: my mother and father and brother and grandparents, cousins, aunts, uncles, nieces and nephews; and my eleven children who've made me so proud and feel so loved, as well as their children and their children's children. There is my St. Paul's family, men I knew as boys and who always remained close to me even as we went our separate ways and grew older. There is my Navy family—the men of USS LST 530 whose friendship did not end when the war did. We've had many reunions over the years, including one in 1990 when my crew hunted through my cellar for the old boxing bell and had it mounted and presented it to me in a touching ceremony.

And there is the largest of them all, my Harbor family. In the late 1990s, someone at the Harbor calculated that more than 40,000 children had been touched in some way by our various programs over the years. I was astounded when I first heard the number. We had started, after all, with just a handful of kids on Duck Island in 1937.

Seventy years later, I am still close to countless Harbor alumni, and regularly encounter many others who have come through over the years. I receive calls and visits all the time, and one of the pleasures of my life is walking on the street and running into someone who spent time at the Harbor as a child. It might be someone I knew sixty years ago or someone who graduated last year. Several times, I've hailed cabs and found the driver to be a Harbor alumnus. Here's my favorite story of all: One

day in the early 1990s, I was heading across the Triboro Bridge into Manhattan when a large African-American cop stepped in front of my car at
the toll booth. "I'm afraid I'm going to have to pull you over," he said
firmly but politely, motioning for me to park off to the side. I complied,
of course, though I couldn't imagine what I'd done. The cop followed me
over and bent down to look into my window. "You're under arrest, Tony,"
he said, breaking into a huge grin. It was Ron Jackson, one of my favorite
campers from the Sixties. I hadn't seen Ron for several years, but his
mock arrest marked the beginning of a renewed friendship. When Ron
retired from the police force years later he told me he wanted to give
something back for all he had gotten from the Harbor and from me.
Anytime I needed to get anywhere around the city, he said, all I had to
do was call him. I was tremendously touched and appreciative, and Ron
has been one of my closest friends, ever since.

For Ron and so many others, camp remains the tie that binds the
extended Harbor family. But the reality is that it can no longer be considered the Harbor's focal point. Our mission has always remained the same:
to be on the cutting edge of efforts to reach, motivate, elevate, and educate inner-city youth. But those goals have long been centered around our
building on 104th Street. And as the world has grown more complex and
challenging, we've tried to find new and creative ways to bring children
on the perimeter of our society into the fold. It seems there has always
been something new going on at the Harbor, thanks to the dedication and
imagination of our staff, board members, and benefactors.

Typical was a program begun in 1990 that brought Columbia University graduate students into the Harbor to teach international studies classes to children of various ages. The program was the brainchild
of Ken Lipper, a former deputy mayor of New York who provided the
seed money for the program and made the arrangements with Columbia's School of International Relations. When the program began, our
young Harbor children would make artwork to send, along with food,
clothing, and toys, to children in refugee camps.

"Why is it important to do this?" one of the Columbia students asking
a class of eight-year-olds one day.

"We can help them feel like they are more like us," said one student.

"It helps them feel better about themselves," said another, showing an intuitive grasp of what had always been one of the Harbor's essential missions.

It was a mission I had placed in the sure hands of Lonnie Williams in 1969. Over the next twenty-six years, he proved to be as right for the job of executive director as I suspected he would be almost from the day I first met him when he was a teenager. Lonnie had not only great personal magnetism and natural leadership skills but a remarkable instinct for knowing what kids growing up in the city needed—both intellectually and emotionally. At camp, there was a giant rock outside the mess hall, big enough for two people to sit on or lean against. It became known as Lonnie's "Let's Talk" rock.

In 1995, everyone at the Harbor was stunned and saddened when Lonnie was diagnosed with an aggressive cancer. I visited him in the hospital every day and saw that he was in the fight of his life. It was a battle that he could not win. He deteriorated rapidly, and within only a few months he was gone. Richard Alonzo Williams was just sixty.

It is hard to describe the pain I felt at losing someone whose impact on my life had been so great. Lonnie's passing came less than three months after my brother Angier's equally unexpected death. It was of course a great personal loss for so many of us but it was also a terrible blow to the Harbor and its future. For twenty-five years, Lonnie had been my partner at the helm. He had picked up what I had started and took it farther than I could have imagined. He worked endless hours, sometimes sleeping in his office after a late-night meeting rather than going home to Jersey City. The Harbor was his home and his life as much as it was mine. His shoes would be extremely difficult to fill.

Over the next six years we had two different executive directors. Each had his strengths but neither embodied all the qualities we needed to run such a large organization composed of so many disparate parts. This was especially so in 2000, when we marked a major new turning point in our mission. Two years earlier, the New York State Legislature had passed an act that allowed parents, teachers, and citizens in local communities to establish independent but publicly funded schools. The idea of these "charter schools" was to provide an alternative to local public schools, especially for students in under-performing districts. Certainly there was a need to improve education and achievement in our East Harlem neigh-

Happy reunions have been a big part of my life. Here are two:
The forty-fifth reunion of the St. Paul's School's Class of 1937
and one of the many gatherings of LST 530.

Angier and Lonnie. Both so close to me, their untimely deaths came three months apart in 1995.

With my great friend Ron Jackson, 2006.

borhood, and in the fall of 2000 we opened one of the first charter schools in New York City. The Harbor Science and Arts Charter School enrolled more than two hundred children in grades one through eight. After decades of providing early morning and late afternoon educational programs to complement the public schools, we were now in the business of running our own accredited school. More than at any point since Lonnie's death, we needed a first-rate person to lead the Harbor. An extensive search led us to someone right in our own backyard.

Hans Hageman was a brilliant man with a compelling personal history. It fed a vision that suited the Harbor perfectly. A decade earlier, Hans had given up what certainly would have been a lucrative legal career to serve the children of East Harlem, where he had grown up under unique circumstances. His father, Lynn Hageman, had been a Methodist minister in Nebraska who was denied his own parish in the late 1950s after he refused to end his relationship with Hans's mother, Leola, who was African-American. Seeking an environment that would be welcoming to an interracial family and where they could devote themselves to social action, the Hagemans moved to New York in 1959 and settled in East Harlem. There they started Exodus House, a residential treatment center for drug addicts. They and their children—Hans, his younger brother Ivan and older sister Erika—lived in the building with the program's residents. "It was like having a bunch of older brothers who had a whole lot of profound experience on the streets, in prison, in the Vietnam War," Ivan once recalled.

Though they lived on the mean streets of East Harlem, Hans and Ivan were such academic stars that they were able to win scholarships to Manhattan's prestigious Collegiate School, where their schoolmates included John F. Kennedy Jr. Hans went to Princeton on scholarship, then on to Columbia Law School. He spent several years as an attorney—in the Manhattan district attorney's office and at two major law firms in the city—before moving to Washington to be a ranking staff member on the U.S. Senate Subcommittee on the Constitution. Ivan, meanwhile, had gone to Harvard and then taught in New York City public schools for eight years before taking a job as head of minority recruiting at Collegiate. But both Hans and Ivan felt they wanted to do something more meaningful with their lives. Hans realized that educating children was his true calling, and in 1992 he and Ivan opened a private school in Exodus House, the former drug-treatment center their parents had founded and where they'd grown up. The idea of their East Harlem School was to give local children a chance to have a first-rate education. They started with just thirteen students but by the end of the decade there were sixty. Support came from the likes of Tom Brokaw and Paul Newman. In our search for a new executive director, we couldn't have found a better candidate.

When Hans joined the Harbor at the beginning of 2002, he was undaunted by the prospect of taking over an agency with a complex array of programs and a deeply ingrained internal culture. He brought in some of his own people, and long-time Harborites had to get used to Hans's way of doing things. The transition wasn't entirely smooth, but I supported Hans. I realized that the best thing for the Harbor, for our children, was to give him the independence he needed to do the job the organization and its mission needed him to do. With his humanity, street smarts, natural leadership, and wonderful way with children, Hans brought new light and vitality to the Harbor. Hans respected and admired the Harbor's past and he has high ambitions for its future. And I am behind him a hundred percent.

At the top of his list was his desire to expand the Harbor's new role as a full-time school. He wanted to establish a high school—not a charter school but one that was privately funded, with a sliding-scale tuition policy—that would target students who could benefit most from a small, rigorous, and stimulating environment. With a generous contribution by our old friend Bill Carey, Hans made it happen in the fall of 2005. Within the Harbor building, eighteen ninth-graders became the first class of the Emily N. Carey Harbor High School, named for Bill's sister-in-law, the late wife of his brother Frank. Both Bill and Frank have long been among the Harbor's most reliable benefactors, and Emily—Bitsy as everyone called her—was a mainstay teacher, tutor and advocate, beloved by children and staff alike.

Here is how we express our high school's philosophy: "The emphasis at the school is on reflection and action. There is a strong liberal arts curriculum that enables students to understand the foundations and institutions of Western society as well as to develop a familiarity with the intellectual and cultural foundations of other parts of the world.

Our students learn 'facts but they also learn how to apply these facts to advance their learning and to make decisions. As a result, our students become *deep learners,* able to think creatively, critically and independently. Character development and physical well-being are key components of the school model."

With this philosphy in mind—and thanks to the vision of Arthur and Janet Ross, who are among the Harbor's most generous benefactors—we have taken an exciting international turn. With the Ross's support, Hans has created a relationship between the Harbor and a school in India and initiated a program of trips to various countries in Africa by groups of students from our high school. Our students absorb other cultures and perform volunteer public service to the communities they visit. They create relationships and come back changed. "You're world citizens," I like to tell them.

With all his many responsibilities at the Harbor, Hans has somehow also found the time to start an Emily Carey High School basketball team—and to coach it himself. One Saturday in January 2007, I had a chance to follow our team to an important game at St. Andrew's School

Hans Hageman, the Harbor's executive director and basketball coach, with the team after their victory at St. Andrew's School in Delaware.

in Middletown, Delaware. I'd known of this fine school since way back in my college days, when St. Andrew's sent many of its best athletes to Princeton. I knew our Harbor team would be facing a very strong opponent from a private boarding school whose tuition is $33,000 a year. But Hans had his team ready. He coaches with gusto and deep concern for each of his players, and he's quickly developed a big team at a small school, a squad to be reckoned with. In a close battle from opening tip-off to final buzzer, the Harbor team emerged victorious by four points. But more important than winning the game was the dignity and determination demonstrated by all of our players. I felt a deep sense of pride in our boys and in Hans.

Adding a class a year, the Harbor's goal is to make the Emily N. Carey Harbor High School a four-year school by the fall of 2008, when our initial freshmen will reach their senior year. But as with everything else, our success—our very future—will depend largely on money. Our city-owned building, nearly a century old, is not only cramped but in serious disrepair. The city has condemned some of it and estimates it would take a daunting $132 million to make all the necessary upgrades—money the city is unwilling to spend and which the Harbor certainly doesn't have. This is perhaps the biggest challenge for Hans, who is experiencing the frustration of having my name connected to the Harbor. Foundations frequently turn down our requests for aid because they erroneously assume, as many people have over the years, that I have more than enough money to personally finance the Harbor and its programs.

WITH THE HARBOR'S FOCUS HAVING gradually shifted over the years from the camp that started it all to the many educational programs we undertook in the city, perhaps it was inevitable that we would come to a crossroads in East Hampton. That moment came in 2005. It seems symbolic that as we ran camp that summer, our fifty-third on Three Mile Harbor, something important was missing. In the background stood my family home, empty and charred, children no longer able to stream in and out. Over the winter, an electrical fire had virtually destroyed the house.

It was a sign of things to come. The camp was old, and in an all-too-familiar bureaucratic refrain, the Town of East Hampton insisted that

A bittersweet day at camp, July 2006. Among the esteemed Harbor alumni who came to bid farewell to Three Mile Harbor are (crouching, left to right) Ron Jackson, whose granddaughter is a third-generation Harborite; Tanya Robinson, one of the first to turn Boys Harbor into Boys and Girls Harbor and who went on to become an attorney and president of the Harbor Alumni Association; and New York State Supreme Court Justice Eduardo Padro (Eddie to us), a former camper, counselor, and major force in turning the Harbor into a serious educational institution. And standing to my left is Hazel Williams, widow of the great Lonnie Williams.

Ramon Rodriguez with some of his Harbor Conservatory students. The Conservatory has earned an international reputation.

we make improvements to meet current codes for plumbing, electrical service, and housing. For instance, our cabins had too many beds and were too close to one another. We calculated that it would cost more than $1 million to bring the camp up to the town's standards. Clearly, a decision had to be made. The board took a hard look at the situation and the answer was unavoidable. Fewer children were choosing to go out to camp in the summer—250 from a peak of 500—while our city programs served more than 4,000. My emotional attachment to camp was as strong as anyone's, but even I found it hard to make the case that so much of the Harbor's resources should be committed to upgrading a facility that served a relatively small number of children. It would be a disproportionate drain on our budget at a time when careful management was needed to ensure the Harbor's very survival. To the majority of the Harbor's 36-member board of directors, it was clear that the best course was to sell the land, use the proceeds to support the Harbor's programs in the city, and then reopen camp in a new location, either by buying or leasing a less expensive property, probably north or west of the city. Thus was 2005 the last year of camp at Three Mile Harbor.

Regrettably, but not surprisingly, word of our intentions caused a great uproar among Harbor alumni. I received many letters and phone calls, some of them quite angry, all of them pleading with me to find a way to keep the camp open in East Hampton. The pain was just as acute for me but I couldn't change reality. The property was put on the market. With the arrival of the summer of 2006, the camp was sadly and strangely empty. Our wonderful staff, led by Kathy Flack, the director of our junior education program, felt the moment should not pass without ceremony, and on July 1, 2006, eighty-nine Harbor alumni came out to camp to mark the passage of an era. It was a bittersweet day, to be sure. A day of reminiscences and a day of farewells—not to each other but to this place where we had shared so much. It was a day to take a last walk down to the water, a day for one last lineup outside the mess hall and for one final meal inside, sitting side-by-side at those long tables. A chance to pay a last visit to Lonnie's "Let's Talk" rock. After he died, a plaque was attached to the rock, commemorating the spot, and the man. Lonnie's family came out—his wife Hazel, sons Richie and Stevie, and his brother Franklin and sister-in-law Lillian. They wouldn't have missed it.

"He looks just like Lonnie," Ron Jackson marveled as he looked at Richie, who's a stockbroker.

It was that kind of day. You looked around and everything reminded you of something. Strolling down to the water, I thought of a thousand little voyages and a few long ones. From this spot, I sailed to Newfoundland and Florida. My son John sailed here from Europe. When you were there you felt you had the world in front of you.

Everybody that day had a memory. They talked about Joe Silvey, our salty-tongued jack-of-all-trades who ran the kitchen, gave haircuts, and perhaps most memorably, drove the bus that took the kids into town, rarely without banging something. "The guy was half-blind!" said Peter Corrigan. They remembered the legendary Lagoon Man. One night, a few counselors were walking by a bunk when they heard a strange chanting coming from inside. They went inside and found a young boy named Mario, who told them that some older boys had told them that repeating an incantation—"Owa Tagu Siam"—would keep Lagoon Man away. Of course, saying those words quickly sounds like something else.

Roy Lopez was there. Roy is part of the recent generation of Harbor alumni, a camper and then a counselor in the early 1990s and a close personal friend of mine today. I can't see Roy without thinking of the day he and I took a dozen kids aboard Rum Runner for a boating excursion out into Gardiners Bay. "From here," I told the young people, "we could travel, if we chose, all the way to Puerto Rico, where some of you are from. We can even travel to Europe or Japan." As I was talking, I started to turn and one of the kids lost his balance and bumped my steering arm as he fell to the deck. We struck a channel buoy a glancing blow, sending Roy flying off the bow and into the water. In more than fifty years of running boats and ships of every kind, including my wartime voyage around the world in a 10,000-ton LST, I'd never had anything like this occur. In an instant, I realized that Roy had gone overboard and that I'd put a hole in the boat. We were taking on water, and I had to quickly turn back to pick up Roy and get back to camp before we sank. A few days later, I was informed by a lawyer that a suit might be brought against the Harbor. But Roy came to me and said he would refuse to go along with it. He wasn't injured, but even if he were, he wouldn't dream of trying to get money from the Harbor. "I know this would cause a lot of pain and trouble, and I won't do it," he assured me. "I love Boys Harbor. This place is part of my life, and I have nothing but great respect for you."

Late in the day, we all got together for one last group photo at Three Mile Harbor. (It's on the back cover of this book). Then the command rang out—"Line up!"—just like old times. The grown-up campers—and ten or so Harbor alumni who had never been to camp—formed two lines leading into the mess hall, the oldest taking their spots farthest from the door. Then they made their way between the lines, shaking hands and exchanging hugs until the lines disappeared and everyone was inside the mess for our last meal together at Three Mile Harbor.

As I took it all in, I realized that the faces have changed but the goal remains the same. Way back in my life, I came to understand that a society that gives substance to the term "citizen" harnesses the energy and vision of its people. I became aware of the value of enfranchisement. If someone asked me what my major concern is for our nation, the answer would be the same whether it was 1946 or 1975 or 2006. I would say that for our democracy to survive, its youth at all economic and social levels must be educated. The latest tally is that the Harbor has now helped empower upwards of 45,000 young people. I pray and I believe that we will continue finding ways to help the disenfranchised claim their rightful place at the table.

When I think about my wartime experience, I think of events, of course, and of the men I served with. But I can't help but think, too, about why we fought—for democracy. All these years later—now more than ever—I think about democracy and its future. Most of us do to some extent, forced by world events to consider America's place in the world. But what about the state of democracy in the world's greatest democracy? As ever, the economy is good for some Americans but not for others. But a society that ignores the education of vast numbers of its citizens is a society at risk. To survive, a democracy depends on the will of an *educated* constituency. That's what we were fighting for six decades ago. We do live in a vastly complicated world—even within our own borders. Cultural, racial, religious, and class differences can best be addressed by an educated populace. We're well into our third century and yet our democracy hasn't reached full maturity. To survive, it must.

TWELVE

All My Children

IT IS SUNDAY, THE TENTH OF DECEMBER, 2006, midway through my eighty-ninth year, and I'm sitting in my apartment, thinking about the holidays and my children, wanting to spread some thoughts about them across the empty pages of my new notebook. Having spent so much time over the decades talking about the boys and girls of the Harbor, I'm aware that I may have left some people curious about my own wonderful children. I've had eleven of them, along with—so far—twenty grandchildren and four great grandchildren. A few years ago, in the midst of a long discussion of the Harbor, an interviewer interjected, "You've had eleven children of your own. None of them are in jail, right?" I laughed and assured him that they're all wonderful, all doing good things with their lives. With that in mind, here are a few words about—and to—my crew, in order of appearance.

Tony Junior

Tony has always been industrious and independent. One summer while at St. Paul's School, he worked as a tuna fisherman off the coast of northern Peru. He also boxed at St. Paul's and rowed on the SPS Crew at Henley in England. When he graduated from college, he insisted I not help him get ahead. He was grateful for the education I had provided him, and from then on he wanted to make it on his own. And that he did, eventually becoming managing partner of Bessemer Trust. Tony has a fine son—the third Anthony Drexel

Duke, born in 1972; a daughter, Milena; and two stepchildren, Cristina and Spencer. He and his wife, Olga, both ardent golfers, became grandparents (and I, once again, became a great grandfather) when Mackenzie was born in April of 2005.

Tony has brought much light and happiness into my life. He served diligently as treasurer of the Boys & Girls Harbor Corporation for twenty years. When complications wedged their way between us a while back, I was saddened. But throughout that thankfully brief period, I prayed for that breach to end, and my prayers were answered. So, Tony, when you read this, just know how deeply I appreciate your genuine understanding and support—as a much-loved son and friend. I am so very proud of you for the way you have handled your life. Tony, you're the best and so are you, Olga, Anthony, and Milena.

Nick

Nicholas, my first contribution to the baby boom, has been a devoted son, with all the instincts of a loving and helpful friend. Looking back on a whole string of observations and experiences and well-recalled events and times with Nick is a true pleasure for me. Once, when he was six, Nick got his foot and leg stuck through the floor of a hay wagon I was towing with a truck on our Connecticut farm. I called out to Tony Jr. to go to the work bench in the barn and get my saw so that I could cut a larger opening in the wagon floor to free Nick's leg from its entrapment. Little Nick let out a shriek of fear when his brother handed me the saw: In his mind, Dad was about to saw his leg off in order to free him.

Nick survived that episode to become a very dedicated counselor at Boys Harbor. He brought many of his friends in, and all of them were stars. Nick started out following his uncles, his father, and his brother to St. Paul's, but decided he wanted to go his own way after his second year. I respected his wishes and he transferred to the Salisbury School in Connecticut, where he blossomed. He worked hard, rowed on the crew, played guitar, and went on to Vanderbilt. He pushed himself and made it very much on his own. Nick always had his sights set on a career in education, and now he's associate director for corporate and

foundation relations in the development office of the University of Virginia. As a professional fundraiser, he's always kept his eye out for Boys and Girls Harbor, often introducing me to people who became supporters. Nick has a son, Nick Jr., who is a member of the Class of 2007 at Elon University in North Carolina. Nick and I have had some great experiences over the years, and our mutual love is stronger than ever. Nick, you're the best and so are you, Nicholas Jr., and now Gardy.

Cordelia

Cordelia, my mother's namesake, is my first daughter and the first of my four children with my second wife, Betty. Delia has always been a fantastic and lovable human being—sensitive, intelligent, beautiful. She is petite but very strong and agile, a great dancer. She has a wonderful sense of humor, as well as a strong sense of reality. I love and

Family reunion in East Hampton on my eightieth birthday, 1998.

admire Delia's husband, Reinhold, a great German photographer. They've lived in Berlin and on the Spanish Mediterranean for many years. They have two beautiful girls, Lilian and Cozima, who are both indeed my loving granddaughters, and Lilian has a beautiful daughter, my great granddaughter, Sienna. Delia, you're the best. And so are you, Reinhold, Lil and Coz, and Sienna.

Josie
My love and respect for Josie has always been a huge part of my life, and it always will be. Josie, the leader, the active scholar who protects the needy of the world. She is the rebel of the family. When she was five, she left the mess hall at camp by herself and turned up at the East Hampton Police Department, where she regaled the cops with the saga of her eight-mile journey. Fifteen years later, when she was attending

With the girls in 2001: Left to right are Josie, Delia, December, and Lulita.

Barnard, I turned on the TV to find Josie leading a group that had taken over the Columbia president's office. She was vehemently opposed to the Vietnam War, and unlike some parents, I agreed with her and admired her for taking a strong stand. Josie left school and opened a coffee house outside the army's training base in Fort Dix, New Jersey, where she tried to persuade young recruits that they were headed for a morally indefensible war. It was there that Josie met a veteran named John Brown who had been seriously wounded in Vietnam and opposed the war when he came home. John is a beloved son-in-law and friend and author of several books. Josie is a strong daughter and a strong mother of five wonderful children. Josie, you're the best and so are you, John, Moses, Jack, Earl, Cordelia, and Ben.

December

And now, December, a beauty as well. She inspires my everlasting love because of her very being, her total independence, her way of handling life and all its challenges. She's her own person, always has been, and I'm a lucky father to know fully that she returns my love in spades. She has a terrific sense of humor. She and her husband Lee are successful farmers in central Florida. December's name produces a happy picture in my head. I love her husband Lee and sons David and Luke as well and David's two children, my great grandchildren, Parker and Simon. December, you're the best and so are you, Lee, David and Luke, and Parker and Simon.

John

Son number three in the family parade, John is a leader—tough, strong, a hero to me from experiences we've shared at sea, a ship captain whose humor, knowledge, and action keep his ship happy and safe. Our relationship is close and filled with true love and mutual respect. When I think of John as I get older, I smile at his humor. And I shed a tear thinking of the time at sea when he put his life on the line to secure his shipmates' return voyage to Florida from Cuba in 1980. John and Betty are great parents to Camila and Natalia. I salute you, Son, Captain John. You're the best and so are you, Betty and Camila and Natalia. (And thank you, girls, for your great work at Boys & Girls Harbor.)

Barclay

Such a very special, kind, humane, resourceful boy and man. We were so very close. I marveled at his ability to overrule and overcome his life's hardships and challenges. His humor and philosophy overshadowed his fears. Goodness, selflessness, kindness, and bravery were part of my beloved son Barc. His name produces an emotion unlike any other because he left us all too soon and I will always miss him. His

With the boys: Clockwise from lower left: Nick, John, Doug, James, Washy, and Tony Junior.

decision to leave this world at twenty-eight, though so hard to swallow, was his. So I have consoled myself over the years respecting his accomplishments and knowing his love for all of us lives on. My powerful feelings about him have followed him and I'm sure he knows how much I love and miss him. Barc, you were the best.

Doug

Another purely special boy and man with whom I proudly and joyfully share a very special love and deep sense of appreciation. On snowy days when he was five or six, I would tow Doug and Barc on sleds to Central Park, where Doug loved climbing on my back as we slid down the hills and I pretended to be out of control of the sled. Doug loved boats and the sea from the beginning. At camp when I took Harbor kids out on the Rum Runner or the sail boat he would wait for me at the top of the dock so he could go out. Later I taught him navigation and he accompanied me on a voyage all the way to Florida from East Hampton. I encouraged him to take his first trip alone across Long Island Sound when he was sixteen. Not surprisingly, Doug wound up in the boating business, in North Carolina, as a captain of yachts that he delivers from and to New York City and Florida (and elsewhere). I've shared some adventurous, memorable experiences at sea with Doug and marvel at his knowledge and his skill as a seaman and captain. The word stalwart comes to mind. I love this man, this son of mine, with all my heart. His wife, Bee, and daughters Delaney and Georgianna are close to my heart. Doug, you're the best and so are you girls—all three of you!

Lulita

As a two-year-old she called me "Dobbie" and pinched me when I was affectionate with her mother. An able, self-dependent little girl, my much beloved daughter developed into a devoted counselor at the Harbor camp. Always a remarkably organized young lady, Lulita also loved to help me in the office, answering the phone, opening the mail, finding my glasses. As she got older, she made sure I stayed in touch with all my other children, and took the initiative in organizing holiday gatherings—no small task with children scattered across the country and overseas. I came to admire Lulita's good sense, and as she grew into adulthood I wouldn't hesitate to ask her advice on matters both business and personal. She has told me that knowing that I valued her opinion and would often act on her advice gave her confidence and independence. She married a fine man, John Reed, of whom I am very fond, and gave me two more magnificent granddaughters, Laila and Penelope. Lulita, you're the best, and so are you John, Laila, and Penelope.

Washy

Now here is a very special son whom I admire, love, and respect with all my heart. Washy has a good sense of reality—no illusions about life or the world. I had more father-and-son fun experiences with Washy when he was a kid than a father could ever wish for: an Alaskan adventure, a trip through Scotland, and watching him develop as a hockey and lacrosse player at school. He's taught me more about life than I've taught him. From early childhood Washy showed a remarkable ability to learn music as a drummer. My friend and Duke professor Paul Jeffrey recognized his talent and Washy became lead percussionist with Duke's Jazz Ensemble. He continues to play professionally around the country as well as teaching percussion to an admiring young group of Harbor students in Ramon Rodriquez's Harbor Performing Arts Conservatory. I applaud Washy's vision and tenacity as a musician. He has a real vision of his future, and I'm sure he'll reach his goals. Washy, you're the best.

James

A truly wonderful son, James has been an athlete all his life. He is a master surfer, snowboarder, and professional lifeguard. James was a terrific and dedicated counselor at the Harbor, sharing his love and knowledge of the waterfront. After college, he traveled extensively in South America and wound up teaching surfing in Peru, where he met his lovely wife, Cinthia. James returned home to East Hampton with Cinthia, and on Halloween in 2006 they welcomed their son, Diego, into the world. James has good ideas for expanding his future. I love him for his kindness and decency as a son—and now as a loving father himself. James, you're the best, and so are you, Cinthia and Diego.

They are all my children, and they are all the best!

Acknowledgments

I WISH TO FIRST EXPRESS my heartfelt appreciation to my friend Rick Firstman, who joined me when I was attempting in fits and starts to write this memoir. Rick rescued me from foundering, patiently drawing out the story of my life and skillfully guiding the book to completion over a two-and-a-half-year period. For this I am humbly grateful. I also want to express my appreciation to Rick's wife, Jamie Talan, for her encouragement and friendship. And I would be remiss if I didn't thank Pat Heller for putting Rick and me together, for it is doubtful the book would have ever been written had it not been for that introduction.

I owe a debt of gratitude to two other individuals whose help in the project's early stages was invaluable. My fine young friend Russell Antonacci ferreted out an attic full of papers, scrapbooks, Navy log books, letters, and old diary-like documents that I'd accumulated over the years and might easily have thrown away had he not flushed them out. Next, my highly admired close friend and son-in-law, John M.G. Brown, husband of my beloved daughter Josie, came along and convinced me to bite the bullet, quit stalling, and go ahead with this book. John himself had diligently written and published the results of his relentless research on the subject of American and Allied prisoners of war who disappeared in Soviet captivity from 1918 through the Vietnam War. His extraordinary accomplishment inspired me to take a crack at writing this book. Both John and Russell helped me get the writing started, and I'm deeply appreciative to both of them. I also want to acknowledge and thank Awilda Penney for her detailed research and assistance in compiling material for the book. (It was her great idea to use the maritime map of Three Mile Harbor as a background on the cover.)

Along the way, a number of people at Boys & Girls Harbor were helpful in various aspects of producing the book. They include Hans Hageman, David Hertz, Ramon Rodriguez, Julio Torres, Linda Blake, Kathy Flack, Jane Lindberg, and Julia Donaldson. Many Harbor alumni kind enough to aid my memory by tapping theirs, notably Ron Jackson, Tanya Robinson, Albie Williams-Myers, Fred Cicerelli, Tony Albarello, Roy Lopez, and Tim Gleason. I extend my deepest thanks and appreciation to Joan Harrison for keeping me afloat through busy and sometimes difficult times. Thanks to Chris Eckert for contributing a morning of photography at South Street Seaport, and to Mike Miller for his volunteer photo work for the Harbor, including the picture of me on the flap of the book jacket. Great thanks to Julio Torres for his thoughtful and comprehensive work on the wonderful Tribute book in 2005. Thanks, too, to Steve Cohn, Director of the Duke University Press.

At The Bayview Press, I thank Susan Brenna, Elaine Firstman, Amanda Talan, Dorothy Bonardi, Robert Firstman, and Allison Talan, for their work getting the book ready for publication. Joe Gannon of Mulberry Tree Press did a superb job designing the book and seeing it all the way through to press. His expertise, patience, and extraordinary care with countless details are why the book looks as good as it does.

In addition to thanking all those who were part of making this book a reality, I would like to thank the many people who have been a part of my life over time. Firstly my gratitude and respect to all Boys and Girls Harbor trustees, past and present, for their innumerable contributions of time, intelligence, and financial support. Hundreds of others flash through my mind—relatives, friends, colleagues, acquaintances, some I've known since my youth, others in the decades since. All of them have helped me in one way or another along my uncharted course and left an indelible impression on my mind. Many have left us but their spirits have not.

First, my extended family, each member of which has enriched my life and selflessly helped Boys & Girls Harbor grow: My mother Cordelia Biddle, of course, to whom this book, my life story, is dedicated. No words could adequately express my feelings. My stepfather Tom Robertson, a steadfast and calm advisor early on; my Duke and Biddle grandparents, particularly Granddaddy Biddle, a true American original; my beloved brother Angier and our father, Angier Buchanan Duke, whom we had for far too short a time. And of course all my children: my sons and daughters, sons-in-law and daughters-in-law, grandchildren and great grandchildren, to whom I've devoted Chapter Twelve.

I salute the late Tony Biddle, my much-loved and admired uncle, and equally loved brother Livingston. I lovingly thank Tony and Karen Biddle for their steadfast love and support; Margaret Biddle, whose encouragement has endured; Robin Duke, my sister-in-law, for being a strong and loving friend; my beloved cousin Mary Biddle Semans, who brought me back to Duke University and nominated me for a trustee-ship, and who has always been a loving and stalwart supporter; my cousin and beloved friend Nicholas Duke Biddle, and God bless Nellie, too; my wonderful friend Pat Hoban; Nancy Biddle, a great friend and advisor; my cousin Fay (Fuzzy) Neville, a long-time Harbor counselor; my younger cousin Toby Biddle; my niece Meg Biddle, a supreme coun-selor and everlasting friend. My much loved nephew Biddle Duke, a former counselor; my aunt Mary Duke Biddle, cousin Virginia Thaw Wanamaker, my beloved and wonderful niece Pandora Biddle Hentic and Yves, and my superb nephew Dario Duke, who served as a coun-selor, and my esteemed nephew George Biddle.

I cannot think of the Harbor without first thinking of the late Lon-nie Williams. To me, Lonnie *was* Boys & Girls Harbor, and we all miss him deeply. I thank Lonnie's wife Hazel and sons Steve and Richard for their everlasting friendship. Cutting to the present, I extend my deep appreciation to Hans Hageman for the beautiful job he is doing bring-ing the Harbor into the future. Going all the way back to the beginning, I think of old friends such as Roger Schafer, Bob Fowler, and David Challinor, all early counselors. In recent years, Luly Duke deserves much credit for organizing countless fundraising events for the Harbor.

The following are friends, many of long duration—schoolmates, shipmates, Harbor mates, and others I've loved. They've all helped me in a variety of ways and at different times. (If you don't see your-self on this list, it's my fault. I am more than a little scatterbrained at this stage.):

The late Larry Drake, my roommate at both St. Paul's School and Princeton, who personified friendship. Colton and Carley Wagner—Wag was early on a Harbor counselor and still holds our SPS class together, seventy years after we graduated. The late Walter McVeigh, who started the Harbor with me and became the abbot of the Trappist order. Quigg's brother Newt was also a lifelong friend and fellow Har-bor counselor. Lonsdale Stowell both counselor and close friend as was the late Paul Moore, who became the Episcopal bishop of New York. The late Dr. S.S. Drury, headmaster of St. Paul's School, and Dr. John Crocker, Episcopal rector at Princeton, later Rector of Groton School.

I salute the crew of my U.S.S LST 530, particularly Lts. Ragle, Sul-livan, Pierce, Bromfield, Mahoney, Geiger, Sinnett, Seiders, Benson, and Shepherd, and the stalwart crew: Tom Tegeder (what a friend!), Harold Palm, and Bob Reed. Vital as our chief motor machinist mate during the war, Bob worked tirelessly in the decades that followed to keep us together and our memories alive. He served as the 530's unofficial historian and tracked down many crew members for a reunion at the Harbor camp in East Hampton in 1990.

When it comes to exemplary Harbor alumni, I couldn't have asked for better people than Professor Albert Williams-Myers, Justice Eduardo Padro, and Tanya Robinson, among many others. Fred Cicerelli and Tony Albarello were early campers and have devoted so much of their lives to the Harbor, providing a wonderful example for the generations that have followed. My children have all been Harbor leaders and supporters, and that tradition continues through their children. My granddaughter Camila ably and effectively teaches second grade at the Harbor and her sister Natalia has taught and tutored preschool. Louie Alcebo was a great counselor. Joe Silvey was a Harbor institutions. Having been a part of the community for more than half a century, I want to thank the people of East Hampton, and that certainly includes the town's police department and fire department and everyone at Sam's Garage, especially Denise Gorgone and Brian Raab, and my good friend and attorney, Jeff Bragman.

I give my heartfelt thanks to Boys & Girls Harbor board members Stephen Dannhauser, David Knott, Mark Axelowitz, William Ackman, Richard M. Asche, Robert Barbanell, Lyor Cohen, Edward Conard, Beth Dannhauser, Richard Davis, Barry Friedberg, Dr. Vivian Gaman, Stewart Gross, Frances Hayward, David Hodgson, Kevin Kenny Jr., Merrick Kleeman, Harold Koplewicz, Sylvester Miniter, Robert Morse, Ilse Nelson, Craig Overlander, Deryck Palmer, Joe Perella, Bill and Pat Pickens, Peter Rizzo, Jane Ross, Tom Tuft, Michael Vranos and Lynn Wheat, Niathan Allen, Peter Duchin, Ben Holloway, Greg Armstrong, Janice Becker, Barbara Brannen, Michael Cinque, Lisa deKooning, Odette Duggan, Bob Horton, Warren Goins, Dr. Paul Jeffrey, Paul Johansen, Ron Lawson, Felipe Luciano, Lisa Fox Martin, John Roche and Chris Williams.

Aside from the many who have selflessly served on the Harbor's board, I give special thanks to some of our most generous benefactors: Robert Tishman, Arthur and Janet Ross, and Julian and Josie Robertson.

Others I want to thank, in no particular order: Christy Alcebo, Tom Hollyman, Mary Birch, and Nick Rutgers; my much-loved godsons Lang Phipps, Tony Kiser, Monty Waterbury, and Josh Warner; John Kiser, Bill Carey, Frank Carey, John and Joyce McGinn, Socrates Ortiz,

Larry Williams, my friend and helper Valerie Smith. Next, Colin Fraser, and most generous Ellen Fraser, Jerry Murray, Rory Corrigan, Peter Corrigan, Townsend Grey, George Vietor, Eddie Indellicati, Chee Holder and her children, Alice Connick Ryan, Peter Connick, Tom Bancroft, George Bodman, Mary Brock, Lisa Stewart, Jim Karish, Dick Mead, Pam LeBoutillier, John LeBoutillier, Bartlett Goble, Joe Dolan, Frank Dixon, Whitney Stevens, Tommy Phipps, Sally Phipps, Mary Phipps, Warner Griffin, Betty Ordway, Diane Douglas, Alice Rutgers Dodge, my younger cousin John Biddle Brock, Joe McCoy, Cotty Jeffcott, Esme O'Brien, Karen Aromi, JoAnne DiPasquale, Dale Netter, Otis Andrews, Karen Collins, Paul Lambermont, Raymond Frazer, Lee Carney, Dale Miller, Joey Miller, Avie Clark, Shot Warner, Mary Ellen McGuire, Bob McGuire, Terry McGuire, Fred Overton, Joe Dolan, Guy Rutherford, Peter Grace, Michael Grace, Peter Smith, Miley Smith, Joe McCoy, John Coleman, Mike Marrone, Tom Bancroft, Eden Foster, Donald Walsh, Cord Meyer, Julian McKee, Chris Herter, Dr. Stanley Mirsky and Sue, Jennifer, and John Mirsky, Drs. Annie and Nina Qu, Dr. Hector Castro, Dr. Michael Poon, Paul Kulakowski, and my barber for fifty years, Cesar.

Also Charlie Dean, Howard Dean. Andre Dean Kathleen Gerard, Dina Merrill Hartley, Valerie Hoagland Smith, Rees Jones, Jack and Elizabeth Kennedy, Alec and Judy Laughlin, Ann LeConey, Mimi Meehan, Yves and Pat Robert, Cliff Robertson, Dudley Roberts, Dan Rose, Eden Foster, Stan Rumbough, Charles and Colette Russell, Anita Salembier, Joe and Nancy Scheerer, Idoline Scheerer, Warren Schwerin, Cooky Dixon, Bill Simon, Jarvis Slade, Peter and Miley Smith, Alix Smith, Phillip Grucci and Family, Joey Annunzio, Socrates Ortiz, Charlie Burg, Gabe Wilder, Larry Williams, Edwin Gibson, Luiz, Gloria Schwartz, Mayors John Lindsay, Bob Wagner, Abe Beame, and Mike Bloomberg, Presidents Roosevelt, Kennedy Eisenhower, and Clinton. Winnie Hatch and her sister Courtia; Peter and Marie Minnick.

Colin Ambrose and Jessica, Andres and Ines Bausili, Albert and Kay Bellas, Michael and Helen Bellas, Tony Boalt, Gavin and Kathryn Breckinridge, Dan and Patricia Breen, Henry and Joanne Breyer, Geoff and Roxanne Briggs, Bill and Natalia Brinkerhoff, Charles and Mary Jane Brock, the whole Arthur Ross family, Tony and Leelee Brown, Polly Bruckman, Kathleen Buddenhagen, George & Joyce Bullen, Chuck and Sue Bullock, Robert and Dale Burch, Mark and Paula Butler, Ingrid Burns, Russell and Anne Byers, Ward and Pat Carey, Doug and Leslie Chambers, Ann Chapman, Ned and Lynn Chase, Chevy and Jayni Chase, Peter and Catherine Connick, Philipe and Deborah

Dauman, Bill Doyle and Kathleen, Spencer and Sara Davis, Mary Deliagre, Bob and Betsy DeVecchi, Alfred and Barbara Decendorf, Bill Draker, Charles and Mary Durkin, John and Josephine Eastman, Albert and Eleanor Edelman, Sally Edwards, Elizabeth Fondaras, Helena, Colon and Rebecca Fraser, Richard and Susan Farland, Anthony Gerard, John Hersey, John and Errol Giordano, George and Marcie Gowen, Bill and Adele Grant, Dr. Joseph and Alexandra Kazickas, Joe and Lucy Kazickas, James and Bridget Lamb, David and Brooke Laughlin, Gary and Carolyn Lind, Dick and Cassandra Look, Bob and Betty Loughead, James and Marianne Lowery, Frank and June Larkin, Walter and Jane Maynard, James and Judy Makrianes, Frank Mansell, Dr. William Anlyan, Mimi Meehan, and Carl and Cordelia Menges, Doug and Patricia Mercer, Rev. Francis Mercer, Jim and Marianne Lowrey, David and Lee MacCallum, James and Judy Makrianes, Frank Mansell, Dr. Charles Miner and Claire, Dr. Ollie Moore, Alfred and Virginia Morgan, John and Natalie Spencer, Katherine Sutro, Henry and Martha Murray, Tom and Maurine Murtagh, Morgan and Jennifer Moyer, Joan and Owen McGiver, Dr. David and Diane Paton, Billy and Kathryn Rayner, Yves Robert and Pat, Jaquelin and Anya Robertson, Julian and Josie Robertson, Stanley and Leah Rumbough, Charles and Colette Russell, Allan and Alice Ryan, Anita Salembier, Angel and Caterine Santamarina, Joe and Nancy Scheerer, Warren and Virginia Schwerin, Jimmy and Julie Sykes, Ted and Barbara Terry, Terry and Betty Teryazos, Roger and Florence Thiele, Mary Tiedenman, Hugh and Helen Tilney, James and Sharon Tompkins, Senen and Joy Ubina, Lew and Diane von Amerongen, Jonathan and Candace Wainwright, Stuyvesant Wainwright II, III and IV, Maud Walker, David & Lisa Walker, Ted and Jane Walkowicz, Ira Washburn and Calista, Anne Washburn, Hope and Susan Waterbury, John and Beth Werweiss, Anne Williams, George and Linda Yates, Mike Womer, Remar Sutton, Phillip Rush, Edwin Gibson, Daphne Richards, Bernard J. Keller, and Will and Lu Robeson.

Lastly, I would like to thank my canine companions, four generations of labradors and a whole bunch of other breeds, all much loved by me and all of my kids and grandkids and Harbor kids: Balogna, Duchess, Sailor, Bang Bang, Chief, Coltrane, Chulo, Peaches, Sampson, Buddy, Monkey, Tucker, and Penny.

Index

italicized page numbers indicate photographs

A Bell for Adano, 181
A.D. Duke Realty, 232, *233*
Absecon, New Jersey, 162
Agency for Child Development, 242
Air Coupe, 196
Air Force One, 243
Albarello, Tony, 111, 119–20, *216–17*
Allen, John F., 28
Allen, Naithan, *189*
Alliance of New York State Arts
    Organizations, 282
Alongi, Tom, 106, *216*
Amaden, Jim 197–199, 201
American Camping Association, 196
American Can Company, 183
American Expeditionary Forces, 20
American Tobacco Company, 29, 32,
    56
Andrews Air Force Base, 244
Andrews, Steve, *216*
Angier Buchanan Duke Scholarship,
    285–6
Aphrodite, 265–67
Arkansas Bear, The, 190
Arizona State University, 231
Arlington National Cemetery, 247
Astaire, Fred, 265
Astor, Colonel John Jacob, 261–262
Astor, Brooke, 261–62, 264, 289, 298
Astor, Vincent, 261–62
Atkinson, Brooks, 254

Atlantic City, New Jersey, 16, 18–19,
    22, 25
Austrian Alps, 89, 128

Baldridge, Tish, 240, 246
Baldwin Auditorium, 49
Baldwin, Hanson, 168
Ball, Tom, 110
Baltimore, Maryland, 40
Bankers Trust, 183, 283
Basset, John Spencer, 32
Bates, Richie, 191, 213, *220*
Batista, Fulgencio, 235, 291–92
Battle of Tarawa, 160
Battles, Mickey, 227
Bauer's Drug Store, 63
Bay of Pigs, 293
Beame, Abe, 278
Beatrix, Princess of the Netherlands,
    248
Beauvais School, 58, 104
Beck, Jozef, 129
Belgium, 130, 134–35
Belleau Wood, Battle of, 20, 162
Ben Nevis mountain, *100*
Berkeley Square, 135
Berlin, Germany, 86, 127, 324
Bessemer Trust, 322
Bianco, Paul, 197
Biddle, Anthony Joseph Drexel
    (maternal grandfather), 9–10,
    13–20, *21*, 22–24, 35, 36, 37–40,

Biddle, Anthony – continued
44–45, 56, 63, 80, 82, 88–90, 92,
102, 113–14, 159–60, *161,*
162–163, 179–80, 192, 253–255
Biddle, Anthony Joseph Drexel Jr.
(uncle), 22, 24–25, *36,* 39, 41,
43–44, 46, 50, 55, 58, 63, 78–80,
87–88, 93, 94, 97, 128–136,
145–148, *164,* 166, 180, 235–36,
238–39, 242, 248, 253, 286
Biddle, Cordelia Bradley (maternal
grandmother), 16, 19, 24, 35, *36,*
37, 44, 160, 254
Biddle, Craig, 13
Biddle, Edward, 11–14
Biddle, Emily Drexel, 12–13, 193
Biddle, Livingston, 15, 21, 24, 26, *36,*
58, 76–77, 80, 179–80, 231, 256
Biddle, Nicholas, 109, *110, 123,* 163,
164, 166, 217–18, 290
Biddle, Sarah, 10
Biddle, William, 10, 12
Big Apple Circus, 285
Big Brothers of New York, 101, 111,
115, 119
Black Panthers, 273, 275
Black, Roy, 140
Blackwell, W.T. and Company, 28
Blue Book of the American
Automobile Association, 19
Boca Raton, Florida, 234
Bonsack, James, 28–29
Boothe, Gardner, *216*
Boyd Theater, 255
Boys (and Girls) Harbor, 118, 183,
200, 202, 204, 206–08, *209,*
210–11, 214–19, 221–23, *224–25,*
226–29, 232, 242, 249, 252–55,
257, 260, 263, 265, 268–70, 273,
276, 289–90, 301, 305, *318,* 324
Boys and Girls Harbor Alumni Society,
216–17
Bradley, Alexander, 18

Breen, Doc, 70
Brereton, William D., 127–28, 137
Brock, John Biddle, *266*
Brokaw, Tom, 315
Bromfield, Geoffrey, 142
Bronx, New York, 101, 262
Brooklyn Bridge, 106
Brooklyn Dodgers, 218
Brooklyn Navy Yard, 142, 163, 186
Brooklyn, New York, 106, 143, 165,
169, 186
Brown, Josephine Duke (daughter), 6,
170, 178, 208, 230, *233–34,* 257,
325–26
Bryn Mawr, Pennsylvania, 23
Buckingham Palace, 25
Buckner Bay, 168
Buenos Aires, Argentina, 126–28, 235,
249
Bullitt, William, 130, 132, 147
Bullitt, Logan, 12
Bundy, McGeorge, 245
Burlington, New Jersey, 10

Cambodia, 268, 295
Campagna, Matty, 219
Cape Cod, Massachusetts, 82–83
Capote, Truman, 261
Carey, Bill, 231, 315
Carey, Emily, 315–16
Carey, Frank, 315
Carey, Hugh, 298
Carey, W.P. & Company, 231
Carey, W.P., School of Business, 231
Carter, Jimmy, 295–96, 299
Caruso, Dorothy, 43
Caruso, Enrico, 17, 43
Casale, Tommy, *216*
Casey, Jim, 137–38
Catholic Worker Movement, 187
Cedarhurst, Long Island, 56
Challinor, David, *110*
Chaplin, Charlie, 65

Charlottesville, Virginia, 33
Cherbourg, France, 149–50
Chesapeake Bay, 139, 148
Chesebro, Mary, 261
Chicago White Sox, 284
Chicago, Illinois, 42, 141
Churchill, Winston, 139, 147, 149, 153, 158–59
Cicerelli, Fred, 111–12, 115, 120, *216*
Circulo de Armas, 127
Civil War, U.S., 11, 26, 28, 76, 194
Clarke, Dr. Kenneth, 217–18
Clarke, Mamie, 218
Amory, Cleveland, 253
Cold Spring Harbor, New York, 73
Collegiate School, 314
Collier's Weekly, 251
Colonial Housing Project, 276
Colonial Trust Company, 125
Columbia University, 108, 310, 314
Concord, New Hampshire, 24, 80
Confederate Navy, 26
Cooper, Gary, 65, 153, 218–19
Cornwells Heights, 194
Corrigan, Paul, 163
Corrigan, Peter, 320
Council of American Ambassadors, 299
Crichton, Kyle, 17, 250–51, 253–54
Cromwell, Oliver, 10
Cross Cut cigarettes, 28
Cuban National Bank, 234
Czechoslovakia, 135

D-Day, See World War II
Dalmores, Charles, 18
Danbury, New Hampshire, 101
Darin, Bobby, 268
Davidson, John, 254
Daytona Beach, Florida, 39
Dean, Charlie, 268
Dean, Howard, 268
Death of a President, The, 245–48

De Gaulle, Charles 245, 247
Delphians, 82, 84
Dempsey, Jack, 20
Denmark 71,130, 248
Deutsche Bank, 127, 158
Diamond, Legs, 65, 66, 67
Diario Las Americas, 293
Disney, Walt, 10, 254
Dollfuss, Englebert, 90, 93–94
Dorset Hotel, 51
Drake, Larry 81, 82, 104,
Drexel Biddle Publishing Company, 20
Drexel, Anthony, 13, 16
Drexel, Francis, 11,
Drexel, Francis Jr., 11
Drexel, Katherine, 193–95
Drexel, Mary, 23
Drexel, Morgan and Company, 11
Drury, Samuel Smith, 80, 85, 101
Duchess of Windsor, 65
Duck Island, 109–10, 113, 120, 124, 141, 170, 185, 190, *216*–17, 220, 309
Duke Blue Devils, 77
Duke Endowment, 32, 49, 286
Dukes of Durham, The, 9, 27
Duke Power Company, 32, 49, 50
Duke Tobacco Company, 30, 35, 109, 287, 294
Duke University, 32, 48–49, 56, 76, 175, 286, 288, 294
Duke of Durham cigarettes, 30
Duke, Angier Biddle (brother), 45–46, *47*, 48–50, 52–53, *54*, 55–58, 60, 69, 81, 85–87, 91, *92*, 93–98, *100*, *123*, 159–60, *164*, 166–67, 168, 174–75, 200, 235–248, 255, 288, 295–96, *297*, 298–300, 303, *313*
Duke, Pony, 298, 300
Duke, Angier Buchanan (father), 5, 9, 15, 28, 33, *36*, 38, 40, *41*, 44, 175–76, 230, 235, 254, 286

Duke, Anthony Drexel,
  at Greenvale School, 69–75
  at Okinawa, 166–69
  at St. Paul's School, 79–81, 84–85,
    99–100
  at St. Paul's School camp, 101–05
  at Princeton, 108, 120, 122, 124
  Boys Harbor, early years of,
    196–215
  camp at Duck Island, 106–21
  celebrating end of war, 170–72
  childhood in New York and Old
    Westbury, 60–77
  commanding USS LST 530, 139–73
  D-Day invasion, 148–56
  family background of: Biddles,
    9–10, 14–26; Drexels, 11–13;
    Dukes, 26–33
  father's death, 53–56
  friendship with Mayor Wagner,
    219–21
  friendship with George Plimpton, 5,
    283
  fundraising, 260–66, 270, 283–85
  gorilla prank at camp, 116–20
  growth of the Harbor (1950s),
    215–27
  growth of the Harbor to Heckscher
    Building, 277–79, 282
  held by Nazis at age 16, 94–98
  in real estate business, 232–35
  in Navy intelligence in Argentina,
    126–28
  in U.S. Navy, 125–28, 136–59,
    162–73
  in South Pacific, 165–73
  incident with Black Panthers,
    272–75
  interest in world events as teenager,
    85–99
  learning to fly, 137–38
  Lagoon Man legend, 201–03, 320
  Lord's Highway Camp, 178–93

Mariel boatlift, 295–96
  marriage to Alice Rutgers, 124–25,
    176–77
  marriage to Betty Ordway, 178, 230
  marriage to Didi Douglas, 257
  marriage to Luly Alcebo, 291
  meeting General Eisenhower,
    145–46
  military surplus business after war,
    177–78
  on board of trustees of Duke
    University, 285–90
  philosophy of Boys Harbor, 221–23
  relationship with John F. Kennedy,
    82–84, 240–43
  relationship with Lonnie Williams,
    227–29, 269–70
  parents' courtship and marriage,
    34–42
  parents' divorce, 51–52, 175–76
  suicide of son Barclay, 305–09
  trip to Austria, 1934, 89–98
  trip to Europe, 1932, 86–88
  trip to India, 1954, 210–11
  visits to Durham as child, 48,
    56–58
  setting up camp in Southampton
    (1936), 105–06
Duke, Anthony Drexel Jr. (son), 138,
  165, 220, 233–35, 248–50, 257,
  283, 307, 322–23, 327
Duke, Barclay (son), 6, 232–33,
  257–259, 268, 277, 301, 303–05,
  306, 207–08, 327–28
Duke, Benjamin Newton (paternal
  grandfather), 29, 30, 31–33, 47, 48,
  50, 56–57, 76, 296
Duke, Betty Alcebo, 291, 294–95, 300
Duke, Betty Ordway (wife), 178–79,
  203, 208, 211, 227, 230–32
Duke, Biddle, 303
Duke, Brodie, 28
Duke, Camila Alcebo, 291

Duke, Dario, 240
Duke, Diane Douglas ("Didi," wife), 232, 255, 257
Duke, Doris, 11, 45, 58, 109, 199, 288–90, 296
Duke, Douglas (son), 6, 232–33, 257, 277, *326, 327*–28
Duke, James (son), 294, *297,* 307, *327,* 329
Duke, James Buchanan ("Buck"), 28–29, *31,* 32–33, 44–45, 48–50, 56, 58, 76, 89, 288, 294, 296
Duke, John (son), 6, 230, *233*–34, 257, 277, 291, 298, 320, 327
Duke, Lulu, 240, 255
Duke, Luly (wife), 291–295, 299, 300
Duke, Maria–Luisa, 240
Biddle, Mary Duke, 33, 40, *41,* 44, 89
Duke, Nanaline Buchanan, 296
Duke, Natalia Alcebo, 291
Duke, Nicholas (son), 6, 177, 208, 218, 230, *233*–34, 255, 257, 290, 323, *327*
Duke, Robin, 53, 131, 240–*41,* 246, 248, 299
Duke, Sarah Pearson Angier ("Ga-Ga," paternal grandmother), 12, *31,* 38, 44–45, *47,* 48–50, 56–57, 76–77, 286
Duke, W. and Sons and Company, 28
Duke, Washington, 6, 11, 26–27, 29, *30,* 31–32, 57, 288
Duke, Washington ("Washy," son), 6, 294, *297,* 307, *327,* 329
Dunkirk, Battle of, 98, 139, 150, 153
Durden, Robert F., 9, 27, 33
Durham, North Carolina, 27–29. 31–33, 38, 44, 49, 56–58, 76, 285–90
Dutchess County, New York, 126, 177

East Hampton, Long Island, 197–98, 202–07, 211–12, 219, 232, 239, 256, 259–60, 264, 276, 283–84. 286, 297, 305, 317–18, *322–23,* 324, 327
East Harlem School, 315
Ebbets Field, 218
Einstein, Albert, 237
Eisenhower, Dwight D. 84, 146–48, 152–53, 163, *164,* 167, 180, 236, 247, 265, 292
El Colegio de Belén, 292
El Museo del Barrio, 279
El Salvador 235–37, 299
Emily N. Carey Harbor High School, 315–17
English Channel, 145, 166
Estonia, 130
Exodus House, 314–15

Felix Estate 284–85
Fiat Company, 33
Fiduciary Trust Company, 283
Finland, 130
Fishers Island, 249
Fitzsimmons, Bob, 17–18
Flack, Kathy, 319
Florida Everglades, 10
Flushing Meadows, 196
Flying Point Beach, 286
Flynn, Errol, 115
Forbes, 261
Ford Foundation, 214, 264
Fordham University, 140, 190
Fort Lauderdale, Florida, 232–234
Fort Schuyler, New York, 139
Fowler, Bobby, 82, 162
Franco, Francisco, 98
Friendship Foundation, 300
Froggy Fairy Tales Do or Die, 18
Fruenther, Alfred M. *164*

Gandhi, Mahatma, 210
Gardiners Bay, 64, 197, 320
Garson, Greer, 254

Garvin Estate, 72
Gehres, Bob, *110*
Gehrig, Lou 218
Gerard, Betty 59
Gerard, Juilian 59
Gibbons, General, 153–155
Gibson, Charles Dana, 260
Gibson Girls, 260
Gibson, Irene, 260
Giller, Susan, 303
Ginter, Lewis, 28
Gladstone Hotel, 15
Global Economic Forum, 299
Glück, Gustave, 127–28, 158, 296
Gold Beach, 156
Goldberg, Arthur, 244
Golden, Frankie, 188, 227
Goodman, Ray, 230
Gould, George, 25
Gould, Jay, 25
Gould, Marjorie, 25
Grace Church, Newark, N.J., 187, 213
Grace, Michael, 75
Grant, Ulysses S., 11–12, 245
Great Depression, 75, 99
Great Society, 270
Greece, 135
Greene, Justin, 226
Greensboro, North Carolina, 28
Greenvale School, 69–70, 72, 76–77
Greenwich Village, 20
Greenwich, Connecticut, 53, 55
Griffis, A. Stanton, 235
Grizzard, George, 254
Grosvenor Neighborhood House, 273
Grosvenor Square, 135, 145, 273
Grucci, Felix 284
Grucci, Felix Sr. 285
Grucci Fireworks, 284–85
Guadalcanal, 140, 162, 185–86
Guam, 166, 168
Guantanamo Bay, Cuba, 166
Guild Hall, 284

Guilford College, 30
Guiliani, Rudy, 285
Gulf of Mexico, 142
Gutherman, Robert, 195

Hackensack River, 190
Hageman, Erika, 314
Hageman, Hans 314–317
Hageman, Ivan, 314
Hageman, Leola, 314
Hageman, Lynn, 314
Haines, Thurston, *220*
Hands Creek 199, 201–02
Hanfstaengl, Ernst 86, 87–88
Hans J. Morgenthau Award, 296, 286
Happiest Millionaire, The, 10, 253–54
Harbor Conservatory for Performing Arts, 282, *318*
Harbor Science and Arts Charter School, 314
Harry's New York Bar, 133
Harlem, New York, 111, 232, 262, 268, 272, 276, 278, 282, 311, 313–15
Harson, Roosevelt, *220*
Harvard University, 34, 83–84, 86–87, 190, 261, 314
Havana, Cuba, 234, 291–95, 299–300
Haydn Foundation, 264
Heckscher Foundation for Children, 278
Heidelberg, Germany, 14
Heimwehr, 95–96
Hell's Kitchen, 101, 226
Hennessey, Dick, 63–64, 74–75
Henry, Ayanna, 276
Henry, Vincent, 275–76
Hersey, John, 181–83
Hindenburg, Paul von, 86–87
Hiroshima, 170, 181, 248,
Hitler, Adolf, 65, 86–88, 90, 94, 97–98, 124, 126–128, 134, 158, 237, 251

Hoban, Pat, 56, *62*, 68, *252*, 286
Holder Hall, 108
Holland, 130, 134
Holloway, Ben, 288
Hollyman, Tom, 181
Hollywood Reporter, The, 255
Holocaust, 129
Holy Trinity Episcopal Church,
    Philadelphia, 19, 40
Hoover, Herbert, 74
Hoover, J. Edgar, 89, 245
Hotel Bristol, 94
Hot Springs, Virginia, 89
House of Lords, 20
Hull, Cordell, 132, 147,
Humphrey, Hubert, 244, 286
Hungary, 131, 237, 295
Huntington, Long Island, 73
Hurt, Harry, 61
Hyannisport, 83

Idlewild Field, 56
Indellicati, Eddie *216*
International Rescue Committee,
    237, 295
Isthmians (at St. Paul's School), 82
Italy 33, 131, 284
Iwo Jima, 168

Jackson, Charles, 267
Jackson, John, 108
Jackson, Ron, 267–68, 311, *313*, 318,
    321
Jacksonville, Florida, 138
James B. Duke House, 298
Janots, Joe, *216*
Jefferson Boat & Machine Company, 141
Jefferson, Indiana, 141
Jeffrey, Paul, 328
Jersey City, New Jersey, 187–191,
    213–14, 226, 228–29, 311
Jessup's Neck, 107, 116, 201
Johnson, Jack, 16

Johnson, Lady Bird, 248
Johnson, Lyndon B., 243, 246–48, 270
Jones, Warner, 175–76
Jung, Cordelia Duke (daughter), 6,
    178, 208, *224*, 230, *233–34*, 257,
    304, 324, *326*
Juno Beach, 151, 155

Kahn, Max, 255
Karish, Jim, *220*
Katsafouros, George, *216*
Katz, Alfred, 210
Kaufmann, Al, 16
Kennedy Airport, 56
Kennedy, Bobby, 83, 242, 244
Kennedy, Caroline, 246
Kennedy, Eunice, 83, 244
Kennedy, Jackie, 239–*41*, 243–46
Kennedy, John F., 82–84, 237–38,
    240, *241*, 242–49, 270, 293
Kennedy, Joseph P., 83
Kennedy, Joseph P. Jr., 83
King Alfonso X111, 90–91, *92*, 93
King, Harry, 300–01
Kingston, New York, 196, 200, 211
Kissinger, Henry, 298
Kliemisch, Rudy, *216*
Koplewicz, Harold, 305
Kresge Foundation, 264
Kristallnacht, 129
Krock, Arthur, 238–39

LCT landing crafts, 139, 142
LCVP landing crafts, 139, 142, 155, 173
LST 530, 5, 139–43, *144*, 148–149, 151,
    152, 153, 155–158, 162, 165, *167*,
    168, 170, *172*, 177, 309, *312*, 320
Lackawanna Railroad, 183
Lagoon Man, 202, 321
Lakewood, New Jersey, 24, 34
Langhorne, Nancy (Lady Astor), 260,
Latvia, 130
Laurel Hollow, Long Island, 73

Lawford, Patricia Kennedy, 298
Lawless, John, 23, 42
LeBoutillier, Marjorie, 69, 74
LeHavre, France, 150
Lebeck, Dickey, 117
Lewis, Freddy, 69
Lexington (battle cruiser), 173
Liebling, A.J, 129, 130, 132–36
Lincoln Hall, 226
Lincoln Hospital for Negroes, 29
Lindbergh, Charles, 69–70
Linden, Patricia, 192
Lindsay, John, 109, 298
Lindsay, Mary, 298
Lipper, Ken, 310
Lithuania, 130
Locust Valley, Long Island, 227, 230
Lombardi, Vince, 140
London, England, 19, 55, 83, 105,
    134–36, 143, 145–48, 159, 178,
    236, 261, 286
Long Beach, Long Island, 45
Long Island Sound 53, 105, 179, 197,
    327
Long Island University, 299
Lopez, Roy, 320–21
Lord Waldorf Astor, 262
Lord's Highway, Connecticut, 179–80,
    183, 200
Lower East Side, New York, 101, 103,
    106, 187–88, 214
Luce, Henry III, 298
Luciano, Felipe, 275
Luxembourg, 135
Lyceum Theater, 254
Lyme Bay, 148–49
Lynn, Jeffrey, 240

MacArthur, Douglas, 25
MacMurray, Fred, 10, 254–55
Machione, Tony, 102
McMahon, Miss Mackie, 52–53,
    55–56, 60, 70–72

Madeira Islands, 14, 19
Madrid, Spain, 133, 235, 238, 248
Maidstone, Chris, 90, 94–96, 98
Malawi, 214
Malcolm X, 268
Manchester, William, 245, 247–48
Manhasset Bay, 53
Manhasset, Long Island, 53, 60, 175, 265
Manhattan Opera Company, 18
Manhattan, New York, 56, 58, 99,
    214, 275–76, 285, 314
Manice family, 72
Mann, Harrington, 52–55, 297
Mansfield, Mike, 247
Mariel Harbor, Cuba, 295
Marshall, George C. ,147
Marshall, Thurgood, 218
Martha's Vineyard, 83
Marx Brothers, 251
Mary Poppins, 254–55
Mary's Deli, 204
Mattituck, Long Island, 115
McCall, Jim, 82–83
McCone, John, 245
McCoy, Joe, 115, 119
McGovern, George, 287
McKee, Julian Jr., 266
McKinley, William, 183
McNally, Jack, 246–47
McNeil, Don, 137
McQuatters, Eugenia ("Genie"), 131,
    135–36
McSherry, December Duke (daughter),
    6, 178, 207–08, 230, 233, 257, 326
McVeigh, Newton, 110
McVeigh, Walter ("Quigg"), 59, 104,
    109, 110, 113, 117, 119, 162, 174,
    191
Meadow Brook Hounds Club, 73
Mediterranean Sea, 248
Mein Kampf 90, 97
Merchantville, New Jersey, 16–17
Metropolitan Club of Washington, 239

Metropolitan Museum of Art, 43
Meyer, Cord, 109, 162
Meyer, John Jr., *110, 216*
Miami Jai-Alai, 293
Miami, Florida, 138
Milford Haven, Wales, 143
Military Manual of Advanced Science in Individual Combat, 18–19
Miller, Gilbert, 90
Minnesota Mining and Manufacturing Company (3M), 178
Miss Walker's School, 23–26, 38, 42
Missionary Society (at St. Paul's School), 101, 109
Montauk, Long Island, 83
Moore, Bill, 82
Moore, Grace, 59
Moore, Jenny, 187
Moore, Paul, 81–82, 104, 109, 117, 162, 183, 187–88, *189,* 191, 208, 213, 226, 228
Morgan family 73, 75
Morgan, J.P., 11, 193
Morgan, John Pierpont, 11
Morocco, 16, 296
Morrison, John, 234
Munich, Germany, 86–88, 158
Murther, Howard, *216*
Muttontown, Long Island, 73
Myers, Kim, 213–214

NAACP, 187, 194, 214, 218
New York University Child Study Center, 305
New York University Law School, 285
Nabisco, 183
Nacional Hotel (Havana, Cuba), 234
Nagasaki, Japan, 170
Nassau County Police Department, 64
National Committee on American Foreign Policy, 296
National Golf Club of Southampton, 218

Nazi Party, 65, 87, 90, 92–97, 126–29, 131–32, 134, 158, 296
Nehru, Jawaharlal 210
Nemy, Enid, 255
Netherlands, 135, 248
Neville, Fay, 231
New Delhi, India, 210
New Garden School, 28
New Hampshire, 24, 44, 80, 98, 101, 105, 121, 184
New Jersey, 10, 16, 23–24, 34, 44, 82, 104, 124, 162, 166, 183, 203, 269, 305, 307, 325
New Orleans, Louisiana, 141–42, 194
Nation, The, 99
New Republic, The, 99
New York Boys Club, 101, 111, 115, 179, 208, 211
New York Harbor, 165
New York *Herald Tribune,* 240, 265
New York *Herald,* 55
New York Times, The, 97, 168, 210, 238, 253, 296
New Yorker, The, 129
New York State Athletic Commission, 20
New York State legislature, 20, 312
New Zealand, 185
Newman, Paul, 315
Newsday, 299
Norfolk, Virginia, 142
Normandy, 55, 140, 148, 150–51, *152,* 153, 158, 169, 193
North Carolina, 9, 26–29, 32–33, 38, 44, 48, 56, 76, 231, 257, 287, 294, 304, 324, 327
North, Bob, 242, 278
Norway, 128–29, 134–35, 299

Office of Naval Intelligence, 125–26
Officer Candidates School, 125
Ohio River, 141
Ohio State University, 210

Ohnishi, Takijiro, 169
Okinawa, Japan, 166–69, 198
Old Hundreds (at St. Paul's School), 82
Old Westbury, New York, 61–63, 65, 68, 99, 252, 256
Olivier, Laurence, 265
Ordway, Lucius Pond, 178
Orient Point Ferry, 105
Oslo, Norway, 128–29
Otis Company, 279
Overton, Fred, 115, 119
Oxford University, 95, 285
O'Biddle, Tim, 19
O'Brien Jack, 18–19, 23
O'Brien, William T., 31

Padro, Eduardo, 277, 285, *318*
Palm Beach, Florida, 38, 104
Palomares, Spain, 248
Pan American Clipper, 135
Pardue, Austin, 205–07
Paris Nights magazine, 69
Paris Review 283
Paris, France, 60, 64, 66, 69–70, 86, 90, 130, 132–33, 164, 178, 283
Parris Island, 20
Patton, William, 156
Peace Corps, 214, 244, 249–50, 257, 283
Peanuts, Johnny, 61, 75
Pearl Harbor, 126–27, 136, 158, 166, 265
Peconic Bay, 83, 106, 111
Pell, Claiborne, 108–09, 116–17, *118*, 120, 162, *220*, 237, 240–41
Penn Station, 108, 174
Penn, William, 10
Perkins, Maxwell, 251
Peru, 249, 295, 321
Petain, Henri Philippe, 134
Philadelphia, 10–12, 14, 16–20, 22, 24, 34–36, 38–39, 41–43, 45, 68,

70, 79, 160, 179, 251–52, 255, 304
Philadelphia Academy of Music, 17
Philadelphia *Evening Bulletin*, 39
Philadelphia *Public Ledger*, 14, 16, 194
Philadelphia Sunday Graphic, 18
Philadelphia Symphony Orchestra, 17
Phipps, Tommy, 68, 73, 261, 289, 302
Phipps, Nora, 260
Pidgeon, Walter, 253–54
Piedmont Mountains, 26
Pierce, Charlie, 140, 163
Pike, Lester, *110*
Pin Head cigarettes, 28
Pittsburgh, 16, 37, 77, 205–06
Place de la Comedie, 133
Plimpton, George, 5, 283–85
Plymouth Harbor, 163
Plymouth, England, 144, 148–49, 157
Pocono Mountains, 35
Poland 129–32, 134–35, 147–48
Police Gazette, 46
Pollier, Justine Wise 219, 221
Polo Grounds, 45
Pompano Beach, Florida, 232
Pope John II, 195
Portugal, 14
Porter, Cole, 65
Potsdam, 147
Powell, Adam Clayton, 268
Powers, James, 255
Presences, 184–85
Princeton University, 34, 58, 108, 120, *122*, 124, 141, 177, 185, 187, 190, 231, 269, 314, 317
Pro Bono Publico tobacco, 26
Prophet's Chamber, 184
Providence, Rhode Island, 166
Puente, Tito, 283

Quantico Sentry 160
Quantico, Virginia 20, 160
Queen Frederika, 248

Racquet Club, *123,* 148, 174, 261
Ragle, George, 140, 150, 154,
Ramsay, Sir Bertram, 150
Randolph County, North Carolina, 29
Reagan, Ronald, 194
Reed, Bob, 172, 332
Reed, Lulita Duke (daughter), 6, *281,* 294, 300, 307, *326,* 328–29
Reynaud, Paul, 132–34
Rhineland, Germany, 87
Richmond, Virginia, 28
Ridgeway, Matthew, 236
Riggs, Bobby, 137
Rittenhouse Square, Philadelphia, 17, 40, 43, 193
River Club, 166
Robertson, Cordelia Drexel Biddle (mother), 9, 12, 14–21, 24–27, 31, 33–35, *36,* 37–40, *41,* 42–46, *47,* 48, 50–53, 55–56, 58–61, *62,* 63–66, *67,* 68–69, 71–72, 74–81, 85–87, 89–94, 97, 99, 106, 109, 115, 145, 165–68, 170, 174–76, 179–80, 191–93, *225,* 235, 249, 250–1, *252,* 253–70, 289–90, 298, 300–04
Robertson, Thomas Markoe (stepfather), 59–61, *62,* 64–66, 68, 75, 85–87, 91, *92,* 93, 97, 108, 165, 167–68, 251, 254–56, 300
Robeson, Paul, 187–188
Robinson, Jackie, 218
Robinson, Tanya, 276, 277, *318*
Rockefeller Foundation, 264
Rodriguez, Ramon, 282, *318*
Rolls-Royce. 26, 33–34
Rommel, Erwin 153
Roosevelt Field, 60, 69
Roosevelt Hotel, 219
Roosevelt Island, 66
Roosevelt, Eleanor, 219
Roosevelt, Franklin D., 82–83, 89, 97, 128–30, 134, 136, 139, 148,184, 265

Roosevelt, Theodore 32, 245
Ross, Arthur, 316
Ross, Janet, 316
Roth, William von, 78–79
Rothschild automobile, 33
Rottenberg, Dan, 11
Royal Marines, 151
Rum Runner, 209, 321, 327
Rumson Country Club, 34
Rusk, Dean, 245
Rutgers, Alice (Allie), 124–27, 138, 142
Rutgers, Henry, 124

St. Andrew's School, 316–317
State University of New York at New Paltz, 214
SS troops, 129
Sag Harbor, New York 117, 197–98
Saipan, 168, 198
Sammy's Beach, 198, 201
San Francisco, California, 11, 64, 173–74, 185
Sands Point, Long Island, 52, 55
Sanford, Terry, 287, 289–290
Santiago del Estero, 234
Saturday Evening Post, 223
Savoy Hotel, 159
Schafer, Roger, 162, *216*
Schultz, Dutch, 66
Schulze, Margaret Thompson, 89–90, 129–136
Scribner's, 251
Seaview Country Club, 162
Selassie, Haile, 247
Semans, James, 286
Semans, Mary, 286
Sennett, Mack, 142–43, 150
Shannon, Herby, 181
Shelter Island, Long Island, 198
Sherman, Richard M., 255
Sherman, Robert B., 255
Showboat, 188

Shriver, Sargent, 244

Silvey, Joe, 321

Sinnet, Cliff, 142

Sisters of the Blessed
   Sacrament,194–95

Slapton Sands, 148

Sloan and Robertson architects, 59

Smith, Julian, 160

Snell, Larry, 148

Society for the Prevention of Cruelty
   to Children, 278

Solace (Navy hospital ship), 185

Solomons Island, Maryland, 139, 141

Somerville, New Jersey, 44

Sonora Electric Phonograph Company,
   50, 175

Sousa, John Philip, 43

South Carolina, 20, 26, 217–18

Southampton Beach Club, 101, 107

Southampton College, 270, 299

Southampton Press, 302

Southampton, Long Island, 60, 63–65,
   75, 78–79, 82–83, 97, 99, 102, 104,
   106, 109, 111, 115, 117, 146, 165,
   185, 218, 226, 235, 237, 242, 256,
   270, 299–302

Southern Power Company, 32

Soviet Union, 292, 299

Spanish Civil War, 90, 98

Springy Banks Road, 198, 200, 202,
   204, 206

St. John's University, School of Law,
   276

St. Matthew's Cathedral, 244, 245, 247

St. Peter's Church, 187

St. Louis 29, 70

St. Paul's School camp 101, 105,
   108–111, 121, 185

St. Paul's School, 5, 24, 43, 69, 79,
   81–82, 84–85, 88, 90, 98–101,
   104–06, 108–09, 127, 174, 183–84,
   186, 222, 263, 309, *312*

Stalin, Josef, 99, 147, 251

Staten Island, New York, 142

Statue of Liberty, 142

Stowell, Lonsdale, 109, 113, *216*

Sweden, 130

Syosset, Long Island, 180

Tammany Hall, 20

Tegeder, Tom, 157

Teheran, Iran, 147

Thames River, 143, 149, 151

Thaw, Bill, 25–26, 34

Thaw, Gladys 25–26, 34

Thomas, George 247

Three Mile Harbor 196–200, 209, 212,
   215, 232, 265, 317–319

Tilton, Newell 106–107, 116–117

Tippett, Cloyce 137

Tokyo Harbor 173

Torresdale, Pennsylvania 194

Total Recoil 251

Town & Country 112, 192, 283

Trent, Josiah, 286

Trenton State Prison, 24

Trinity College, 29, 32–33, 48, 50, 175,
   285

Truman, Harry S., 235–36, 247, 261,
   298

Tunney, Gene 20–21, 102

United States Marines Corps, 9, 20,
   24, 45, 114, 125, 159, *161*, 170,
   185–86, 249–50

United States Navy, 28, 45, 125,
   137–42, 154, 158–60, 162–63, 165,
   168, 172–73, 177, 196, 198, 211,
   217, 221, 235, 250, 269, 291, 296,
   309

Uansa, Toby, 77

University of Havana, 292

University of Pittsburgh, 77

Upper Brookville, Long Island, 73

Upward Bound, 279, 282

Uruguay, 137, 149–50

Vavoulis, George, *110*
Vavoulis, Teddy, *110*
Vienna, Austria, 90, 93–95, 97
Vietnam War, 237, 249, 295, 314, 325
Virginia, 20, 28, 33–34, 104, 159, 260
Vlis, Diana van der, 253

WPBX, 299
Wagner, Robert, 219, *220*, 221
Wagner College, 214
Walker, Jimmy, 20, 65, 74
Wall Street, 82, 177, 193, 265, 270, 283
Walter Reed Army Hospital, 238
Warren Wilson College, 257, 305
Warren, Lesley Ann, 254–55
Warsaw, Poland, 129–31
Washington, D.C., 40, 88, 97, 118, 120, 125, 128–30, 147, 172, 239–40, 243–46, 270, 296, 299, 314
Washington Duke Inn, 288
Washington, Booker T., 29
Washington, George, 32, 307
Weston, Connecticut, 179
Westport Times, 182
Westport, Connecticut, 179, 188–192, 196, 212
Whalen, Ralph, 219
Wharton School of Business, 231
White's Club, 145
Whitney family, 73, 75
Whitney, Cornelius Vanderbilt, 298
Whitney, John Hay ("Jock"), 265–66
Wigram, Father, 184
Williams, Franklin, 319

Williams, Hazel, 270, *318*, 319
Williams, Lillian, 319
Williams, Marvin, 188
Williams, Richard L. ("Lonnie"), 227–29, 231, 260, *266*, 269–70, *271*, 277–78, 282, 311, *313*, 314–16, 319–20
Williams, Richie, 320
Williams, Stevie, 319
Williams-Myers, Albert ("Albie"), 188, 190–91, 212–15, *220*
Williams-Myers, Janice, 214
Wilson, Derek, 261
Wirth, Dick, *216*
Wiswell, George, 223, 226
World War I, 19, 33, 58, 76, 78, 88, 134, 137
World War II, 55, 87–88, 96, 168, 222, 250
D-Day, 144, 146–148, 152, 156, 162, 164, 173, 236, 261
World Wrestling Foundation, 102
Wyndecote, 256

Xavier, New Orleans 194

Yale University, 59, 124, 159, 185, 190, 277, 285
Yalta, 147
Young Lords Party, 275
Young, Leontine R., 210
Yugoslavia, 135

Zambia 214